Learning and Teaching
at M-Level

Education at SAGE

SAGE is a leading international publisher of journals, books, and electronic media for academic, educational, and professional markets.

Our education publishing includes:

- accessible and comprehensive texts for aspiring education professionals and practitioners looking to further their careers through continuing professional development

- inspirational advice and guidance for the classroom

- authoritative state of the art reference from the leading authors in the field

Find out more at: **www.sagepub.co.uk/education**

Learning and Teaching at M-Level

A Guide for Student Teachers

Hazel Bryan, Chris Carpenter and
Simon Hoult

Los Angeles | London | New Delhi
Singapore | Washington DC

SAGE Publications Ltd
1 Oliver's Yard
55 City Road
London EC1Y 1SP

SAGE Publications Inc.
2455 Teller Road
Thousand Oaks, California 91320

SAGE Publications India Pvt Ltd
B 1/I 1 Mohan Cooperative Industrial Area
Mathura Road
New Delhi 110 044

SAGE Publications Asia-Pacific Pte Ltd
33 Pekin Street #02-01
Far East Square
Singapore 048763

Library of Congress Control Number: 2009933700

British Library Cataloguing in Publication data

A catalogue record for this book is available from the British Library

ISBN 978-1-84860-615-9
ISBN 978-1-84860-616-6 (pbk)

Typeset by C&M Digitals (P) Ltd, Chennai, India
Printed in Great Britain by CPI Antony Rowe, Chippenham, Wiltshire
Printed on paper from sustainable resources

Mixed Sources
Product group from well-managed
forests and other controlled sources
www.fsc.org Cert no. SGS-COC-002953
© 1996 Forest Stewardship Council
FSC

CONTENTS

ABOUT THE AUTHORS

Hazel Bryan is Head of the Department of Professional Development and Director of Masters degrees in the Faculty of Education at Canterbury Christ Church University.

Chris Carpenter is a Senior Lecturer in the Education Faculty at Canterbury Christ Church University. He is the subject leader for secondary PGCE Physical Education and teaches on the Masters in Education.

Simon Hoult is the Director of 11–19 Initial Teacher Education at Canterbury Christ Church University and the subject leader for the 11–18 Geography PGCE. He is also a Teaching Fellow of the University's Learning and Teaching Enhancement Unit.

INTRODUCTION

WHAT IS THE BOOK FOR?

Ways of seeing

When you first go into school you will no doubt experience the frenetic pace of the school day. Some things will be familiar to you and some things will be very new. Observing practice in school through the new lens of the student teacher will enable you to experience the richness of the classroom. With so much to take in, however, this may lead to multi-sensory overload! This book will enable you to know *how to look and listen,* and *what to look and listen out for* when looking at schools, classrooms and pupils during the hurly-burly of the school day.

A language for learning

In line with the philosophy of Reggio Emilia we see learners as rich in every way. As such we see you as experts in your field bringing knowledge and experience to your course and new working environment. As a graduate you will have subject-specific language from your field. This book will enable you to develop other languages about learning. An understanding of the vocabularies of learning theories, with the grammatical framework of your educational experiences, will allow you to synthesise your expert subject knowledge. We acknowledge that all language is value-laden and culture-specific and this book will explicitly bring your attention to the ideological and political use of terminology and vocabulary in relation to teaching today.

Meaning making

By developing your skills and insights into practice and developing a professional language, this book will support you in reflecting about learning and teaching. We believe that reflection is crucial in order to learn, and as such this book will support you in asking deep and challenging questions about your practice. As your reflective skills sharpen, you will discover layers of complexity that surround the relationship between teaching and learning. Your skills as a professional will strengthen as you ask questions of your practice; through enquiry you will make familiar aspects of learning unfamiliar. The resulting reflective thinking and discussion will deepen your understanding of teaching and learning.

Theory as kinetic energy

We see theory as an energy, as a food to nourish your practice. By living theory you will bring your practice to life. Just as in order to live healthily we need to consider what we eat and its effect on our bodies and minds, so too should we explore the nature and implications of theories for our practice.

This book will support you in 'theory-using' and 'theory-building' as a powerful, knowledgeable practitioner. All schools are different, all teachers are different and this book will help you in developing your professional self.

WHO IS THE BOOK FOR?

This book is for PGCE students, NQTs and teachers engaged in Masters-level work and other professionals who are seeking to undertake enquiry with integrity in school settings. Additionally, we hope the book will be supportive to our colleagues who are HEI tutors, school-based mentors and class teachers, in their engagement with student teachers.

HOW MIGHT YOU ENGAGE WITH THE BOOK?

This book is intended to support your understanding of, and the links between, theory and practice. It is not a book therefore to be read in isolation of either of these fundamentals. Theory and practice will exemplify, contextualise and situate your learning as a teacher researcher. Although you will all engage differently with the book, the three sections of the text will stimulate thinking and provide support in specific ways.

This book is in three parts:

Part 1:   The importance of enquiry in enhancing learning
Part 2:   Key methods and ways of doing enquiry
Part 3:   Professional development and moving from student to teacher.

In **Part 1** we introduce you to the policy landscape of education, to concepts around learning and to the notion of student teachers as researchers.

In Chapter 1 we introduce the education policy landscape within which you will practise. We explore the terrain of professionalism and professional identity and then set that within the context of an increasingly politicised arena. We map out for you key ideological concepts and policy concepts and explore Modernism and Postmodernism in relation to education.

In Chapter 2 teachers' beliefs about theories are considered in some depth, as is the less than straightforward relationship between teaching and learning.

In Chapter 3 we invite you to consider theories that seek to explain how learning happens, and we have approached this in the kind of critical analytical manner that we see as essential to adopting deeper approaches to learning. We consider the strengths and weaknesses of four key learning theories and the implications for pedagogy and assessment.

In Chapter 4 we argue that research is an integral part of your professional practice. We pick up the themes of learning from Chapter 2 and look at issues relating to research that might help you as a student teacher. We explore the place of reflection and reflexivity in research, learning and teaching and offer complexity theory as a lens through which to look at learning.

In **Part 2** we move the focus to the classroom and look at issues related to observing classrooms and the kind of methods that you might employ in developing your learning through enquiry.

Chapter 5 opens Part 2 of the book and asks you to think about the presuppositions that you will bring to teaching and to reflect on things you observe in teachers. We also ask you to consider the kinds of knowledge that teachers need.

In Chapter 6 we ask you to consider issues related to observing children and in particular how we can make meaningful interpretations about what children learn. We ask you to reflect on how teachers might construct learners.

In Chapter 7 the focus is on the conceptual frameworks that underpin research, such as methodology, and on methods that might be helpful for the student researcher.

In Chapter 8 we support your critical reading and writing – essential at Masters level – by immersing you in words and putting writing under the microscope.

Chapter 9 focuses on field work – we take you step by step through the issues related to the methods of interviews and questionnaires.

Part 3 of the book is designed to support your professional development, as you enter your new profession.

In Chapter 10 we explore ways in which you might work with other professionals, presenting this in a historical context so that you are aware of how this area has evolved, and we also lay out some inherent dilemmas.

In Chapter 11 we invite you to consider your own professional development needs.

We hope you find this book both challenging and supportive.

PART 1

THE IMPORTANCE OF ENQUIRY IN ENHANCING LEARNING

TEACHER PROFESSIONALISM TODAY

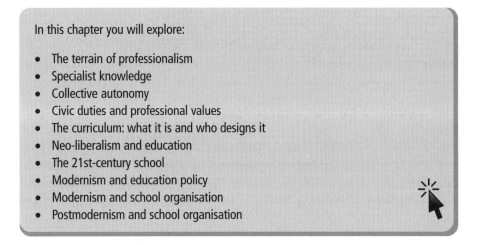

In this chapter you will explore:

- The terrain of professionalism
- Specialist knowledge
- Collective autonomy
- Civic duties and professional values
- The curriculum: what it is and who designs it
- Neo-liberalism and education
- The 21st-century school
- Modernism and education policy
- Modernism and school organisation
- Postmodernism and school organisation

INTRODUCTION

The zeitgeist of the 21st century is characterised by a focus upon education. In England, New Labour came to power in May 1997 with a mantra of 'Education, Education, Education'. Since then the focus has, if anything, become sharper. As you progress through your PGCE year you will become socialised into the professional context of education. This socialisation will take place in school, where, as soon as you enter the grounds, you are caught up in the rich fabric of everyday life, engaging with pupils, teachers, parents and a multiplicity of other professionals who support pupils' development in school. Your process of socialisation will also take place in the University, where you will engage with tutors who will open doors to national and international ideas around education, and who will provide channels for you to engage with the wisdom of past generations of educators whilst simultaneously introducing you to current education theories and practices. Your socialisation will induct you into a new discourse of education, a multi-layered discourse that reflects the complexities of what it is to be a teacher in the politicised landscape of education in England today.

As a teacher you will engage on a daily basis with pedagogical issues and subject-specific issues – all of which have a focus upon learning. This is explored in detail in Chapters 2 and 3. You will interact in an inter-professional context with other professionals, and this is explored in Chapter 10. This first chapter, however, introduces you to the ways in which, at many levels, government policy influences, to a greater or lesser extent, all of your actions and shapes your discourse. By understanding the policy arena within which education decisions are made at national level, you will become empowered to influence what happens at a localised level, in your school and your classroom. In this way, you will enrich and enhance your professionalism. So, what do we really mean by teacher professionalism?

THE TERRAIN OF PROFESSIONALISM

The terminology of professionalism began to develop during the 1950s and 1960s, when sociologists attempted to describe the quintessential characteristics of a profession (Whitty, 2003). It is possible to understand the concept of a 'profession' as fluid in nature, ever shifting along a 'hypothetical continuum' (Hoyle, 1995). As occupations achieve increasing characteristics of socially agreed features, they move along this continuum, gradually undergoing a process of **professionalisation**. Professionalisation relates to the ways in which an occupational group achieves status and standing in society – it is a measure of the 'societal strength and authority of an occupational group' (Englund, 1996, p. 76). Englund's focus here is on the strength of teaching as an occupational group, not a focus upon the qualities or characteristics of good teaching. Professionalisation can be understood as a political project (McCulloch et al., 2000) on the part of teachers to be recognised as professionals. An example of this is the political project the teacher unions have engaged in over the last two decades in enhancing professional status. Alternatively, professionalisation can be understood as a 'professional project' (Whitty, 2003), where teachers strive for status, but in professional terms rather than through political acts such as union action. An example of this is the creation of the General Teaching Council for England (GTCE). You are becoming a teacher at a time when it could be argued, 'after a century of striving, teaching has become a bona fide profession' (Whitty, 2003, p. 65) with a General Teaching Council to represent it.

〰️ **Reflection**

What is the General Teaching Council for England?
In what ways does the GTCE represent teachers?
What is the remit of the GTCE?
In what ways can the GTCE enhance your practice?

If professionalisation is the process the profession goes through to gain occupational capital, then **professionalism** can be understood as relating to 'exceptional standards of behaviour, dedication and a strong service ethic' (Helsby, 1995, p. 320). It could be said that professionalism, as distinct from professionalisation, is inward looking in that it relates to the pedagogical skills teachers need to carry out their duties satisfactorily. Lawn (1996, p. 21) offers a no-nonsense definition of teacher professionalism, stating that 'professionalism is a highly specific, contextualised idea which is used in contemporary educational writing as a commonsense way of describing the work of the English teacher'.

It has been suggested that professionalism carries with it a moral dimension (Carr, 2000), with a concern for standards, behaviour and dedication. Professionals have been described as the 'moral milieu' of society (Durkheim, 1957): if industry had the overriding goal to compete, then this 'moral milieu' was necessary to bring 'cohesion and stability' to society (1957, p. 29). This sense of occupying the moral high ground and in some way being motivated by altruism and commitment are well documented. The nature of professional motivation is not personal financial gain but 'client centredness' and in this sense is linked to morality and community interests.

〰️ **Reflection**

What do you believe are the qualities of a good teacher?
Carr (2000) argues that professionalism carries a moral dimension. Do you believe teaching is a moral undertaking?

The third term to consider here is **professionality**. In relation to education, the term professionality refers to the knowledge and skills needed to undertake the business of teaching. Traditionally, 'professionals' could be characterised as enjoying specialised knowledge that set them apart from other members of society (Perkins, 1989). The specialist knowledge of professionals traditionally took many years of study in Higher Education to acquire, and would include specific skills based on that theoretical knowledge, which was certified by examination. The nature of teacher knowledge today (pedagogical, curricular and socio-educational) has shifted from being the sole preserve of the occupation to a matter for Government, and often public, debate.

〰 **Reflection**

What pedagogical knowledge do you need to be a good teacher?
What curricular knowledge do you need to be a good teacher?
What socio-educational knowledge do you need to be a good teacher?
Where does this knowledge come from?
How can you update your knowledge?
What skills do you need to be a good teacher?
How do you know what skills you need?
What do you know about your Subject Association?

Teachers' professional work, then, embodies the dimensions of professionalism, professionalisation and professionality, that comprise a body of systematic knowledge, professional values, study in Higher Education, a degree of autonomy, prestige and some control over the decoding of policy texts.

TEACHER PROFESSIONALISM

In the past, teachers' work was regarded as the domain of the professional, and certainly not an area that would be of interest to Government. During debate in the House of Commons on the Crowther Report of 1960, the Minister of Education, Sir David Eccles, commented that the findings of the report were 'an irresistible invitation for a sally into the secret garden of the curriculum' (Eccles, 1960, quoted in McCulloch et al., 2000, p. 11). The Minister was swift to point out that 'parliament would never attempt to dictate the curriculum' but that 'I shall, therefore, try in future to make the Ministry's own voice heard rather more often, more positively and, no doubt, sometimes more controversially' (p. 11). It seems extraordinary to us today to think that there was a time when there was little interest, let alone intervention, in the business of education. Then teachers enjoyed curriculum design autonomy – what Lawton termed 'the Golden Age of teacher control (or non-control) of the curriculum' (Lawton, 1980, p. 22). In the past, constructs of teacher professionalism would have involved the following features:

- Specialist knowledge
- Collective autonomy
- Civic duties and professional values.

Specialist knowledge

Traditionally, the occupational group known as professionals could be characterised as enjoying specialised knowledge which set them apart from other members of their respective society. This knowledge is not always necessarily a natural scarcity and as such, the members of that profession may protect it by regulating the supply of expertise. This specialised knowledge would have taken many years to build. Today, the nature of teacher knowledge has shifted from being the sole preserve of the profession to a matter for both the profession and Government. Government intervention can be seen in all stages of education, from the Standards that determine whether or not a student teacher has reached a satisfactory level of competence to move into the NQT year, through a National Curriculum for pupils, sporadic Strategies and a stratified Professional Development offer from the TDA.

Collective autonomy

Professionals regulate entry into their profession. As gatekeepers of their profession they enjoy a degree of protected collective autonomy. This collective autonomy allows them to guard and define the body of knowledge needed within the profession. Professional councils register members of their profession, thereby protecting autonomy and determining their codes of practice. In this sense, the group manipulates the market and employs a 'strategy of closure' (Perkins, 1989, p. 378). Today, teachers enjoy a certain level of autonomy in relation to gatekeeping the profession.

The role of the mentor in school is significant in terms of both supporting the PGCE student but also, in partnership with the Higher Education Institution (HEI), making judgements on the student against the Standards. You will have completed (or are in the process of completing) online tests, without which you cannot progress through your NQT year.

It is unlikely in contemporary society that any profession enjoys absolute autonomy and the way in which you progress through your training to qualified status is a good example. You will be supported in your learning by tutors in the HEI in partnership with mentors and class teachers in school. You will be required to meet the Standards which have been determined by Government and pass your M-level work which is assessed by the HEI. This complex relationship within which you are training is a good example of the subtleties of professional and practitioner autonomy today.

Civic duties and professional values

Professionals have for many years been regarded as the 'moral milieu' of society. As far back as 1957, Durkheim argued that if industry had the overriding goal to compete, then the moral milieu was necessary to bring 'cohesion and stability' to society (Durkheim, 1957, p. 29). This sense of professionals occupying the moral high ground and in some way being motivated by altruism and commitment is well documented. The nature of professional motivation in terms of education is seen as 'client-centredness' rather than financial gain. In this sense, professionalism becomes more closely linked to moral issues and community interests. The personal gain is not financial but rather in the acceptance of status bestowed upon that individual by society, who accepts 'honour and authority' as payment (Nixon, 1997).

From a professional context in 1960, where the Minister David Eccles talked about education as a 'secret garden', to a situation where the Secretary of State, Estelle Morris, comments 'We shall take forward this [education] transformation with vigour, working enthusiastically with those who share our cast-iron commitment to raising standards and who share our vision of creating a trusted, high quality teaching profession' (DfES, 2001, p. 28), there has clearly been a radical shift in the relationship of Government to education. Table 1.1 sets out the changing policy landscape of education since the 'secret garden' comment of 1960 in terms of dominant political ideology and approaches to curriculum intervention.

TABLE 1.1   The changing policy landscape of education

Dates	Political Party	Prime Minister	Dominant political ideology	Curriculum approach
1997–	Labour	Gordon Brown Tony Blair	Moral collectivism; communitarianism	Interventionist
1979–1997	Conservative	John Major Margaret Thatcher	Neo-liberalism; free market ideology	Interventionist
1976–79	Labour	James Callaghan	Diverse	Non-interventionist
1974–76	Labour	Harold Wilson		
1970–74	Conservative	Edward Heath		
1964–70	Labour	Harold Wilson		
1963–64	Conservative	Alec Douglas-Home		
1957–63	Conservative	Harold Macmillan		

As teachers, we live our professional lives through changing political land-scapes. Each political party brings with it an ideology that will shape educa-tion. Table 1.1 shows that between 1957 and 1979 there was, generally speaking, non-intervention in terms of curriculum design from Government. However, after 1979, things changed. These changes have formed the land-scape within which we practise today. As such, it is worth exploring this rela-tionship between Government and education a little more.

THE CURRICULUM: WHAT IS IT AND WHO DESIGNS IT?

The 'great debate' was held at Ruskin College, Oxford, on 18 October 1976, by the then Labour Prime Minister James Callaghan. Amongst the many things discussed (teacher accountability, vocational education), the idea that a curriculum might have a 'core' of basic knowledge was explored. You will see from looking at Table 1.1 that government intervention in education really began in the late 1970s under a Conservative Government. In 1979, with a Conservative Government in power under Margaret Thatcher, the Secretary of State for Education, Mark Carlisle, published the consultative paper, 'A Framework for the School Curriculum', the first in a trilogy of cur-riculum documents. These documents represent the first steps taken by Government in terms of curriculum interest and control:

> a good deal of support has been found for the idea of identifying a 'core' or essential part of the curriculum which should be followed by all pupils accord-ing to their ability. Should the core be defined as narrowly as possible? Should it be expressed in terms of traditional school subjects or in terms of educational objectives which may be attained through the medium of various subjects, appropriately taught? (DES, 1979)

You will realise that these questions were being asked 30 years ago. How would you respond today to Mark Carlisle's questions? What is your profes-sional opinion?

〰️ **Reflection**

Should there be a narrowly defined 'core'?
If so, should the core be taught through subjects or through objectives?
In what ways will rich and deep learning be facilitated?

The journey towards a National Curriculum continued steadily from 1979. It seems incredible today to think that in 1983 the General Secretary of the National Union of Teachers expressed concern that the Conservative Government was intent on controlling the curriculum. In fact, the ideologically non-interventionist (Jenkins, 1995, p. 113) Secretary of State for Education, Sir Keith Joseph, was at that time wary of direct curriculum intervention. He announced his intention to define the objectives of the curriculum for ages 5–16 so that levels of attainment could be met, but resisted direct intervention. In 1984 the White Paper *Better Schools* was published. In this, Joseph determined the principles underpinning the curriculum and the purposes of learning at school.

〰 **Reflection**

What, in your professional opinion, are the principles underpinning the curriculum today?
What are the purposes of learning at school?

By 1987 Sir Keith Joseph's successor, Kenneth Baker, was in post as Secretary of State for Education. Where Sir Joseph was a non-interventionist neo-liberal, Kenneth Baker was pro-intervention. Where Joseph 'tinkered at the fringes' (Jenkins, 1995, p. 113), Baker intervened in the curriculum as soon as he was appointed. Decades of educational laissez-faire were followed by increasing political intervention as the 'passive phase of Thatcher policy' (Jenkins, 1995, p. 115) drew to a close. During this new period, with increasingly energetic interest from the Department of Education and Secretaries of State, a number of highly influential think tanks were also formed.

The Education Reform Act of 1988 represents Government at the heart of educational systems and curriculum policy, although not yet at the stage of intervention or influence on pedagogical practice. The Education Reform Act is a complex cocktail of tension between centralisation and decentralisation: on the one hand, and put somewhat simplistically, finance was decentralised with power devolved to schools in terms of budgetary decision making, where the state was 'rolled back' and individual schools were remodelled as small businesses. In juxtaposition, a centralised curriculum system was conceived with a vigorous inspection system regulating practice.

In 1992 the Conservative Government published *Curriculum Organisation and Classroom Practice in Primary School* (DfEE, 1992), otherwise known as the report of the 'Three Wise Men'. Alexander (himself one of those 'wise men') highlights the fact that the report, an investigation into pedagogical practices at Key Stage 2, ultimately favoured autonomous professional judgement, and words which echo the Crowther Report of 1960. John Major's Conservative Government took over the baton from Margaret Thatcher at the start of the 1990s, and continued in Government until New Labour was elected in 1997 bringing with them the concept of 'Third Way' politics. The period between 1990 and 1997 saw the introduction of the Office for Standards in Education (Ofsted), the Parent's Charter, and the 'back to basics' campaign.

The last 30 years can be characterised, then, in terms of a move to 'marke-tise' education, to apply the principles of the economy to education. Schools today operate along business organisational principles in terms of budgetary considerations, and Head Teachers and Governing Bodies, with Local Authority support, are accountable to parents and Government. The period up to 1997 has been characterised as a time of neo-liberalism, where schools evolved within a free market economy.

Neo-liberalism and education

It has been argued that since 1979, neo-liberal principles have characterised public life, and that 'a new political order of neo-liberal public accountabil-ity was constituted, based upon principles of rights designed to enhance individual choice' (Ranson, 2007, p. 203). In essence, neo-liberalism applies market logic to education, where education is positioned as a key driver of future economic growth. The 'Foreward' in policy documents began to be increasingly introduced by Secretaries of State with a focus upon the value to society of a strong education in economic terms. David Blunkett, in the Green paper, *Teachers Meeting the Challenge of Change* in 1998 stated, 'We recognise the very real challenge facing manufacturing industry in this country and the way in which we need to support and work with them for skilling and reskilling for what Tony Blair has described as the best eco-nomic policy we have – education' (DfEE, 1998). The 1988 Education Reform Act devolved financial power to schools (Head Teachers and Governing Bodies) and in doing so, reconstructed schools along a business model of enterprise. In addition to a focus on the market, neo-liberalism also brings with it the concept of accountability. As schools developed along business lines, so business practices began to emerge in the education system: targets (performance related, pupil attainment, standards) became pivotal to prac-tice. Performance accountability was realised through the publication of Ofsted reports and league tables. The Parent's Charter introduced by John Major's Conservative Government in the 1990s matured into a key policy platform for the Labour Government of 2005, when Prime Minister Tony Blair stated 'We believe parents should have greater power to drive the new system: it should be easier for them to replace the leadership or set up new schools where they are dissatisfied with existing schools' (Blair, 2005). In this way, teachers have become publicly accountable to pupils and parents and this has brought about a 'changing relationship between users and providers' (Ball, 2008, p. 77).

〜〜 **Reflection**

To whom, as a teacher, are you accountable?
What do you believe should be the relationship between parents and the education system?
What performance and accountability measures have you seen in practice in schools?
What do you feel about the publication of league tables in newspapers?

NEW LABOUR

If the Conservatism of the period leading up to 1997 can be characterised as neo-liberal, with a focus on the market economy, then it is possible to characterise New Labour as seeking a 'Third Way' – and this, arguably, has at its heart, moral collectivism and economic responsibility. A plethora of education policies followed Labour's election in May 1997; long gone were the days of Sir David Eccles' 'secret garden'. The first Secretary of State of the new Government, David Blunkett, wanted to be seen to be effective early on. By July of 1997 a White Paper *Excellence in Schools* detailed the new agenda, having six underpinning principles:

- Education will be at the heart of government.
- Policies will be designed to benefit the many not just the few.
- The focus will be on standards not structures.
- Intervention will be in inverse proportion to success.
- There will be zero tolerance of under performance.
- Government will work in partnership with all those committed to raising standards.
  (DfEE, 1997)

A characteristic of New Labour is the desire to develop within society a 'moral collectivism' which is 'essentially the same reservoir of virtues and traditions' that influenced Attlee (Hargreaves, 1996, p. viii). There has also emerged a desire for social cohesion:

Classic themes from the eighteenth and nineteenth centuries — the role of trust in a market economy; the prerequisites of civil society; the meaning of citizenship; the relationship between duties and rights; the need for and scope of a public domain; the threats to and demands of community — have all been discovered. (Marquand and Seldon, 1996, p. 10).

〰️ **Reflection**

In what ways is social cohesion promoted in your school?
How is the concept of 'community' encouraged in your school?

A desire for moral collectivism was at the heart of the introduction of citizenship education into the curriculum in September 2002 – a curriculum based upon humanistic ideology, where moral priorities are understood in terms of human need.

If moral collectivism is one defining feature of New Labour, a second is the way in which there has been continuity between the former Conservative policies and New Labour. Indeed, this was reflected by Prime Minister Tony Blair in the statement 'Some things the Conservatives got right. We will not change them' (Labour Party Manifesto, 1997, p. 3). It has been argued that Prime Minister Blair endorsed virtually all of the Thatcher reforms. This idea of a direct line of continuity between the Conservatives and New Labour suggests that there has been a 'paradigm convergence' (Ball, 1999).

A third feature of New Labour policy that is directly relevant to you is the way in which the concept of 'new professionalism' has emerged. Estelle Morris, Secretary of State in 2001 stated 'we need to be clear about what does constitute professionalism for the modern world. And what will provide the basis for a fruitful and new era of trust between government and the teaching profession' (DfES, 2001, p. 20). This concept had been further developed in *Higher Standards, Better Schools for All* (DfES, 2005b).

A New Professionalism:

8.7   A thorough reform of all teachers' professional standards will set out what can be expected of teachers at every stage of their career. This will include the need for teachers to have good up-to-date knowledge of their subject specialism as part of a clear commitment to effective professional development. We will introduce into this framework more stretch at all levels.

8.8   We will make performance management more effective. The greatest rewards and promotion throughout a teacher's career will go to those who make the biggest impact on pupils' progress and who show commitment to the development of themselves and their colleagues. The best training will be delivered in schools by our best teachers and we will ensure classroom observation and feedback are improved.

8.9 For our best and most experienced classroom teachers, access to the Excellent Teacher grade will be dependent on having been assessed as meeting demanding Excellent Teachers standards, showing that they have developed themselves professionally, including demonstrating excellence and up to date knowledge in their specialist area, and providing regular coaching and mentoring of other teachers.

8.15 We will ensure that the school workforce is able to play the wide range of roles set out in this White Paper, through:

- a group of leading teachers in every school to coordinate catch up and stretch activities, within and beyond the normal school day. This is essential for one-to-one and small group tuition;
- more support staff trained to a high level in literacy and numeracy; and more staff trained in vocational areas, like catering, to come into our schools and colleges to deliver the 14–19 diplomas;
- health and welfare staff ready for the new roles they will play in full-service and other extended schools;
- trained sports coaches, music tutors and modern foreign language assistants to enrich the primary curriculum;
- professionals with the credibility, recent practical experience and workplace knowledge to provide high-quality vocational education. Some of these will be school employees; some will be brought in from employers, work-based learning providers or colleges;
- trained specialists able to deal with disruptive behaviour, truancy and pastoral issues; and
- trained bursars and other administrative staff, freeing teachers to teach and ensuring the best use of resources to improve outcomes for children. (DfES, 2005b 8.7, 8.8, 8.9, 8.15)

This White Paper was published in 2005. Since then what have you experienced in your school in terms of:

- Support staff – in what ways do they support the pupil and teacher?
- Diplomas – how are they operating? Who is teaching them?
- Health and welfare staff – when do they come into school? In what ways do they work in school?
- Coaches, music tutors and language assistants – have you worked with them in your primary school?
- Pastoral managers – in what ways have you seen them working?
- Administrative staff – in what ways do they work? With whom do they work?

THE 21ST-CENTURY SCHOOL SYSTEM

In his 'Statement to the House', Secretary of State for Children, Schools and Families, Ed Balls, announced on 30 June 2009 his intentions for 21st century schools. It is interesting to identify key policy drivers that have been tracked further back in this chapter. There is a clearly articulated commitment to keeping parents at the heart of the education system:

Mr Speaker, our new Parents Guarantee will ensure:

- regular online information about their child's progress, behaviour and attendance;
- access to their child's personal tutor;
- that parents' views will be listened to and reported on the School Report Card so parents know what other parents think when choosing a school.

Personalised learning is at the heart of the pupil offer:

- every secondary pupil has a personal tutor;
- all pupils get 5 hours of PE and sport every week and access to cultural activities too;
- gifted and talented pupils get written confirmation of the extra challenge and support they will receive;
- all pupils with additional needs get extra help, with 4,000 extra dyslexia teachers;
- all pupils in Years 3 to 6 falling behind in English or maths get one-to-one tuition to help them get back on track;
- we will now extend the offer of one-to-one or small group tuition to all pupils at the start of secondary school who were behind at the end of primary school. (Balls, 2009)

Secretary of State Balls also makes a commitment to ensuring the standard of teaching is monitored:

Mr Speaker, because a world-class schools system needs a world-class workforce, we are making teaching a Masters-level profession.

And we will now introduce a new 'licence to teach' similar to that used by other high-status professionals like doctors and lawyers.

Teachers will need to keep their practice up to date to renew their licence – and they will be given a new entitlement for continued professional development. (Balls, 2009)

Secretary of State Balls concludes his statement by framing his commitment in terms of the two overriding New Labour ideological principles – economic and moral drivers:

Mr Speaker, with this White Paper we match continued investment with reform and higher expectations so that:

- we meet the economic imperative by ensuring every young person gets the qualifications they need;
- and we meet our moral imperative by ensuring that every child can succeed, whatever barriers they face.

And I commend this statement to the House. (Balls, 2009)

POSTMODERN SCHOOLS FOR POSTMODERN TIMES?

It is possible to understand the period within which you are currently training as the Postmodern era – that the education policies articulated by Secretary of State Ed Balls are in essence a Postmodern position. In order to understand this, it is useful to begin with a consideration of Modernism, and its implication for schools.

MODERNISM

Based upon the premise that scientific progress will improve the human condition, Modernism has its roots in Enlightenment ideals. Technical advances are at the heart of Modernism and are viewed as the means through which progress will be made. Mass production and profit are key drivers in this social condition and it follows that factory models of working – that is, specific tasks allocated to individuals or teams are seen as the most profitable way of working. Factory workers on a production line will attend to whichever element of the product they have been allocated – no one worker attends to, say, the production of a car from start to finish – specialist workers focus on different elements of production in an attempt to increase profitability, efficiency and expertise.

In this system, hierarchy is essential to maintain order, and promotion and seniority are systematised – control from the centre is seen as the means to ordering this entire system and intervention and even regulation from the centre are commonplace.

MODERNISM AND EDUCATION POLICY

If we look at education policy initiatives in recent times, it is possible to read these through a Modernist lens. The 1988 Reform Act is a study in centralising, on a vast scale, the curriculum entitlement for young people in England and Wales. Decision-making in terms of curriculum content was taken away from individual teachers, departments and schools, and moved to a centrally determined offer. In terms of regulation and intervention, an inspection system was developed in the form of Ofsted. More recently, the National Literacy and Numeracy Strategies were developed around a centrally determined construct of subject matter, accompanied by a suggested pedagogy.

In this sense, the process of determining subject-specific material appropriate to pupils in a given classroom was taken from the teacher and determined by a remote body. In this way, it can be argued that production-line processes were applied to classrooms – the subject matter was remotely determined, the pedagogy was remotely determined, the Strategies were sent into schools where teachers 'delivered' their part. Interestingly, the National Strategies have now been phased out by Secretary of State, Ed Balls (June, 2009) exactly 10 years after their introduction.

MODERNISM AND SCHOOL ORGANISATION

It has been argued that secondary schools are the ultimate expression of modernism (Hargreaves, 1995). The scale of secondary schools changed in the light of comprehensivisation – a Labour initiative of the 1970s when Secretary of State Shirley Williams sought to restructure secondary education. This proved a contentious initiative and one that was never resolved. It resulted in a patchwork of school structures. However, the comprehensive schools that were established were often vast in size, with a specific hierarchy in terms of Senior Management (or the Senior Leadership Team) and a structure of subject-based departments. Hargreaves argues that such balkanised structures of complexity failed to 'engage the emotions and motivations of many of their students and considerable numbers of their staff' (1995, p. 158).

POSTMODERNISM

In recent times, Western society has seen a decline in industrial activity. The global oil crisis in 1974 provided a backdrop against which further industrial unrest was to develop. The miners' strike of the 1980s and the subsequent battle between the Thatcher Government and the mining industry is one example of the painful process of industrial decline. As large industries faded away, the Modernist model of factory-floor production systems increasingly lost their relevance. In place of large-scale production, services emerged on a smaller, more personalised scale. Advances in technology resulted in a situation where workers could be relatively autonomous, linked through mobile technology and instantly contactable.

Rapid results and instant, personalised communication characterise Postmodernism. The result of these changes is to put the individual at the heart of the system – the production line has largely disappeared, and control is decentralised. Hand-in-hand with this change comes uncertainty – where Modernism created standards and structures that provided benchmarks, Postmodernism rejects these standards resulting in a more personalised but ultimately more uncertain condition.

Postmodernism and school organisation

The 1944 Education Act provided the blueprint for education in the post-war era. Based upon Judaeo-Christian principles, this influenced subsequent developments in education. As Britain has recognised and embraced its multicultural heritage, uncertainties have emerged in terms of faith-based perspectives. This uncertainty and multiple faith perspective is characteristic of Postmodernism.

⌇ Reflection

In what ways do the schools you have experience of reflect multi-faith, multi-cultural perspectives?
How do schools articulate their values and principles?

The structure of comprehensive schools has undergone continuous change since their development in the 1970s. In recent times, large schools have established structures to facilitate a more personal approach to learning and teaching. You may find that in the schools in which you work there are:

- mini schools within schools
- faculties that focus on curriculum
- houses that have a pastoral focus
- vertical groupings that are developed around houses
- curriculum departments
- schools of learning
- Key Stage groupings.

〰️ **Reflection**

What have you experienced in terms of structures within schools that aim to personalise learning and teaching for pupils and teachers?

Whereas Modernism provided structures and stability in terms of working practices, the Postmodern state breaks down such structures, allowing for a more flexible approach to the workplace. This can be seen in particular in the way in which, following the National Agreement *Raising Standards and Tackling Workloads* (DfES, 2003), Higher Level Teaching Assistants began to assume greater responsibility in the classroom when teachers were allocated planning, preparation and assessment (PPA) time. This raised complex issues around the professional identity of the teacher, the place of the para-professional in the classroom and the right of pupils to access a curriculum provided by qualified teachers. This is explored in depth in Chapter 8.

In 1988 the Education Reform Act provided a National Curriculum that offered a mass curriculum experience for all pupils. This expression of Modernism has since had a layer of Postmodern complexity laid upon it in the form of personalised learning. The consultation document *2020 Vision* (DfES, 2007) offered a detailed personalised vision for pupils. This is a good example of the way in which Modernist and Postmodernist approaches overlap in education – schools may be operating according to Modernist organisational principles whilst simultaneously attempting to implement personalised learning. As you can see, deep complexity lies at the heart of education.

CONCLUSION

In this chapter we have introduced you to the terrain of teacher professionalism, to issues of status as an occupational group, moral duty and knowledge and skills. From a consideration of teacher professionalism we have then contextualised the professional within the policy landscape, considering issues of curriculum design and control. We have introduced you to the neo-liberal policies of the Conservative government, and the moral collectivism of New Labour. Finally we have explored the way in which education can be viewed through a Modernist and Postmodernist lens.

📖 *Recommended further reading*

Ball, S.J. (2008) *The Education Debate*. Bristol: The Policy Press.
This book tackles policy issues in detail – it will introduce you to key concepts in education and provide a critique of current education policy.

Lingard, B. and Ozga, J. (eds) (2007) *The RoutledgeFalmer Reader in Education Policy and Politics*. London: Routledge.
If education policy analysis appeals to you, then this challenging and wide-ranging Reader introduces you to the complexities of policy within education.

Olssen, M., Codd, J. and O'Neil, A.-M. (2004) *Education Policy: Globalisation, Citizenship and Democracy*. London: Sage.
We recommend this book if you find education policy fascinating and want to really deepen your understanding of policy – how it has evolved and how we can understand policy in a global context.

Scott, D. (2000) *Reading Educational Research and Policy*. London: Routledge.
This book takes you through the relationship between research and policy-making. It is accessible and well structured.

Trowler, P. (2003) *Education Policy*. New York: Routledge.
This book provides the reader with a comprehensive account of recent education policy. Trowler provides commentaries on the policies which enable the reader to classify policy text and to begin to understand how policy is made.

2 DEVELOPING A DEEPER UNDERSTANDING OF LEARNING

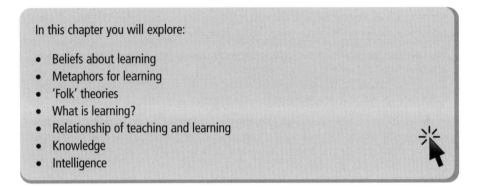

In this chapter you will explore:

- Beliefs about learning
- Metaphors for learning
- 'Folk' theories
- What is learning?
- Relationship of teaching and learning
- Knowledge
- Intelligence

INTRODUCTION

We are all familiar with the concept of 'learning' although it has been suggested by Athey (1990), Claxton (1999) and Marton and Booth (1997) that sometimes even teachers' conceptions of learning are often more closely aligned to what might be described as 'folk theories'. Folk theories are a reference to those conceptions that are commonly held and espoused but often bear little resemblance to knowledge that is based on the conclusions of more robust empirical research. These 'folk' theories are referred to by Furnham (1988) as 'lay' theories and often exist at an implicit or tacit level, in other words they are conceptions that we are not necessarily aware of ourselves but that are likely to impact on the ways that we see situations and that even underpin our practices as teachers. In order to learn more about these implicit theories, they need to be discovered or revealed (Sternberg, 1990).

> It is not so important that you show that you know that this week but it will be critical next week. (Student teacher talking to year 9 class).

The quote above is an example of an implicit personal theory about learning. Thestudent teacher's comment to the class might be seen as sympathetic and intending to be reassuring, which no doubt was the intention. However, it might also be seen as supporting the view that the essence of assessment, and indeed learning, is about high stake events where the key is for the pupil to 'raise' their game at key moments, rather than about prolonged engagement with knowledge that has intrinsic value and is therefore worthwhile in its own right.

While at first sight it might seem strange to suggest that many teachers may not hold sophisticated understandings about learning, which is something that might be seen to lie at the heart of their work, there is considerable support for such a contention:

> Not enough attention is paid to how children learn most effectively and consequently, how teachers can teach most effectively. (Athey, 1990, p. 8)

> We find the lack of communication between these fields [theories of learning and teaching] extremely surprising and puzzling ... it seems to us that the practice of instructional design must be based on some conception of how people learn and on what it means to learn. (Duffy and Jonassen, 1992, p. ix)

> In the context of education in schools, there appears to be an almost complete ignorance of any critical debate about 'inductive procedures', and very little critical discussion of the logical basis of learning theory at all. (Swann, 1999b)

How has this situation come about? Chapter 1 has mapped out the ways in which teachers' work has been shaped by successive governments since the 1988 Education Reform Act and it could be argued that teachers have been marginalised in relation to their agency and relationship with the curriculum. We argue that as an 'extended professional' (Ruddock and Stenhouse, 1995), you will need have a secure understanding of the process of learning and its relationship to teaching.

Examples of 'folk' theories

- Children are noisy on windy days.
- Skills learned in one context transfer readily to others.

Often these 'folk' conceptions are dearly held and buttressed from many sources and if espoused enough times become 'accepted knowledge'; we feel that there is a tendency to dwell on the *nature of the knowledge* rather than taking a step back and considering the *basis* upon which the claims are made. We would see the essence of 'masterly' learning as the capacity to *question* perspectives that are presented to you as in some way, the 'truth'. Caroline Cox (in Hargreaves, 2000) suggests that the grounds we use to justify our practices may be defined as:

- Tradition – how it has always been done
- Prejudice – how I like it done
- Dogma – this is the right way to do it
- Ideology – as required by the current orthodoxy.

BELIEFS ABOUT LEARNING

> 〰️ **Reflection**
>
> - Consider a deeply held belief that you have about learning.
> - Now take a step back and consider the possibilities that it might be described as tradition, prejudice, dogma or ideology.

Claxton (1999) identifies a number of notions regarding beliefs about learning:

- Learning is for the young.
- Learning progresses smoothly.
- We can predict what will be learned.
- Knowledge is 'true'.
- A person's intelligence is fixed.

Learning is for the young

That 'learning is for the young' may seem an obviously flawed perception yet we know there are problems for adults coming back into education (Mezirow, 1991). Perhaps this is connected in professional contexts to mature professionals feeling they need to present themselves as the 'finished article' which then prevents them adopting a more open and tentative approach which might be seen as vital when learning. There is also the notion of the way that we defend ourselves in new situations, and being seen not to know things can be very undermining to self-confidence, especially if the adult is operating in a culture where not to know or to be shown to be mistaken is seen as a weakness rather than a focus for learning. We would support Linda Darling-Hammond et al.'s (2005) notion that we need 'teachers who learn through teaching rather than teachers who have learned how to teach'. This concept of 'learning through teaching' is one that is at the heart of this book and resonates with Heidegger's (Rogers and Freiberg, 1994) assertion that the essential difference between the learner and the teacher is that the teacher realises that there is *more to learn* and therefore needs to be more 'learnable' than the learner.

Learning progresses smoothly

The idea that learning progresses smoothly is also to be challenged. Twomey-Fosnot (1996) and Bailey (2000) both talk about the need for the learner to experience some kind of disequilibrium where their expectations are confounded in some way, which then causes them to reconsider their beliefs and personal theories. Personal theories refer to the notion that as we live our lives we develop schemata or constructions that help us organise our worlds and give meaning to our experiences (Dweck, 1999).

This process of reshaping of personal theories may be seen as a synonym for learning (Claxton, 1984). For example a student teacher might believe that the way to help children learn is to tell them things ('there is so much to get through') and then realises that this is less helpful than engaging them in tasks that allow the children to develop understandings for themselves at their own pace. In other words *meaningful learning takes as long as it takes* and we tend to learn best when we feel relaxed and secure (Claxton, 1998). This illustrates the need to see personal theories as malleable and capable of change as well as the importance of seeing ourselves as learners in the way that Heidegger envisaged.

We can predict what will be learned

If we see that learning is some sort of personal meaning-making process where knowledge is created rather than 'given' then the idea of predicting learning can be seen to be problematic. This notion will be examined more closely in Chapter 5 when we look in more depth at classrooms, but may be seen as problematic as we can never be quite sure what learners will 'make' of any concept or phenomenon. This can make the concept of 'learning outcomes' problematic as in effect the author of the learning outcomes is trying to predict what the learner will make of any particular episode of teaching. We asked a group of Secondary PGCE PE students to e-mail in response to the question 'what struck you about the gymnastics session that you have just undertaken?'. Four of the responses are below:

Student 1

One of the things that struck me most about the gym lesson was the approach to feedback that we were utilising. Many people assume that the best approach to feedback is to provide criticism and then follow it up with examples of how to improve. What we learnt, however, was the importance of reflection and encouraging people to assess their own performances. We found that this not only encourages people to learn about their performance for themselves but it also encourages them to think of ways to improve without prompting.

The importance of asking questions like: How did you find it? Why did you do that? What do you think would happen if you tried it this way?

We all learnt how difficult it is to introduce equipment and incorporate it within an existing sequence. Discussing how easy/hard we found it.

The importance of reflection and watching the performances of others. Learning new things from others and also using other people's mistakes to ensure that you do not do the same.

We all found that it is much easier for people to work in pairs. We automatically feel safer and this makes us more likely to try more adventurous moves. Working individually leaves us more open to criticism. When working in pairs it is far easier to accept negative analysis.

The importance of letting people know that they are capable of improving.

The significance of recognising good performances.

Student 2

What struck me most this morning was how small subtle changes to our often innate ability to communicate what we want others to learn, can have substantial benefits e.g. voice tone, thinking time etc. I was also struck by the literal explanation of divergent learning and how we are so quick to limit learning through glass roofs, rather than to sit back and allow pupils to explore and maximize their learning.

Finally, I found the idea of feedback not being homogeneous as an intriguing and interesting concept. Although often innate, we quickly look to feedback to say what is wrong and how to make it right, rather than to use subtle prompts and explore learning through reflective thinking and open ended discussions.

Student 3

At the start of the lesson I believed these to be the aims of Gymnastics: balance, co-ordination, flexibility, movement, being creative and fun. I now realise that there is more to the aims of gymnastics such as: being comfortable trying and not succeeding, that you can recognise a good performance in gymnastics and to be able to create and improve movements and sequences of movements.

There is more to Gymnastics than just learning skills. It is about progression and improving by trial and error. It is about learning by doing. I discovered that gymnastics is not about being able to do the right sequence or have the right balance. It is about everyone giving it a go at a level that they feel most comfortable with. By supporting each other and raising the difficulty of the challenge you begin to learn more.

The process of learning was formed by group performance and then group reflection. We had groups watch and give us some constructive criticism. We then had time to try improving our sequence and then we had group analysis again. Thereafter one piece of apparatus was incorporated into our sequence and we had groups help us reflect on our sequence again.

I discovered the importance of questions as a form of feedback. It is so important to reflect on each process and by asking questions it will enable the person to learn more. I had to avoid using the words 'you could, you should ...' this was hard at first but then ... I understood the better way of asking questions. For example 'What do you think about your performance?' What would you change about the sequence if you could do it again? If you had a different piece of apparatus would that have affected your sequence? How could you incorporate that apparatus better into your sequence? Did you find it harder this time? All of these ways of asking questions became a new skill for us to master. They promote self learning and independence. These questions do not inform you of what you should do but merely help you come up with the answers yourself.

I really learned from the group reflections. The group asked me 'what way could I incorporate the apparatus throughout our sequence and not just at the end?' I was enlightened by this as I had not even realised that we had just added the new piece at the end of our sequence and not smoothly throughout our sequence. I found this method a valuable way of learning.

Student 4

The use of 'agency' will be very helpful in both teaching and learning.

I have learnt to question with more openness and not to dive in.

I also learnt to view others work with an open mind with no preconceptions. This became apparent when you and my group discussed how an onlooker expecting new movements possibly missed out on more refined movement because their mind was pre-occupied with looking for something else when in fact the gymnastic performance ran smoother as we had worked on transitional parts.

To my surprise I realised today that you can develop a small sequence over a period of time/weeks and this is probably more beneficial to the pupils as they are not beginning from scratch every lesson and they have something to grasp and practice. (EXPLORE—SELECT—REFINE)

Perhaps not as important as the above points I have learnt a few silly things such as it's better to begin work in pairs rather than intimidating individuals and that trust can be established quickly when working closely with another person you do not know very well.

I was apprehensive about today's session as I didn't really know many of the guys on the course and was worried my gymnastic knowledge wouldn't be sufficient but I enjoyed my day and relaxed into the tasks.

As we can see from the responses above, the aspects that struck the four students are similar in some ways but also contain some very different emphases. This is not surprising as each of the four will have come to that situation with very different expectations and past experiences in teaching and gymnastics. Of course in such an exercise there may well have been aspects that they felt able to disclose and there may have been more significant ones that they did not feel able to reveal. This illustrates the difficulty with pre-determining the learning that will take place.

Knowledge is 'true'

'Knowledge' is often seen to be 'true' and something that can be 'given' rather than something that is created and is always provisional. Of course it is tempting to think of knowledge as fixed or fossilised, as this means that once we feel we have some mastery over a particular concept we can put it aside and then move on to new areas.

For example, for many years it was thought that the earth was flat and then Eratosthenes, who lived between 276 and 194 BC noticed that light fell straight down into a well in Syene during the summer solstice, but at an angle in Alexandria on the same date. Knowing (roughly) the distance between the two cities, he concluded that the Earth was round. He further calculated that the diameter of the earth would be approximately 252,000 stadia, although this too proved to be provisional, as subsequently it was found that the distance was nearer to 292,000 stadia, a difference of about 16%. Although given the relatively unsophisticated nature of the tools he had to work with this may be viewed as an exceedingly good attempt!

This story serves to illustrate the notion that knowledge is provisional and that as teachers we need to be able to navigate our way through situations where there are often few fixed points. We would see the capacity to deal with and even relish such uncertainty to lie at the heart of masterly thinking about helping children to learn.

Intelligence is fixed

There can be a feeling, often deeply held, that intelligence or our capacity to learn is fixed: this is often supported by external factors such as the 11-plus examinations, media and literature. This is well illustrated below in an extract from *A Study in Scarlet*, a Sherlock Holmes story written by Sir Arthur Conan Doyle:

> His ignorance was as remarkable as his knowledge. Of contemporary literature, philosophy and politics he appeared to know next to nothing. Upon my quoting Thomas Carlyle, he inquired in the naivest way who he might be and what he had done. My surprise reached a climax, however, when I found incidentally that he was ignorant of the Copernican Theory and of the composition of the Solar System. That any civilized human being in this nineteenth century should not be aware that the earth travelled round the sun appeared to be to me such an extraordinary fact that I could hardly realize it.
>
> 'You appear to be astonished,' he said, smiling at my expression of surprise. 'Now that I do know it I shall do my best to forget it.'
>
> 'To forget it!'
>
> 'You see,' he explained, 'I consider that a man's brain originally is like a little empty attic, and you have to stock it with such furniture as you choose. A fool takes in all the lumber of every sort that he comes across, so that the knowledge which might be useful to him gets crowded out, or at best is jumbled up with a lot of other things so that he has a difficulty in laying his hands upon it. Now the skilful workman is very careful indeed as to what he takes into his brain-attic. He will have nothing but the tools which may help him in doing his work, but of these he has a large assortment, and all in the most perfect order. It is a mistake to think that that little room has elastic walls and can distend to any extent. Depend upon it there comes a time when for every addition of knowledge you forget something that you knew before. It is of the highest importance, therefore, not to have useless facts elbowing out the useful ones.
>
> (Extract from Conan Doyle, *A Study in Scarlet*, 1887/2006)

By using the metaphor of the mind as an attic, we would see that Conan Doyle is supporting the 'mind as a container' metaphor which suggests that the brain has a definite capacity, a classic 'folk conception' because we can be fairly sure that the more we think, the cleverer we become and that in fact there is little in the way of a fixed capacity (Black et al., 2003; Sternberg 1999). We find Hoy and Murphy's (2001) idea that knowledge requires belief but belief does not require knowledge to be helpful. In other words to have a deep knowledge of how steam trains work requires a belief that the various systems and their interplay will be able to produce enough pressure to move the train. However, it would also be possible to believe in the possibility of steam trains yet have no knowledge about how they work. In an educational context we argue that sophisticated knowledge of how children learn requires belief but equally we may be able to accommodate folk theories as beliefs without any form of sophisticated knowledge. In this case we need to be clear that intelligence is not fixed and therefore student teachers need to consider the theories they hold about intelligence carefully.

It can therefore be possible to operate in the classroom applying a repertoire of strategies which are based on sometimes shallow notions of 'what works'. We have also found that student teachers sometimes 'borrow' strategies in the classroom without being too clear about why they are doing what they are doing – a phenomenon occasionally referred to as 'caught impersonating a teacher'. This is perfectly understandable as student teachers will come to Initial Teacher Education (ITE) courses with well-established notions about the kinds of things that teachers do in classrooms and there is always a possibility that they may apply them without understanding why they are applying them (Green, 1998).

This notion of intelligence not being fixed has resonance in neuroscience where 'plasticity' of the brain has been well established. Blakemore and Frith (2006) report stories of deaf people whose auditory cortex (the part of the brain that usually processes sounds) no longer deals with sounds but over time will begin to process mouth movements. Similar adaptations have been noted in the visual cortex of blind people who start to respond to other sensory signals. So we are suggesting that domains of competence such as 'intelligence' and 'ability' are not limited by fixed capacities like an attic but are capable of change. In other words, the more we think the cleverer we become or the more we practice the more competent we become. We see this as a key idea that student teachers need to apply to both to themselves and their own learning in addition to how they perceive pupils. The latter will be considered in more depth in Chapter 6.

Because we are all familiar with the concept of learning it is important to have some understanding of, and even challenge, our own conceptions of learning. The questions below are intended to help you reflect on your beliefs about learning.

Reflection

- What is learning?
- What are your beliefs about learning?
- What is there that is worth learning?
- What do you feel it takes to learn?
- To what extent do you see personal attributes such as 'intelligence' and 'ability' as fixed or subject to change?
- Do you feel that you are more intelligent now than you used to be?
- Do you feel that the more you think the cleverer you become?

METAPHORS FOR LEARNING

Metaphor is a powerful tool for understanding our world. Metaphors in general and more specifically metaphors about learning are more embedded in our language than we realise. Words may be seen as symbols or little packets of meaning and there are two principal ways that they become absorbed in our language. Firstly there is the notion that words are not necessarily what they represent, but shapes and sounds that we use to signify what we intend. In a metaphorical context they can also be used to explain something that we don't have the specific vocabulary to describe, by using a 'known' to explain the 'unknown'. When shared with others, we can thus communicate. Secondly, as language is imitative, certain words and phrases can also become conversational 'set pieces' that we may use in a given situation in a relatively unthinking manner. When considering learning it is worth considering the nature of the metaphorical language that is employed to represent it.

The following are some commonly used metaphors for learning and teaching:

- Soak it up
- Grasp it
- Give them knowledge
- Cover the ground
- Switching on a light bulb
- The penny drops
- Chew it over
- I didn't get it
- Getting it across

The language we use to describe our thinking about learning and teaching is never completely neutral and therefore has meaning, even if at an implicit level (Bruner, 1986). We argue that the metaphors we tend to use will at some level be representative of how we see learning and we have included some examples in the points above. As can be seen there is a strong underlying sense that we tend to see learning as a process by which knowledge is 'acquired' or 'transferred' from teacher to pupil, rather than a process by which knowledge is actively created by the learner. If we saw learning in this way we argue that the nature of language and associated metaphors would be qualitatively different. This is illustrated by the following examples of alternative ways of talking about learning:

- I wanted the children to build their own understandings.
- I wanted to see how the children saw their world.
- I wanted to see what sense they made of the activities.
- I wanted the children to create their own meanings and understandings.
- I wondered what they would make of it.
- I wanted the children to grow their own understandings of the topic.

〰️ **Reflection**

- What metaphors do you use to represent learning?
- What metaphors do you hear teachers use in your placement school?
- What metaphors have you heard children use to describe learning in your placement school?

In a study with science students, Thomas and McRobbie (1999) asked them to describe themselves as learners and the learning processes they use. They found that the metaphors used were credible expressions of tacit knowledge, or implicit theories about learning that the student teachers brought to the course. Furthermore the metaphors enabled the students and teachers to develop a common language about learners' processes and their roles as learners. We argue that attending to metaphorical language is a very useful tool for student teachers learning at Masters level as it gives clues as to the implicit understandings that we have about learning.

WHAT IS LEARNING?

In a sense the question 'what is learning?' may seem so obvious that we fail to really consider it. There is a tendency to see learning as 'remembering' and as to do with mastering skills that are well known to others. We have no argument that such conceptions are valid definitions of learning but we feel that 'learning as recall' is just a part of it.

Different academics have conceptualised this question in different ways. Illeris (2007) talks about learning being processes of 'cumulation', 'assimilation', 'accommodation' and 'transformation'. Marton and Booth (1997) drawing upon an earlier 1993 study by Marton, Beaty and Dall'Alba, propose a twofold division between learning as reproducing and learning as seeking meaning. They see learning as reproducing as involving activities such as memorising sections of the periodic table in science or increasing one's knowledge about the repeal of the Corn Laws. An example of learning as applying would be a maths lesson where the teacher demonstrates an algorithm and then the children have to practise it on new data.

In learning as 'seeking meaning' the learner seeks understanding, and that might mean understanding that you don't like a subject! Learning as seeing something in a different way might be seen as exemplified by the experience of a secondary teacher newly arrived in a school with a predominantly affluent, middle-class intake who found that the children in their tutor group thought that homeless people 'deserved to be homeless', but through carrying out some research and reading case studies in preparation for an assembly many of the children came to see homeless people in a very different way. Changing as a person may be seen as congruent with Mezirow's (1991) notions of 'transformative learning' which he describes as a process of becoming aware of one's tacit assumptions and often involves powerful emotions that are evidenced by actions. This may be exemplified by the story of the Year 10 boy who is present at an assembly where a teacher is talking to the children about the characteristics of learners who demonstrate mastery and performance orientations to learning and this serves as a catalyst to encouraging him to redouble his efforts in school.

Table 2.1 gives a summary of conceptions of learning based on the work of Marton and Booth (1997).

TABLE 2.1 Summary of conceptions of learning (based on Marton and Booth, 1997)

Learning as ...	
A. Increasing knowledge	
B. Memorising and reproducing	Learning primarily as reproducing
C. Applying	
D. Understanding	
E. Seeing something in a different way	Learning as primarily seeking meaning
F. Changing as a person	

Finally, we would urge you to see learning as a heterogeneous phenomenon which embraces a number of facets and is far from just being a matter of remembering.

CONCLUSION

We find that student teachers often associate 'learning' and 'teaching' to the point where they feel that 'teaching' is an indispensable factor in bringing about 'learning'. Indeed Illich (1970, p. 35) somewhat ironically says that 'School is an institution built on the axiom that learning is the result of teaching'. We would urge you to see the relationship between teaching and learning, not as a causal one, that is to say one where it is possible to say that learning during a particular episode of teaching was 'caused' to happen, but as a form of idiosyncratic, personal sense-making or construction by the learner. Without wishing to underplay the role of the teacher in bringing about learning, especially as this is a book aimed at student teachers, it is important to consider the relationship of teaching and learning as less than straightforward.

When we interview PGCE candidates we ask them to identify essential ingredients for effective learning. Typically they will propose aspects such as, 'a teacher who has good subject knowledge', 'a teacher who is supportive' or a 'teacher who is able to motivate learners'. Of course this may be in part due to them wishing to be seen in a good light at an interview! Wood (1988) reminds us that in some societies there is no such verb as 'to teach', yet presumably the children in those societies manage to learn and grow to become valued members of those communities. It is also worth considering that when a person has, for example, learned how to put formulae into a spreadsheet on their own they might well say, 'I taught myself' rather than just saying 'I learned it on my own'.

So from the outset we urge you to consider the personal theories that you may hold about the relationship between teaching and learning and seek to interrogate these as closely as possible in order to develop deeper insights.

📖 *Recommended further reading*

Illeris, K. (2007) *How we Learn: Learning and Non Learning in School and Beyond.* London: Routledge.
Knud Illeris is a professor of life-long learning from Denmark. In this book he examines key factors that take a holistic view of how we learn. He considers questions such as what learning is, the content dimensions of learning and barriers to learning. Throughout he draws upon key literature and issues, providing the reader with a good overview of the field.

Jarvis, P. (2006) *Towards a Comprehensive Theory of Human Learning.* London: Routledge.

A well-structured book by a well-respected academic in the field of learning. In the first section of the book he explores learning from a number of different perspectives such as philosophical and experiential. In the second part he provides a very clear overview of learning theories and then reflects on the implications of these.

Marton, F. and Booth, S. (1997) *Learning and Awareness.* Mahwah, NJ: Lawrence Erlbaum Associates.
This extremely scholarly text examines issues related to learning in great depth and draws upon philosophical ideas to help throw light on the key issues. Key themes include the consideration of what it takes to learn and the experience of learning.

3

CONSIDERING THEORIES FOR LEARNING

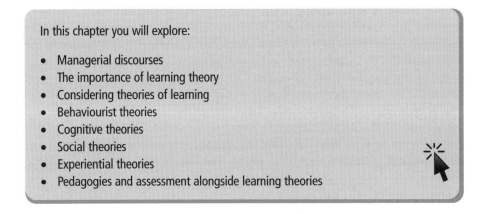

In this chapter you will explore:

- Managerial discourses
- The importance of learning theory
- Considering theories of learning
- Behaviourist theories
- Cognitive theories
- Social theories
- Experiential theories
- Pedagogies and assessment alongside learning theories

INTRODUCTION

In Chapter 1 we saw that the 'managerial' discourses that underpin the current educational policy may frame our thinking about learning in a way that can be unhelpful. At first sight it may seem tempting to import such notions into education. The point of manufacture is to produce goods, the point of schools is to produce learning, although given the manner in which schools are expected to demonstrate their effectiveness this may be problematic, and we will look more closely at the nature of 'school output' in Chapter 5.

However we would argue that the aims of education and industry are qualitatively different and to focus on end product rather than the activity misses the point and can lead to us to taking a very instrumental view of learning. For example, we find that student teachers will suggest we need learning that is 'efficient', which we would see as a very utilitarian perspective. Learning should be joyful, take the time it needs, be spontaneous, led by the learners' curiosity, and foreground the learner in whatever process is employed. There is also this idea that we tend to talk about learning in terms of 'work' (Langer, 1997). So we end up making statements such as 'get on with your work' rather than 'get on with your learning' or 'please start work now' rather than 'please start learning now'.

THE IMPORTANCE OF LEARNING THEORY

In Chapter 5 when we examine issues related to the classroom we will examine the relationship of theory and practice more closely. At this stage when considering theories about learning we have noticed that students tend to see theory as removed from practice, as something that is esoteric, complex, impenetrable and 'academic'. However, theory represents a succinct description or a way of representing something in terms of something else so as to render it less complex (Claxton, 1984, p. 2). Far from being irrelevant, theory has no meaning outside of practice (Popkewitz, 1984, p. 11). Practice is the site where theory is developed and therefore cannot exist in isolation.

A distinction between 'theorists' and 'practitioners' is unsound and unworkable – the 'theory–practice' dichotomy is untenable as such a distinction is epistemologically unstable. Educational theory in textbooks may be a more codified abstracted form of thinking about universal processes, but it is not different in kind from the understandings embedded in our own local decisions and actions (Brookfield, 1995). 'Formal theory' acts as a sounding board for the development and refinement of the more informal theories that we hold and crucially can be seen as a way of bringing critical analysis to bear on the latter (Usher, 1989). As I articulate my own 'lay' theories about learning I can test them against established theories and that process enables me to develop deeper understandings.

Example

A primary teacher has got into the habit of giving children 10 words to learn to spell overnight, and then decides to ask the children to copy down words in a story that they don't understand or know how to spell. The teacher then looks at cognitive theories of learning and is able to locate a rationale for their new practice within that.

Practices in school are shaped by local cultural factors, policy directives and notions of what teachers feel 'works'. That is not to say that we downgrade the possibilities offered by tacit understandings, but many issues related to pedagogy and assessment are not based on thinking about how children learn, partly because there tends to be little time in school for reflecting on such important matters (Pye, 1988).

CONSIDERING THEORIES OF LEARNING

A key element of learning at Masters-level is that students learn to engage criticality with issues in order to develop deeper understandings. When it comes to considering learning in human beings there are many different ways to consider and explain how learning happens (Jarvis, 2006) that in effect represent a range of 'babbling voices', none of which has privilege (Findlay, 2003). We are aware that this may not be of any comfort to you but an engagement with uncertainty and competing perspectives lies at the very heart of Masters learning!

We are about to give an overview of some learning theory and then, in what we would see as a 'masterly style', we have deconstructed each of the theories in order to make visible their strengths and inadequacies. Later, in order to demonstrate the integrated nature of theory and practice, we have explored what pedagogies and assessment underpinned by each theory would look like. This will enable you to see learning theory, pedagogy and assessment as key ideas that are inextricably linked and to be able to develop holistic understandings, as well as to see the critical process in action. As a result we would hope that far from being daunted by the 'babbling voices' you feel excited by the challenge of considering the complexity and consequently empowered to look critically at classrooms.

Introduction to learning theories

For many years there has been an interest in establishing just how we learn and many theories have been advanced, but there is still much more to be learned about the process (Jarvis, 2006).

At this stage a clear distinction must be made between theories that seek to explain how we learn and theories about how we teach. This may seem like an obvious separation, but over years of working with PGCE and Masters students we have found that students tend to conflate the two in a manner that is not always helpful to their learning. For example, it might be that theory X is seen as the definitive way to explain how we learn (as if we were even close to such a thing!). If that were true then that would mean that no matter the modes of teaching that teachers employ, the learner will learn in this way. Knowing that X is our best explanation of how learning happens might mean that this causes the teacher to teach in a manner that is congruent with that theory.

Often our practice is based more on ritualised aspects of teaching that we borrow from our experiences of schools – as learners, from the teachers we observe, and from the media. We often operate in the classroom in a relatively unthinking manner, but it is an essential process to 'take nothing for granted' and be free from supposition before critical work can begin (Carr and Kemmis, 1986). In Chapter 5 we will explore notions of how teachers construct their identities and consider their role in the classroom and how this influences their classroom practices.

Theories to explain how learning occurs can be classified in various ways. We have drawn upon a structure suggested by Jarvis et al. (2003): behaviourist, cognitive, social and experiential (see Table 3.1). We urge you not to see each of the theories that will be presented in the next section as discreet or alternative explanations. Rather, these are sets of principles that have different emphases about how learning happens and in many cases demonstrate high levels of congruency with other theories.

TABLE 3.1 Overview of theories of learning

Behaviourist	Cognitive	Social	Experiential
Behaviourism focuses only on the objectively observable aspects of learning. There is an assumption that a bond develops between the stimulus and the response.	Cognitive theories look beyond behaviour to explain brain-based learning.	Social learning theory focuses on the learning that occurs within a social context. It considers that people learn from one another, including such concepts as observational learning, imitation and modelling.	Experiential learning focuses on the learning process for the individual. Thus, one makes discoveries and experiments with knowledge first hand, instead of hearing or reading about others' experiences.

BEHAVIOURIST THEORIES

For an overview of behaviourist theories of learning, see Table 3.2.

TABLE 3.2 Overview of behaviourist theories of learning

Main characteristics
- Behaviourism focuses only on the objectively observable aspects of learning.
- There is an assumption that a bond develops between the stimulus and the response or between the desired action and the situation.
- Learning is viewed as something that can be readily seen and quantified.

Issues/dilemmas
- Pedagogies underpinned by behaviourist notions of how children learn are characterised by clearly defined structures.
- Learning can be seen as linear as the teacher can go through stages with the learners.
- Behaviourism at best marginalises the cognitive dimension and so does not seek to develop understanding.
- Behaviourism treats the learner as a blank slate and while experience might be an issue it does not seek to ascertain it.
- Behaviourist pedagogies may be seen as excessively centred on the teacher.

(Continued)

TABLE 3.2   *(Continued)*

- As the teacher tends to be in charge there may be a tendency for the learner to be positioned as passive.
- Learners are not required to develop critical and reflective skills.

Related pedagogies
- Direct instruction or objectivism. Carefully planned curriculum.
- Purpose of instruction is to help the learner interact with the world in a pre-determined way.
- Learners should be directed by instructors, who make the decisions about the content and sequence of the learning.
- Breaking down a subject area (usually seen as a finite body of knowledge) into assumed component parts, and then sequencing these parts into a hierarchy ranging from simple to more complex.
- Rewards are given for 'correct' responses.

Assessment
- Tests of recall.
- Focuses on observable behaviours.

Main characteristics

Behaviourism as a way to explain how learning happens was a theory developed by researchers such as Pavlov, Skinner and Watson, who carried out much of their work with animals. They developed the idea that in learning a bond develops between the stimulus and the response. So in Pavlov's well-known experiment he noticed that the dog salivated when it saw the food. He then rang a bell when the food appeared and then when he felt that the bond was established he rang the bell and brought no food and the dog still salivated. Thus he concluded that the dog had made an association between the bell and salivating. When seeking to explain how learning happens in humans there are a number of problems with such a theory, one of which is that it assumes that humans have no agency in their responses. However it might be argued that some of the strategies we use as teachers are in line with such thinking.

Examples

A teacher who insists on 'hands up' before children are allowed to speak and then only speaks to children who do have their hand up might be seen to be employing a strategy in line with a behaviourist theory of learning. When we ask children to take their coats off when they enter the classroom and then reward the children who do with a team point we are in effect hoping that the reward will strengthen the link between the desired behaviour and the particular situation.

Issues and dilemmas with behaviourism

Behaviourism assumes that a strong link develops between the learner and the object of learning and thus has simplicity that is appealing. In thinking about learning in humans however it has largely been superseded, not least because behaviourism was developed in the early days of psychology and much of the field work was carried out in laboratory conditions on animals.

Much of the criticism of behaviourism centres on its inability to accommodate reflective and affective dimensions of learning. Maslin concludes that: 'behaviourism maintains that statements about the mind and mental states turn out, after analysis, to be statements that describe a person's actual and potential public behaviour' (2001, p. 106). This highlights a weakness with behaviourism which is that it denies the possibility that one might have private thoughts but choose not to disclose them (Jarvis, 2006). A related limitation of behaviourist theories is that they assume there will be a strong correlation between learning and behaviour and therefore they tend to marginalise the possibility that a person might learn something but then might choose not to adapt their behaviour. Behaviourism also seems to marginalise the possibility that mastery of an activity might hold deep-seated intrinsic appeal or that it engenders a love of learning (Winch, 1998), although it might be argued that primary school children can develop a deep love of team points and that Pavlov's dog 'loved' the food put out for him.

Pedagogies related to behaviourism

Pedagogies that are congruent with behaviourism are characterised by this notion of repetition or drills. A classic example might be the way that children were taught multiplication tables in the past. In this the key idea would be that the learner knows that seven sixes make 42 through some kind of association rather than understanding that multiplication is a form of multiple addition and therefore seven lots of six total 42.

So, within a pedagogy based on behaviourism, direct instruction would be a central feature, as would the possibility of having a carefully planned and essentially convergent curriculum. In essence, the purpose of instruction is to help the learner interact with the world in a manner that is not only pre-determined by the teacher, but has pre-determined outcomes as well. Another characteristic is that because the subject area is usually seen as a finite body of knowledge, there is an assumption that it can be broken down into its component parts, and then the parts can be sequenced into a hierarchy ranging from simple to more complex.

Assessment practices related to behaviourism

Because behaviourism assumes that learning is about the learner developing a bond with whatever is to be learned, assessment may be seen as relatively straightforward. The assessment can consist of presenting a situation where what has been learned has to be demonstrated.

Example

In an examination the learner sees a question about ox bow lakes and is able to recall the details and even draw on a carefully rehearsed sketch to illustrate their answer. A possible limitation of such an approach is that it might encourage shallow approaches to learning based solely on recall, which is just one kind of learning, and may not invite the learner to engage with the content in a manner that might promote deeper understanding.

It can be argued that much of our examination systems are based on this principle. Given the current concern with measuring learning outcomes within the current policy landscape, behaviourism has an enduring appeal (Jarvis, 2006).

COGNITIVE THEORIES

For an overview of cognitive theories learning, see Table 3.3.

TABLE 3.3   Overview of cognitive theories of learning

Main characteristics

Piaget
- Learning is related to human development.
- Children learn through being active.
- The child needs to discover for itself.
- The teacher provides the 'artefacts' that the learner requires.
- Cognitive growth has a biological, age-related, developmental basis.
- Piaget assumed steady incremental development whereas Bruner saw it more in terms of fits and starts.

Vygoksky
- Children learn through being active.
- Learning is socially mediated.
- Emphasis is placed on the teacher to act as a 'scaffolder'.
- Development is fostered by collaboration and is not strictly age-related.
- Learning is an internalisation of social experience.

(Continued)

TABLE 3.3   *(Continued)*

Other characteristics of cognitive theories
- The learner actively 'constructs' knowledge.
- At higher levels one has the ability to theorise about one's own theories and processes (meta-cognition).
- Adults think in dialectical operation terms *(Dialectic – of, pertaining to, or of the nature of logical argument)*. This demands the ability to tolerate and even welcome contradiction.
- People deal with past experiences and construct new experiences based upon their past experiences, both conscious and unconscious (implicit learning).
- There is an explicit acknowledgement of the affective domain.
- Learning relies on the relationship between one's inner voice, meanings and articulated speech.
- Meaning is seen as an interpretation of experience.

Issues/dilemmas
- Piaget assumed that the closer the content matched the stage of development the better.
- Piaget's theory may be seen as reductionist as it is too concerned with mental processes and relation to age rather than their relationship to the wider world.
- Is human development more related to the learner's experience?
- With cognitive theories there is a danger that we focus on 'understanding' as articulated and ignore tacit and intuitive forms of knowing and competence.
- Piaget felt that learning was highly age-related and that there was less consideration of outside influences.
- It may be argued that cognitive theory concentrates on the individual too much and not enough on the process and influences involved.
- Mezirow's definition of learning, as the process of using prior interpretation to construct a new or revised interpretation of the meaning of one's experience as a guide for future actions may be seen to convey an assumption that learning is not a single process but a complex set of processes (Jarvis et al., 2003).
- A criticism of cognitive theories may be that they marginalise the importance of a love of learning (Winch, 1998).

Related pedagogies
- Cognitive theories seek to develop understanding.
- They seek to match task to learner capability.
- They draw upon learning mentors and buddies.
- 'Scaffolding' learning is a key strategy.
- Teacher interaction with children individually or in small groups is important.

Assessment
- Teacher seeks to establish what the learner knows.
- Understanding is important in assessment.
- Cognitive theories are characterised by essentially divergent approaches.

Main characteristics of cognitive theories

Cognitive theories have been seen as highly influential as they can be seen to combine the romantic elements of Rousseau and the more explicitly scientific theories of Chomsky. In addition they can be seen as explanation of both how we learn and how we think (Winch, 1998). Cognitive theories of learning are extremely heterogeneous. Piaget's work may be seen as significant as he developed the notion that the learner 'constructs' knowledge about the world. Its main insight is that learning cannot be 'given' but that the learner needs to actively engage with what is to be learned in order to construct knowledge and, in effect, 'discovers' things for themselves.

Piaget saw cognitive growth as a biological, age-related, developmental process and he assumed that there was a generally steady incremental nature to it, whereas Bruner saw it more in terms of progressing in fits and starts. The key concept here is that it is the child who makes sense of their environment and the inputs they receive, by constructing links with their prior knowledge. It is assumed that the construction of links is an active intellectual process involving the generation, checking and restructuring of ideas in the light of those already held. Construction of meaning is a continuous process and this view of learning is often referred to as 'constructivist' (Bennett and Dunne, 1994).

Issues and dilemmas with cognitive theories

Piaget saw the child as a lone scientist whom, he concluded, actively hypothesises about the world and then constructs meaning. He also set great store by biological age and it is important not to confuse biological processes of development and cognitive ones. However his work was based exclusively on young children, which may be seen as a limitation. If cognitive development is a natural process then it might be argued that the relationship between the learner and their life world would be insignificant (Jarvis, 2006), and this seems a difficult position to sustain. In building on Piaget's work, Vygotsky suggested that language was key to learning and also felt that the key was for the learner to work with a more knowledgeable other, therefore suggesting that in effect learning was related to age but not dependent on it.

Whilst we see constructivism as a powerful way to describe how learning happens, it is not without problems. For example, the idea that learning requires active engagement on the part of the learner ignores the possibility that not only do learners acquire knowledge by acting upon the world but they are also acted upon. There is also the notion of implicit learning as developed by researchers such as Seger (1994) and Reber (1993) which suggests that often we are aware of the world but in an almost subconscious manner. In other words, we process information but do so at the periphery of conscious thought.

Example

Clark and Squire (1998) reported that people can acquire a conditioned eye blink response even when unaware of the relationship between the conditioned stimulus (CS) and the unconditioned stimulus (US). In their procedure, one CS, a tone, predicted a puff of air to the eye while another, a white noise, did not. Participants watched a silent movie while the conditioning trials were presented. It was found that there was a relative increase in the likelihood of making a preparatory eye blink response to the tone compared to the white noise even though the practice trials were randomised and the participants were not told the purpose of the experiment.

Pedagogies related to cognitive theories

Cognitive theories focus on how the learner builds knowledge or seeks to make sense of their world by 'constructing' meaning. In a pedagogy that matches cognitive theories, the teacher seeks to match learning tasks to the learner's capability. A key strategy associated with cognitive theories is the notion of 'scaffolding' the learner.

The concept of scaffolding in teaching serves a similar purpose to the scaffolding constructed around a building to make it safe and accessible. When the job has been done, the scaffolding is removed and the new or reconstructed building stands in its own right. The idea of a scaffold is that teachers adopt such an approach to teach a specific aspect where they construct a 'scaffold' around the area so that learners have direct access to the chosen focus, with minimal interference from outside allowed to get in the way. To be of benefit, scaffolding must be temporary. When the learner shows signs of handling the task in question, the 'scaffolding' can then be removed gradually until it is no longer needed. In this way, 'handover' is achieved; without this part in the process, scaffolding would breed dependence and helplessness. The idea is that scaffolding enables learners to reach beyond their current competencies and explore new understandings and skills.

Example

When learning to ride a bike, a child often begins with stabilisers. After a while these might be removed. The child might need someone to stabilise the bike by holding the saddle intermittently. After a while the child learns to balance and peddle on their own.

~~~ **Reflection**

Think of situations in your life where your learning has been scaffolded.
Think of situations in school where you have scaffolded learning.

Within a cognitive theory of learning, teachers will draw upon learning mentors, buddies and open-ended tasks. In behaviourist pedagogies the teacher will tend to operate by giving the learners drills to do, whereas in cognitive ones the teacher will seek to interact with children individually or in small groups. Cognitive theory requires teachers to encourage learners to be inventive and to have some control over task design. Where possible learners need to raise their own questions and test their own theories.

Disequilibrium facilitates learning. 'Errors' need to be perceived as a result of learners' misconceptions and therefore not minimised or avoided. Challenging open-ended investigations in meaningful contexts, or, as Perkins (1992) refers to it, the potential to work beyond the guidelines, is important. Learners need to allow time for reflection in order to help them make meaning, and central to the process is that dialogue is seen to engender further thinking.

In this way classrooms need to be seen as 'communities of discourse' where learners are responsible for defending, proving, justifying and communicating their ideas and where learning is about developing cognitive structures. As learners struggle to make meaning, progressive shifts in perspectives are therefore constructed (Twomey-Fosnot, 1996). In this way we can see that learning is very much a trajectory or work in progress.

Assessment practices related to cognitive theories of learning

In assessment that is linked with cognitive theories of learning, the teacher seeks to establish what the learner knows and then uses this information to match their teaching accordingly. Because the learner is said to be constructing knowledge, the assessment seeks to establish 'what' the learner understands rather than 'whether' they know (Torrance and Pryor, 1998).

Attending to what children and young people say and do will provide you with rich insight into their construing and this will be an invaluable source of assessment information. Individual constructivism is a form of cognitivism in the sense that it regards the outer (acts, behaviours) as being in need of explanation and the inner (mental acts) as explanatory (Marton and Booth, 1997). Within a constructivist model the individual's idiosyncratic sense-making is seen as key. Therefore, assessment needs to be divergent and seek to establish what children know or are making of a situation.

Example

Undergraduates were asked to explain why it is hotter in the summer and colder in the winter. Many of them said that it was because the earth is closer to the sun at that time of year. The correct explanation has to do with the angle of the sun's rays as they slice through the earth's atmosphere. However, this sort of misunderstanding is very useful to the teacher as it provides them with an appreciation of the learners' construing and the outer acts. In this case the idea that the sun is closer to the earth in the winter is an external act that helps explain the inner understanding or construction.

Table 3.4 illustrates some questions that establish 'whether' or 'what' the learner knows.

TABLE 3.4 An example of a misunderstanding

Questions that seek to establish 'whether' the learner knows	Questions that seek to establish 'what' the learner knows
Teacher: Who can tell me the difference between a reptile and a mammal?	**Teacher**: What can you tell me about reptiles?
John: Is it that a reptile … has scales and a mammal has fur?	**John**: Well, they have scales they eat other animals to get energy and they like to lie in the sun.
Teacher: Mmm no that is not right. Anyone any ideas?	
Margaret: Is it that mammals reproduce by having their young alive and reptiles lay eggs?	
Teacher: Yes, well done, Margaret!	

SOCIAL LEARNING

For an overview of social learning theory, see Table 3.5.

TABLE 3.5   Overview of social learning theory

Key points
- Historically the study of learning has been located within psychological paradigms, however learning also has a social dimension.
- Learning at school has many social dimensions, e.g. teacher–pupil, pupil–pupil.
- Learning may have a social purpose, e.g. to learn to write allows the child to be able to text which connects them to their friends.
- Learning is socially constructed through interaction with others.
- When people talk they construct their world.
- Learning allows participation in a social milieu.
- Knowledge is contingent on circumstances?
- Learning centres on the meaning and significance of the process itself rather than the accumulation of knowledge for externally imposed reasons.
- Evidence of the mind can only be manifested socially.
- Learning can only be social because mind and self are constructed through the social process of habit and response.

Issues/dilemmas
- May be seen as active if learner is seen as an active agent assimilating information and then translating it to others.
- Sees learner as agent of social action and interaction.
- Can position people as passive receivers of predominant cultural practices.
- If learners act within a social context and are reinforced or not then this may be seen as behaviourist?

Related pedagogies
- Characterised by use of local contextual features.
- Teacher employs open-ended tasks.
- The class is seen as a group by the teacher and strategies to enable group cohesion are employed explicitly.
- Problem-solving activities where the process is a key assessment construct are used.
- The power of the group is actively harnessed to help individuals as well as to develop collective foci.

Assessment
- Collaborative tasks.
- Collaborative problem solving.
- Discussions.
- Seminar-type discussions.
- Learners must adopt different roles.

Characteristics of social theories of learning

Social learning theory focuses on the learning that occurs within a social context. It considers that people learn from one another, and includes such concepts as observational learning, imitation and modelling. Among others, Bandura (1969) is considered the leading proponent of this theory. Initially learning was considered to be essentially a process of individual internalisation or accommodation, and was considered from a predominantly psychological perspective.

However, with the development of Vygotsky's work in which language was seen to play a major part in learning, the social dimension has been increasingly recognised. At the heart of the social dimension of learning are the interactions between teachers and learners as well as between learners with other learners. Therefore it may be seen that social factors can inhibit or promote learning. There is also a sense that historical, social and cultural factors will inevitably determine the nature of learning, so in this way the social aspect may be seen as being central to effective learning.

It is worth drawing a distinction between learning to be social and learning socially, which we find student teachers sometimes conflate. Of course cognition plays a role in learning. Over the last 30 years social learning theory has become increasingly cognitive in its interpretation of human learning. Awareness and expectations of future reinforcements or punishments can have a major effect on the behaviours that people exhibit. Social learning theory can be considered a bridge or a transition between behaviourist learning theories and cognitive learning theories.

In adult learning Lave and Wenger's (1991) work has been an important development. Their work looked to reinvent the notion of apprenticeship and also moved the focus of learning from the predominantly psychological to the social. Their work was based on learning as participation and they developed the idea of the newcomer to a setting being what they term a 'legitimate peripheral participant'.

Issues/dilemmas associated with social theories of learning

Over the years we have found that students often confuse 'learning' with 'behaviours'. For example, a pupil might leave a Physical Education programme at 16 knowing a great deal about the key ideas in health education. However, this might not necessarily affect their behaviours. This is in stark contrast to a behaviourist perspective which would be to say that learning has to be represented by a permanent change in behaviour. In contrast, social learning theorists say that because people can learn through observation alone, their learning may not necessarily be shown in their performance. Learning may or may not result in a change in behaviour.

There can be confusion between personal constructivism and social constructivism. Individual constructivism is a form of cognition in the sense that it regards the outer (acts, behaviours) as being in need of explanation, and the inner (mental acts) as explanatory, whereas in social constructivism the inner mental acts are in need of explanation and the outer acts serve as explanations (Marton and Booth, 1997).

In Table 3.6 we have summarised an example. In individual constructivism we listen to a child describe how the sun 'goes out' at night and we can infer that their 'inner' understanding is of the sun as being a light bulb and capable of being switched off, and as they can no longer see the sun they assume it has 'gone out'. So, in this way we can explain the outer act, the description of the sun 'going out', by inferring the inner construction or understanding. In social constructivism the reverse is the case. The teacher seeks to explain the inner acts of constructions regarding the cause of the Second World War and asks the children to work together to produce a poster. In this way the outer, the poster, serves to explain the inner acts.

TABLE 3.6   Comparing Individual and social constructivism

Type of constructivism	Explanation	Example
Individual constructivism	Outer acts are in need of explanation. Inner acts as explanatory.	Child thinks that the sun 'goes out' at night. They do not understand that the sun is a mass of burning gases that continues to burn even when not visible from the observer's position on the earth's surface.
Social constructivism	Inner acts are in need of explanation. Outer acts as explanatory.	Teacher seeks to explain children's understanding of the reasons for the start of the Second World War. Children are asked to work on a poster that presents reasons for the start of the Second World War.

Pedagogies related to social theories of learning

Teachers employing a pedagogy that is linked with social learning theory will typically see the class as a group. Strategies that seek to enable group cohesion will be employed explicitly. Student teachers often confuse 'learning socially' with 'learning to socialise' or with learning to get on in the classroom. Lessons will characteristically employ local contextual features.

> **Example**
>
> In a History class, the focus might start on the history of the local area to promote deeper understandings about the lives of the children's ancestors.

Typically teachers will employ open-ended tasks and problem-solving activities where the way in which the children engage with the process is a key assessment construct. Because the teacher sees the class as a group of a number of smaller groups and the learning is social in nature, the power of the group is actively harnessed to help individuals as well as develop the collective. There is also an argument that children will learn to collaborate best through having really authentic and engaging tasks which force them to collaborate. This notion of the situation shaping collaborative behaviours is exemplified by Brookfield (1995) who cites a story told by Myles Horton of a farmer who, in a field where he had black and white workers toiling in the sun, provides one bucket of water and one ladle, thus forcing the members of the gang to share the ladle or go thirsty!

Assessment related to social theories of learning

Any assessment of learning needs to acknowledge the assumption of social learning theory that the learner learns through interacting with others. In summative assessment this can cause problems with assessing group work, as, whatever the situation, the contributions made by individuals in groups will be different. In general assessment activities that are congruent with social learning would be collaborative tasks that require a problem to be solved. Ideally the task should require all in the group to make a contribution.

> **Example**
>
> In a primary setting, a group of about four children are given an imaginary budget and have to organise a stall at a school fair. The children have to buy the goods to go on the stall and then decide roles on the day, for example, setting up, serving, creating a tariff, cashing up, etc. Teachers can then make judgements about how the children are doing through observation and asking the children to reflect on the process. Adopting different roles and reflection are seen as key elements of social learning and therefore, as well as being central to the pedagogy, also allow the teacher to make judgements about what is being learned.

EXPERIENTIAL LEARNING

For an overview of the characteristics of experiential learning, see Table 3.7.

TABLE 3.7   Summary of characteristics of experiential learning

Key points
- Learning from experience has a long tradition.
- Experience is an existential phenomenon (*Existential – of, relating to, or dealing with existence. Based on experience; empirical*).
- Learning is seen as a holistic phenomenon.
- Experience may be primary, secondary or simulated.
- Experience is the foundation and the stimulus for learning.
- Learners actively construct their own experience.
- Learning is seen as 'transformative'.
- Incorporates non-reflective and reflective learning.
- Learning occurs when individuals are consciously aware of a situation and respond to what they experience and then seek to reproduce or transform it.

Issues/dilemmas
- 'Experience' is subjective and we are continually re-authorising our past.
- Awareness of the external world is not constant.
- Disclosure of experience will vary according to context.
- We don't always learn from experience – cost–benefit analysis.
- How can we learn about events that we can have no experience of?
- Important to distinguish 'biography' which includes life-long experiences from past experiences. Biography includes the hidden and unconscious while past experience conveys the impression only of those experiences of which we are conscious.
- If all learning is experiential does this mean that the term is superfluous?

Related pedagogies
- Teacher encourages reviewing and reflection.
- Field trips, laboratory work, practical learning at the centre.
- Learning journals and reflective logs are often a feature.
- Learners are encouraged to re-interpret the past, e.g. 'What if ...'.
- Characterised by open-ended tasks.

Assessment
- Learning journals.
- Reflective logs.
- Biographical.

Main characteristics of experiential learning

Experiential learning tends to be seen in two contrasting ways (Brookfield, 1983). It can be seen as learning undertaken by students who are given the opportunity to acquire knowledge, skills and feelings in a relevant setting. This 'experiential' learning is seen as learning through direct interaction with the phenomenon that is to be studied.

> **Example**
>
> Children going to a beach in order to develop understandings of beach profiles and issues related to tidal action and longshore drift.

The second type of experiential learning might be seen as education that comes as participation in life (Houle, 1980).

> **Example**
>
> Through knowing what it is like to be loved, we learn that this is a pleasant state of being, and so this second dimension of experiential learning takes a more existential turn.

It might be argued that all learning is experiential, in which case the term would in effect be superfluous. However there is a substantial body of theory that has grown over the years that would suggest that experiential learning has specific connotations which we will explore in this section.

There is considerable support for the notion that learning is a process rather than an outcome (Claxton, 1984; Kolb, 1984) and in no other theory is this more evident. Experiential learning is inevitably associated with high levels of subjectivity because its grounding is that the learner interprets or makes sense of their experience in some way. Miller and Boud (1996) propose that the key elements of experiential learning are that experience is the foundation and also the stimulus for learning. Experiential learning is founded on the notion that learners will make sense of their experience, so there are strong links with constructivism. It is worth considering the distinction between biography, which includes the hidden and unconscious, while past experience conveys the impression only of experiences of which we are conscious (Jarvis et al., 2003).

Within an experiential paradigm, learning is seen as holistic. We are part of what we learn (Claxton, 1984) and in this way learning is seen not as the result of development, but as development (Twomey-Fosnot, 1996). Within an experiential paradigm, we may see that learning will be influenced by the socio-economic context within which it occurs. In other words, if learning is to be related to experiencing the environment then the predominant cultures and practices that exist in that social milieu will inevitability have a profound effect on the learning experience.

Issues and dilemmas in experiential learning

It might be argued that, in a sense, all learning is experiential (Jarvis et al., 2003) and there have been times when this view has attained a strong following. However, there are possible problems and limitations.

Example

If we start with the premise that all learning is experiential then it might be argued that anyone born after 1918 would not be able to learn about the First World War, which is clearly not a sustainable argument. However this may be addressed by considering experiential learning as emerging from primary, and or secondary experiences. In this First World War example, a primary experience would be that of a veteran who had been there, while secondary experiences might be available through reading accounts of people who had been there, visiting the battlefields and looking at news reels.

Kolb's work on experiential learning is a major study. In this the process of learning 'experientially' is said to follow the stages shown in Table 3.8. The learner undergoes a 'concrete experience' that they then reflect upon and as a result of that reflective process the learner then theorises about what they have learnt from the experience, which leads them to actively experiment. This then informs a new concrete experience, and so the cycle is said to continue.

TABLE 3.8 Summary of Kolb's phases of experiential learning

Stages in Kolb's model of experiential learning	Definition of stage
Concrete experience	Learner undergoes an experience.
Reflective observations	The learner then reflects on the experience.
Abstract conceptualisation	Having reflected on the experience, the learner then theorises about what they have learnt from the experience.
Active experimentation	The learner then uses their reflections as a basis for informing future 'trial and error' type engagement.

A possible weakness of Kolb's cycle might be the whole notion of a 'concrete' experience. It assumes that learning will be generally explicit or that the learner is well aware of what is happening, whereas we know it is quite possible to learn implicitly. Kolb also assumes that we necessarily learn from our experiences!

Pedagogies consistent with experiential learning

A key feature of pedagogies that match experiential theories of learning is that the learner has to be committed. They cannot learn in a passive manner (Illeris, 2007) or in a manner referred to by Freire (1970) as 'banking' – an approach by which learning is seen as passive and as the filling up of empty vessels.

A key element of pedagogies based on experiential learning is **reviewing**. The potential of this is that children can become more aware of themselves as learners and also develop a deeper appreciation of learning processes (Fisher, 1995).

A key strand within this is that the teacher must allow the children to take the lead. We have found that student teachers often end up reviewing an activity themselves with the children present. The danger here is that the student subconsciously regards the children as simply the audience, rather than treating it as a process where the children are reviewing the lesson themselves and their conceptions are actively sought by the teacher. Therefore it is vital that the student teacher does not dominate the verbal space in such activities.

In addition to reflection, the **emotional** or affective domain cannot be discounted. Experience will inevitably have an emotional dimension and it may be that until the learner has come to terms with or accommodated the emotional impact of the experience (Boud et al., 1985b), it is only then that they are able to develop new perspectives and move on. So within an experiential learning context it is especially important for the teacher to attend to the emotional state of the learners.

Assessment practices linked to experiential theories

If experience and reflecting on experience are the central notions in experiential learning, then assessment consistent with such theories would need to focus on helping the learner to become reflective. It would therefore need to take account of both the content of the learner's reflections as well as focusing on how effectively the learner reflects.

Example

Learning journals encourage learners to take the time and space to build reflection on their experiences through writing a journal. However if the contents of the journal are to be 'measured' through assessment, this may inhibit what learners write, whereas if the journal entries are seen by supervising professionals as a window into the learners' 'construing', then this can be a very powerful tool to stimulate dialogue.

We would view the key to assessment linked to experiential learning as an interest in 'what it is like for the learner'. This may be seen as a phenomenological approach, and so questions that you might employ when considering the entries in reflective writing must have a genuine enquiry at their heart.

Example

Think of questions such as 'Why do you think that made you feel so frustrated?' and 'What do you feel you learned from that?'

CONCLUSION

We have seen how theories about learning can be helpful to you. Once the student teacher is on the 'inside', they can form a kind of educational shorthand. For example, a teacher operating in a manner consistent with constructivist theories of learning, can convey quite complex meanings simply and easily.

These theories should not be seen as 'fixed' or complete in any way – with each there are dilemmas and inadequacies which the chapter has outlined. As learning is always about learning 'something' and does not occur in a vacuum, it is best to consider theories of learning alongside assessment and pedagogy as this sets learning within a context.

Recommended further reading

Fox, R. (2005) *Teaching and Learning: Lessons for Psychology*. Oxford: Blackwell.
This book is ideal for beginning teachers as it provides psychological insights into what happens in classrooms and then looks at different areas of research that have contributed to our understandings of teaching and learning. It tackles a range of topics such as assessment and gender and ethnicity.

Jarvis, P., Holford, J. and Griffin, C. (2003) *The Theory and Practice of Learning*. London: Routledge.
This book provides a comprehensive survey of a wide range of theoretical issues related to learning. It includes a comprehensive overview of learning theory, culture and learning, as well as problem-based and work-based learning.

Thomas, G. (2007) *Education and Theory: Strangers in Paradigms*. Maidenhead: Open University Press.
This is a very well written book that challenges the value of educational theory in a very reflective and often witty manner. The author provides a thorough and critical review of many theoretical positions. It provides an ideal counter perspective to many established texts.

THE STUDENT TEACHER AS RESEARCHER

In this chapter you will explore:

- Deep and shallow learning
- Critical thinking
- Why do research?
- Research as enquiry
- The value of reflection
- What is reflection?
- Questioning and reflection
- Types of reflection
- Reflection in and on action
- Reflexivity
- Classrooms as places of complexity

INTRODUCTION

Why should research be important to you as a PGCE student and as a teacher? In this chapter we will develop the notion that research is synonymous with deeper learning and critical engagement, and build upon some issues related to learning that were considered in Chapters 2 and 3. The false dualism of theory and practice (Pring, 2000) is explored, asking what we really mean by theory, by practice, and moving to a position where these two elements are seen to be inexplicably entwined.

You may or may not have undertaken a wide range of different forms of research as part of your undergraduate degree. Either way, research in and around classrooms is likely to be relatively new to you. This chapter will introduce you to why research is important to undertake, and how adopting an enquiry approach associated with reflection will enable you to develop a deeper understanding of your practice and issues about pupil learning. As your approaches to enquiry and critical reflection are honed, so your capacity to enhance teaching and learning will be strengthened, as will your ability to acknowledge your own predispositions and the possible constraints of a school's culture and/or wider policy.

This chapter supports you in developing an understanding of the complexities of learning. Complexity theory will be drawn upon as a means to support you in developing a rich understanding of the nature of learning, teaching and classrooms.

DEEP AND SHALLOW LEARNING

The nature of the learner's engagement with learning has long been of interest. Of course in a culture where the 'rewards' of education are often presented as high stakes to learners, there is a natural tendency for learners to adopt strategic approaches whereby they are more concerned with the qualification than being open to the opportunities offered through engagement with the ideas.

The notion of 'deep' and 'shallow' learning was developed by Marton and Saljo (1976). In learners adopting 'deep' approaches, the learner is not content with mastery of the surface features of content but instead seeks deeper meanings.

Example

A pupil reads a poem and looks beyond the surface features of rhyme and the appealing images that the poem invokes to seek to understand the metaphor used, as well as being keen to understand what the impulses for the poem were.

In deeper approaches the learner seeks to relate ideas to previous knowledge and will interrogate the logic of arguments. In shallow approaches the learner tends to be accepting and is happy to memorise facts and routines without seeking to probe any deeper. We would argue that the characteristics of deeper learning might describe a PGCE student learning at M-level!

Table 4.1 summarises the principal characteristics of deep and shallow approaches to learning.

TABLE 4.1   The characteristics of deep and shallow approaches to learning

Shallow approaches to learning	Deeper approaches to learning
• Intention simply to reproduce parts of the content • Accepting ideas and information passively • Concentrating only on assessment requirements • Not reflecting on purpose or strategies in learning • Memorising facts and procedures routinely • Failing to recognise guiding principles or patterns.	• Intention to understand material for oneself • Looks beyond surface features of content • Interacting vigorously and critically on content • Relating ideas to previous knowledge/experience • Using organising principles to integrate ideas • Relating evidence to conclusions • Examining the logic of the argument.

CRITICAL THINKING

In Chapter 2 we considered the notion of 'folk theories' or 'lay' theories. Often the personal theories that we hold can become entrenched or fossilised. If knowledge is always provisional, openness or being prepared to be tentative is an essential predisposition to ensure that our knowledge does not become fixed. The notion of being critical is an important cognitive tool which can address the danger of knowledge becoming fixed and synonymous with the easily accessible – your classroom observations, ideas discussed in your University-based seminars or prevailing literature.

> it becomes apparent that a primary task for any research activity is to emancipate teachers from their dependence on habit and tradition by providing them with the skills and resources that will enable them to reflect upon and examine critically the inadequacies of different conceptions of educational practice. (Carr and Kemmis, 1986, p. 123)

Of course Carr and Kemmis are referring to experienced teachers but we feel the point stands in that developing the capacity to be critical is an essential aspect of being a PGCE student, especially one engaged in Masters-level learning.

Differing however from Carr and Kemmis, and to an extent Brookfield, we see criticality as an attitude underpinned by curiosity – the desire to seek the truth or the motivation to understand at deeper levels. This makes it more than a 'skill set'. The place or appropriateness of criticality in student teachers is not unchallenged. McIntyre (1993) suggests that it is not appropriate for student teachers and that the best they can achieve is a kind of induction into a critical way of being. We encourage a more situated approach – being critical is in effect being interested in learning and in order to be critical we have to have something to be critical of. There is a tendency that student teachers often see being critical as being negative. This is not necessarily the case. Poulson and Wallace (2004) suggest the following as characteristics of being critical in an academic enquiry:

- Adopting an attitude of scepticism
- Habitually questioning the quality of your own and others' specific claims to knowledge
- Scrutinising claims to see how convincing they are
- Respecting others as people
- Being open-minded to other perspectives
- Being constructive by using your scepticism to find better ways or interpretations.

Wallace and Poulson (2004) also say that in their experience as teacher educators, they have found that many students are unsure of what is involved and are reluctant to speak out as they feel they should know. Scott (2000) proposes four dimensions to critical thinking – see Table 4.2.

TABLE 4.2 Dimensions of critical thinking (based on Scott, 2000)

Dimensions of critical thinking	Definitions
Indentifying and challenging assumptions	Those assumptions may be taken-for-granted notions about education, accepted ways of understanding educational matters or habitual patterns of behaviour.
Challenging the importance of context	Being aware of these contexts allows the reader or practitioner to transcend them. It allows the practitioner to develop alternative ways of understanding and alternative modes of practice.
Imagining and exploring alternatives	The thinking of the practitioner goes beyond the merely conventional or accepted way of thinking and behaving. Thinking about practice becomes rooted in the actual context of teaching and learning and it allows the practitioner to experiment within their own practice.
Developing reflective scepticism	This involves being sceptical to all claims of knowledge unless the claims for that knowledge have been evaluated. (Brookfield, 1987, pp. 7–9)

Over the years we have found that student teachers often separate the academic and teaching. So from time to time they will say things like 'my teaching is fine, it is the academic side I find hard'. In their mind there is some kind of separation between the 'doing' of teaching and the reading or they see them as existing in parallel dimensions. However, a central feature of Master's-level engagement will be your capacity to integrate literature as a means to inform practice. Pring (2000) refers to the theory–practice divide as a false dualism: 'Making this distinction is epistemologically and practically untenable. Like it or not, we are all theorists and all practitioners. Our practice is informed by our implicit and informal theories about the processes and relationships of teaching'.

Vignette

Consider ways in which you have developed your own understanding of your practice and how you have helped yourself to develop as a teacher.

Now read the following vignette about Sally.

Sally is a Primary PGCE student teacher undertaking a Key Stage 2 placement. She has just taught a Geography lesson to a Year 4 class where she used ideas that she had seen modelled in a PGCE session which focused on using children's own stories to develop pupils' connections to, and understanding of local weather conditions. Theories of socially constructed learning seemed to make good sense to Sally and she was also keen to include aspects of social and emotional learning that she had discussed in Professional Studies.

She planned for her pupils to write their own stories following group discussions and a common stimulus from a series of photographs of people experiencing extreme weather conditions including Monsoon rain, hurricane-force winds and hot desert sun. She had a writing frame prepared to support the pupils' story-writing.

Her lesson, however, did not go to plan. Sally's mentor asked her to reflect on the lesson. The discussion between Sally and her mentor identified that the lesson did not engage the pupils as expected and the pupils' thinking and resulting work was limited in depth. The mentor suggested that the planned objectives for learning were fine but that in the lesson she seemed muddled in terms of what she wanted the pupils to achieve – her instructions were much more about what tasks the pupils should be undertaking. Sally had noticed that the pupils' responses to the weather photographs had caused some hilarity about the difficulties which the people were facing. The pupils did not empathise well with the people in the photographs. The pupil discussions about extreme local weather produced some good stories, often about the last time it snowed heavily, however, Sally found it very hard to enable the pupils to say how they felt about the weather apart from how playing in the snow was fun and the resulting stories reflected this and the writing frame was not fully used. The mentor suggested that to unlock the pupils' feelings about weather there needed to be more support for this and perhaps different photographs of weather might help.

- What has Sally learnt?
- How did asking questions and reflecting on practice help in this situation?
- How did the use of theory help in developing the thinking about the lesson?

WHY DO RESEARCH?

What is the value of undertaking your own research into learning, teaching and issues related to schools and young people? David Hopkins notes that by asking this question, 'one is raising a whole series of issues around topics of professionalism, classroom practice, the social control of teachers and the usefulness of educational research' (Hopkins, 2002, p. 31). We have seen in Chapter 1 that to be a professional is to build your autonomy as a teacher. This is not to say you declare unilateral separation from the rest of your school but it does mean that you know:

- why you approach pupils' learning in particular ways
- how and why you apply particular policies
- how you develop your understanding of pedagogy by observing and reflecting on practice, and reading and talking to colleagues about these matters.

This position assumes that education research is educational in that it has an application as part of the findings of the work and that there is some relationship between the research and future policy and practice. However, it should be noted that there are many forms of research which do not have these.

It's easy, during the hustle and bustle of the school day, to focus purely on the operational business of teaching. Often experienced colleagues will know intuitively that for them, there is a right way to approach an aspect of teaching. Without unpacking the reasons for this action it is harder to critique it and to learn from it, whether you have 20 years or 20 days of teaching experience, but it is this 'unpacking' and development of your understanding that all PGCE students are asked to undertake in order to develop their professional and pedagogical knowledge and to develop as a teacher.

It is often through post-lesson or post-seminar reflections that your thoughts are shared and *developed* through discussion of the reasons for the way an aspect of a lesson went or what a theory means to you. This suggests that pedagogical knowledge of practice is not a fixed commodity (such as say the name of a capital city or a mathematical equation) that may be transmitted to others in order that they too can possess this knowledge. This information–transmission form of knowledge presupposes it is objective and absolute (Brew, 2006) and that power lies with those who hold the knowledge. However the knowledge about your practice is constructed by you, your peers, tutors and mentors, as well as by published authors in the field. In other words, the epistemological landscape is flat (Wenger, 2008). Sense of this is made only in the context of, and enquiry into your own practice – it is 'situated'. As such, 'theoretical knowledge which is the traditional preserve of universities, has been subject to attack in favour of knowledge which can be of practical use' (Brew, 2006, pp. 22–3).

No practical activity is approached without some underpinning theory (Carr and Kemmis, 1986). This may relate to a published theory from a journal or it may be a personal theory, and, of course, the more you involve others (peers and/or published works) in the discussion about an issue the more interpretations of that issue will be suggested.

This is exemplified by Powell et al. (2004) through their systematic review of research into managing pupil behaviour in classrooms (see Table 4.3). A common occurrence is described as 'off task behaviour'. We can consider the reasons for this, and therefore the different appropriate actions, through a wide range of theoretical lenses:

TABLE 4.3   How off-task behaviour might be explained and addressed (from Powell et al., 2004)

Frequent behaviour	Theory	Explanation examples	Action
Off-task	Behavioural	Child is getting more attention by being off-task	Reward on-task behaviour
Off-task	Cognitive	Child thinks he is unable to do the task	Encourage child to reappraise task, identify what parts of the task he can do, etc.
Off-task	Affective	Child fears failure	Circle time to build self-esteem; offer increased adult or peer support
Off-task	Social/environmental	'He has a brother who is just the same'	Possibly nurture group or work with parents
Off-task	Biological	Perhaps the child has ADHD?	Refer for medical assessment
Off-task	Developmental	Child is not ready to work independently	Allocate learning support and set more suitable learning challenge

Although it is tempting to try and provide a 'one size fits all' theory to answer all your questions or to solve all your problems, it's clear from this example that an appropriate action for one pupil in one particular context is unlikely to work with another pupil in a different one.

Additionally, you will find that different teachers see the 'problem' and the 'solution' quite differently (this is further developed in Chapter 5). You might see this as frustrating, or acknowledge this as one reason why teaching is a profession and not merely a technical pursuit. You will hopefully see the complexity of these issues as something into which you can immerse yourself. Whatever your stance, this is one of the reasons why as teachers we should always be enquiring and reflecting about practice and related policy, and by doing this we develop our professional knowledge.

⌇ **Reflection**

Consider a situation where you have discussed an element of a lesson that you have taught or observed.

- What theories about learning or teaching were suggested?
- Did the discussion help you make some meaning of what happened in the lesson? If so, in what ways did it help?
- In what ways did this reflective process change your professional knowledge?

There is clearly room for many forms of research, however, the research you will undertake during your PGCE is most likely designed to enable you to understand pedagogy further and therefore to help improve your pupils' learning in the classroom, i.e. it is applied educational research undertaken by classroom practitioners with an outcome designed to enhance understanding *and* inform future practice.

There have been various debates about the nature and quality of education research over the years. Quite often the timescale between the undertaking and publication of research does not match the preferred pace of policy change. In some cases criticisms have been made that research does not relate to, and therefore help, practice at all. In the case of learning to teach at Masters-level, we will focus on the possibilities for your research to make visible the underlying principles that underpin practice, within the policy landscape.

Classroom-based research that digs deep into learning and teaching in a small but significant way has much to contribute to our understanding of these complex pedagogical processes. As we have seen in Chapter 1 the political landscape of teacher education and education more generally can be described by a series of nationally based policies. More recently policies have suggested ways that teachers in different phases and subjects should teach. Stronach et al. (2002) highlight the trade-off that teachers make in their professional practice between the 'ecologies of practice' and the 'economies of performance'. The economies of performance are indicated by a 'language of indicators' such as Ofsted inspection data, SATs and performance tables, or by nationally driven policies that are adopted in school. The ecologies of practice however, lie in what teachers take to be their 'personal/professional orientation' such as 'my preferred style of teaching; pupils' preferred style of learning; my approach to teaching'. It is in considering these issues that you can utilise small-scale research to its advantage. You are not trying to find answers that will give general insight into the world of education but by focusing on a small issue you will be able to understand issues related to learning and teaching more deeply and so adapt your practice and possibly influence policy in the future.

It is quite possible that your responses to Reflection 4.1 would not be considered as an account of research, but however small the matter into which you have enquired, you have used ideas or theories to scrutinise the issue (or vice versa) and ventured some tentative explanations. As such it is a piece of small-scale, albeit informal, research.

〰 **Reflection**

Consider times when you have used small-scale research (either formally or informally) in order to investigate a matter:

- What was the focus of your questioning?
- What provoked you to ask these questions?
- How did you find out about these matters?
- What were your findings?
- How did this change you or your practice?

Some academics would argue that small-scale, highly focused research is more appropriate to the complexity of the real world than the sweeping findings (e.g. the grand narrative cited by Lyotard, 1984) used by research with an extensive scope and which aims to provide general themes to be applied over a large scale. Small-scale research is most useful in this Postmodern approach.

It is likely that you are asked to reflect on your own learning as a teacher as well as consider the learning of your pupils. In order to do this you will be drawing on at least two important methods of research – observation and reflection. Hopkins (2002) suggests there are two key research methodologies that teachers may use to undertake classroom-based research. The first is associated with sociological and anthropological research (e.g. ethnography). The second is associated with action research. These are linked to research in the social sciences and include action research. This is a 'form of self-reflective enquiry undertaken by participants in social (including educational) situations in order to improve the rationality and justice of (a) their own social or educational practices, (b) their understanding of these practices, and (c) the situations in which the practices are carried out' (Kemmis, 1983 cited in Hopkins, 2002, p. 43). As such action research and other such methodologies have links to critical theory through their emancipatory potential or in other words to liberate the learner.

David Hopkins (2002, pp. 53–4) develops six criteria for classroom research by teachers. These are:

1. The research methods that are chosen should not impinge on the classroom teaching.
2. Data collection should not be too time demanding but teachers need to be clear about data collection techniques to be used.
3. The chosen methods must be reliable enough to allow teachers to formulate hypotheses.
4. The teacher must be committed to the research focus in order for it to be given sufficient priority to succeed.
5. The approach to the research must meet high ethical standards.
6. The research should be 'classroom exceeding' and relate to wider educational discussions and priorities in the school and beyond.

In later chapters you will explore a range of approaches that will enable you to meet the criteria regarding data collection, ethical considerations and setting the research question in a wider setting. The key aspect which will drive this research forward, however, is going to be your desire to find out about the focus of the research, and to help keep your focus we will consider the research process as an enquiry, just in the way that you might approach your pupils' learning.

RESEARCH AS ENQUIRY

We can approach research in a multitude of ways and you will read about some of them in Chapter 5. The wider we define research the more it is not seen as a hierarchical, elitist activity undertaken by university professors, but rather as something that we can all engage in at various scales and levels. Whatever form of research is decided upon they all have something in common – making meaning by learning through enquiry.

Some of you may be familiar with enquiry-based approaches to learning. Enquiry is not just about a way of teaching, or a framework for developing your pupils' thinking about issues. It can be a common approach to research whether you are planning a Year 3 lesson on mapping the different spaces used in the classroom or researching in relation to your teaching practice. The power of this approach brings teaching and research potentially together through a common approach to learning.

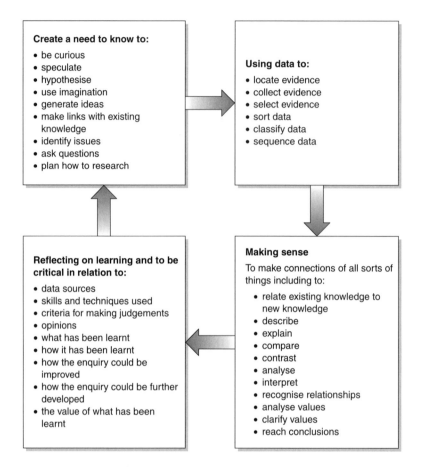

FIGURE 4.1 A framework for learning through enquiry (from Roberts, 2003, *Learning Through Enquiry: Making Sense of Geography in the Key Stage 3 Classroom*, Geographical Association. Reproduced with permission of the Geographical Association (www.geography.org.uk))

Approaches that use enquiry as a common approach to teaching and research illustrate the success of such ways of thinking in higher education (Healey, 2005). Asking questions about teaching and learning and reflecting on practice, policy and theory in the consideration of these questions all relate to good enquiry processes. Figure 4.1 illustrates the cyclical approach to classroom enquiry where reflection based on analysis of data from enquiry enables learning from this research to inform future thinking and practice. This model for approaches to classroom practice can also provide a framework for our research. As you can see from this approach, research is not an unfamiliar activity and perhaps forms the basis of what you expect your pupils to undertake regularly as enquiring learners.

This cyclical approach also forms the basis for action research which has itself formed the basis for a lot of small-scale research undertaken by teachers (see Chapter 7).

THE VALUE OF REFLECTION

'Throughout the 1990s the overwhelming majority of those leading teacher education programmes ... claimed that their courses were explicitly informed by a notion of reflection' (Furlong and Smith, 1996, p. 22). Stephen Rowland notes that the 'importance that reflection is currently held to play in learning relates to the Platonic idea that knowledge and understanding are to be gained by questioning and thinking in depth about what we know, rather than being presented with new facts' (Rowland, 2005, p. 93).

The need for questioning to uncover the truth or seek new meaning is a critical aspect of learning, particularly when, in the context of learning to teach, the answers are seldom easy to find and are often heavily situated in the context. Perhaps early on in your PGCE you, or your peers, may well have asked your tutor questions expecting responses that would universally guide you in your practice. It can be frustrating when responses are framed by a series of questions, but it is this way that reflection is stimulated and as we have seen in learning through enquiry, this reflection is integral to learning.

The model below illustrates a four-phase model of reflection showing how reflection is at the heart of the professional development process.

Phase 1: Develop awareness of the nature of current practice
What is your current work practice with reference to this subject matter or these skills? For example, how do you currently promote or educate for health?

Phase 2: Clarify the new learning and how it relates to current understanding
What is it that you have learned here/on this course that can improve your practice? For example, what have you learned that is useful to you for the promotion of health?

Phase 3: Integrate new learning and current practice
How does this new learning relate to what you knew and did before? For example, what are the general implications of the new knowledge/skills for your practice?

Phase 4: Anticipate or imagine the nature of improved practice
How will you act in such a way that your practice is improved (as a result of the learning)? For example, what will you do that represents improvement in your promotion of and education for health – what will you do differently?

(Schema to guide reflective activity in professional development towards improvement of professional practice from Moon, 1999, p. 180.)

WHAT IS REFLECTION?

'Reflective practice' is probably a well-known term to you and emanates from Donald Schön's work on reflection as a way to developing as a professional in the 1980s (Schön, 1983), however ideas of reflection in professional learning have been debated much earlier than this (e.g. Dewey, 1933; Habermas, 1971).

Reflection is a commonly used term and has an ambiguity of meaning. With relation to educational reflection three elements of reflection are suggested by Moon (1999). Firstly, reflection is associated with the learning process and the representation of that learning. Secondly, in relation to study, reflection needs to have an implied purpose to be significant. And thirdly, reflection about learning is about complexity and it involves complex cognitive processes that consider complex issues for which there is no obvious conclusion (Moon, 1999, p. 4).

Written reflection can serve a number of purposes, such as: facilitating learning from experience; developing critical thinking or the development of a questioning attitude; encouraging meta-cognition; increasing active involvement in and ownership of learning; and increasing ability in reflection and thinking and enhancing reflective practice (Moon, 1999).

We see the role of reflection in learning as a means by which your personal theories can be made visible and reconstructed. As we saw in Chapter 2, the process of reforming personal theories is viewed by Claxton (1984) as representing learning. We believe all practical activity is approached with some underpinning theory (Carr and Kemmis, 1986) and that the relationship between theory and practice is dialectical rather then merely applicative (Usher and Bryant, 1987). This is not to suggest that the knowledge developed through reflection replaces bodies of theoretical knowledge, but rather it is used as a guide to develop deeper insights into personal situated theories to support your practice.

The 'panoramic view from the high ground of education' (Schön, 1987, p. 3) is uncomplicated by detail, and although it is possible to solve more simple problems through research-based theory and technique, it is when the practitioner is in the more emotive 'swampy lowland [that] messy, confusing problems defy technical solution' (Schön, 1987, p. 3). This concurs with the complexity of practice faced by you with the multiple variables at play in your classrooms and is the area you are often asked to consider cognitively and emotionally through reflection.

Reflection in the 'swampy classroom' is not as Dewey suggested, a 'chain of linked ideas that aim at a conclusion' (Dewey, 1933 cited in Moon, 1999, p. 12) but is more a case of considering an issue without trying to come to fixed conclusions about it (Claxton, 1999). Your consideration of the issue will be influenced by the professional context you find yourself in and your personal theories which in turn are influenced by cognitive and affective responses to this learning situation.

The lack of conclusive outcomes within reflection is, at times, hard to contemplate when you might feel bound to come to hard conclusions in your work in order to prove your competence as a teacher and/or a researcher. This can cause anxiety in developing your reflective skills. It is, however, through questioning of practice, policy and theory and the problematising of issues, that reflection enables some sense to be made of the complexity of these links, their cognitive and affective situation within this, and thus where and how their identity and practice can be developed.

Morrison (1996) suggests that the term reflection includes action research, professional development, personal development and teacher empowerment, and this links well to the ideas explored in Chapter 1 and later in Chapter 5. Whichever form of reflection you wish to consider they all stem from the need to ask suitable questions about practice in order to consider and learn from these questions.

QUESTIONING AND REFLECTION

Questioning as a means to coming to a deeper understanding has a great heritage in approaching learning. The Socratic method, explained by Plato was based on 'posing only critical questions, rather than solutions and in this fashion leading the student towards a better understanding of the subject in question' (Rowland, 2005, p. 93). This 'better understanding' may be influenced by a variety of matters. In an enquiry-based approach to learning the teacher will pose questions to provoke the student to consider the matter in question at a deeper level without directing them to what they consider as the 'correct answer'. The openness of this reflective discussion will clearly depend on the power relationship between teacher and student and how they construe the development of knowledge.

So, in an open, enquiry-based approach the teacher will not provide answers to their student, which can appear frustrating when seen at a superficial level, however, the discussion which follows will develop the reflective powers and understanding of the student. As Angela Brew notes, 'the scholarship of teaching and learning requires a dialogic, constructivist view of practice as socially and historically constructed as reconstituted by human agency and social action' (2006, p. 114).

~~ **Reflection**

Review a recent lesson you taught:

- What went well/not so well in the lesson?
- Why was this so?
- Did you teach the lesson just as the plan indicated?
- If not, what did you change and why?
- What questions do you need to ask of yourself and your practice in order to consider these points?

In the light of this lesson, think about a relevant piece of school or government-level policy:

- What does this policy mean to you as a professional?
- How does it help or hinder your teaching?

There are many questions that may be asked in order to reflect on issues of practice. Table 4.4, adapted from Johns (1994), illustrates such a series of questions to develop practice through reflection. Using these guiding questions can enable the practitioner to identify an issue, describe it and consider aims, feelings and influences on the situation before considering how the issue could be improved, and to identify learning from this. The criticism of this model is that it tends to focus the learning in the situation, without consideration of how the reflection has been undertaken, how it could be developed, and the personal assumptions and beliefs that underpin the reflection (Moon, 1999). We will now consider differing levels of reflection and introduce the idea of reflexivity.

TABLE 4.4 Questions to develop practice through reflection (based on Johns, 1994)

Core question
What information do I need access to in order to learn through this experience?

1.0 Cue questions
Description of experience
1.1   Phenomenon: Describe the experience
1.2   Causal: What essential factors contributed to this experience?
1.3   Context: What are the significant background factors to this experience?

2.0 Reflection
2.1   What was I trying to achieve?
2.2   Why did I intervene as I did?
2.3   What were the consequences of my action for myself, the pupil(s) and colleagues?
2.4   How did I feel about the experience when it was happening?
2.5   How did the pupil(s) feel about it?
2.6   How do I know what the pupil(s) felt about it?

(Continued)

TABLE 4.4   *(Continued)*

3.0   Influencing factors
3.1   What internal factors influenced my decision making?
3.2   What external factors influenced my decision making?
3.3   What sources of knowledge did/should have influenced my decision making?

4.0   Could I have dealt better with the situation?
4.1   What other choices did I have?
4.2   What could be the consequences of these choices?

5.0   Learning
5.1   How do I feel about learning?
5.2   How have I made sense of this experience in the light of past experiences and future practice?
5.3   Has this experience changed my way of knowing these matters?

(Adaptation of Johns' model for structured reflection taken from Moon, 1999, p. 71)

TYPES OF REFLECTION

If the need for questioning is paramount in initiating reflection about our practice then the nature of the questions is going to be important in helping determine the resulting reflection. There are a range of ways of recognising the different levels of reflection related to the nature and scope of the reflection (see Table 4.5). This relates to the depth of reflection and also to its scope depending on whether it regards your own practice or considers wider matters that have the potential to empower or emancipate you (see Kreber and Cranton, 2000).

See Table 4.5 for levels of reflection and their focus.

TABLE 4.5   Types of reflection (adapted from Brew, 2006, *Research and Teaching – Beyond the Divide,* Palgrave Macmillan. Reproduced with permission of Palgrave Macmillan)

Level of reflection	Focus	Types of questions asked
Instrumental or technical	Orientation to understand the facts in order to control the situation. Learning occurs through solving problems related to specific tasks	How can I improve pupil behaviour? What is the best way to support my pupils' writing?
Communicative	Learning about and sharing others' ideas and perceptions, including negotiating meaning with them	How does my mentor's views of differentiation relate to my own – what can I learn from critiquing these?

(Continued)

TABLE 4.5 *(Continued)*

Level of reflection	Focus	Types of questions asked
Emancipatory	Intention to go beyond the existing situation through a process of critical reflection and reasoning. The goal is to overcome the limitations of self-knowledge and the social constraints on one's thought and actions	What does critical reflection theory mean to me and how does it support my classroom reflection? How can I interpret Every Child Matters to improve inclusion in my classroom?

Asking the most appropriate questions, in our experience, is not always an easy practice to learn and can cause a certain resistance as it can expose your perceived lack of knowledge to others. We see in Table 4.6 that knowledge should always be viewed as provisional (see Chapter 2) and not seen as a given fact, but negotiated depending on the context and situation within which you are operating.

Your situation is unique but by asking questions and helping you to delve deeper into the situation, your tutor and peers can help you to understand it in a richer way. To reach this deeper understanding the need to resist coming to easy conclusions can be a hard thing to master as a student teacher, however, the understanding of complexity that is gained from this is a feature of Masters-level engagement (critical reading and writing are explored in detail in Chapter 8).

It is not just the depth of your reflection that will affect your ability to consider theory, policy and practice in different lights but also the nature of the questions that are asked. Table 4.6 illustrates the orientations to reflective practice.

TABLE 4.6 Reflective orientations (adapted from Wellington and Austin, 1996)

Reflective orientation	Defining the orientation
Immediate	Emphasis upon pleasant survival. Tendency to focus on immediate demands of the task in hand, pedagogy often eclectic, but shallow.
Technical	Emphasis upon development and perfection of teaching methodology and deficient delivery of prescribed results. Typically emphasises behavioural techniques.
Deliberate	Emphasis upon discovery, assignment and assessment of personal meaning within an educational setting. Accept given ends but negotiate the process.
Dialectical	Emphasis upon political emancipation, questioning educational ends, content and means. Tendency to focus on political and social issues. Pedagogy involves continual questioning, revision and internal validation, stressing empowerment and personal responsibility.
Transpersonal	Emphasis upon inner self-development and relationship of internal to external self.

We understand that the immediacy of developing classroom practice will most probably be uppermost in your mind on the PGCE. Being a technically competent teacher is an important aspect of becoming a professional practitioner. In Chapter 1, we argued that being a professional is much more than this. Reflection that is dominated by technical or immediate orientations does not readily invite a consideration of the wider social, economic, political or environmental factors that influence the situation you find yourself in or are reading about. Consider the following reflection.

∿ Reflection

Review a series of your reflections in a learning journal (or similar document). Consider the nature of your reflections in relation to Wellington and Austin's 'Reflective Orientations' (Table 4.6).

- How have your reflections changed over the course of your PGCE?
- What is your dominant orientation? Does this differ depending on the issue upon which you are reflecting?
- If your reflections currently dominate immediate or technical orientations, what other approaches might you take in order to develop a wider range of reflection?
- Are there any barriers to this happening? Consider how they can be overcome.
- How can your reflections become part of your research data?

REFLECTION IN AND ON ACTION

Schön (1983) refers to two key types of reflection: that which is *'in action'* and that which is *'on action'*. Reflection in action occurs while still engaged with an activity and reflection on action is a retrospective activity. But as Moon (1999) points out there is some ambiguity in their relationship to each other. For example, is reflection that is overtly undertaken as part of a lesson planning process reflection in action or on action?

Bolton (2010) notes that 'Reflection in action is the hawk in your mind constantly circling, watching and advising on practice. Reflection upon action is considering events afterwards'. It is the latter with which we feel you – as a PGCE student engaging at M-level – should be primarily concerned. Overt reflection, conducted because of the need to reconsider an element of practice (a problem-solving or problematising approach) has direct links to forms of action research and other methodological approaches to research.

REFLEXIVITY

Reflexivity and reflection are strongly related. However, it is the acknowledgement of one's own predispositions that distinguishes reflexivity from reflection. The term 'reflexivity' comes from 'reflecteur' meaning to bend back on oneself. As Bolton notes, 'reflexivity' is considering: 'what are the mental, emotional and value structures which allowed me to lose attention and make that error?' She adds that reflexivity provides a deep questioning approach that can be missed (or avoided) 'if the practitioner merely undertakes reflection as practical problem-solving: what happened, why, what did I think and feel about it, how can I do it better next time?' (Bolton, 2010).

Being reflexive in learning to teach is to open oneself up to much deeper questioning with the potential to understand one's values and beliefs in relation to the situation. A reflexive approach will require you to avoid general assumptions that influence your practice as a teacher or researcher: 'The reflexive thinker has to stand back from belief and value systems, habitual ways of thinking and relating to others, structures of understanding themselves and their relationship to the world, and their assumptions about the way that the world impinges upon them' (Bolton, 2010). It is only then that we are able to see ourselves and the situation in a new, unfamiliar way, enabling us to question '*one*'s own actions, thoughts, feelings, values, identity, and their effect upon others, situations, and professional and social structures' (Bolton, 2010).

Vignette

Review the following vignette of a lesson noting examples of Tom's reflection in and on action. How could you provoke Tom to be reflexive about his teaching? What questions would you ask him to support this process?

Tom, a Secondary History PGCE student teacher planned a lesson on the Battle of Hastings for his Year 7 Humanities lesson. The lesson started with Tom dressed as King Harold in a hot-seat situation being quizzed by his pupils about why he had lost the Battle of Hastings. There were some good questions initially but he sensed these were drying up quickly. He decided to change plans and get the pupils into small groups to quickly devise some further questions. After re-grouping as a whole class the questions went very well.

Pupils followed the hot-seat by writing an account of the Battle of Hastings or drawing a storyboard explaining why the Battle was lost by Harold. Pupils opted to do either task, thus taking some responsibility for their own learning. Tom liked this but noticed that some were struggling with the written account and asked the Teaching Assistant to focus his attention on these pupils whilst he

(Continued)

(Continued)

challenged those drawing the storyboard to ensure they included explanations of why Harold lost the battle in their work. This went well although Tom forgot to ask pupils to critique each others' work. In order to complete the work Tom decided to abandon the plenary and to work up to the end of the lesson.

After assessing some of the pieces of work he found that some pupils had not been able to develop explanations into their work and they remained descriptive. He thought that perhaps he should have stopped the class and shared some good pupil practice. He noted perhaps it is better for pupils to understand a point of learning and for him to know this rather than complete a task.

Given the nature of this approach, the more scientifically trained student teacher may well be sceptical (or indeed a little frightened) of reflexivity. How on earth can such a process reveal certainty about an issue? Do I really need to be so introspective in order to know how to teach effectively?

Much of what is being discussed in this book is about taking a subjective approach to enquiry – we are aware of this and explicit in our discussions about it. Hunt and Samson note that the central tenet of reflexivity is 'a particular kind of 'engagement with an "other" whether another person or oneself as "other"'. Where reflection could be said to involve taking something into oneself – a topic, an event, a relationship – for the purpose of contemplation or examination, reflexivity involves putting something out in order that something new might come into being. It involves creating an internal space, distancing ourselves from ourselves, as it were, so that we are both 'inside' and 'outside' ourselves simultaneously and able to switch back and forth fluidly and playfully from one position to the other, giving ourselves up to the experience of 'self as other' whilst also retaining a grounding in our familiar sense of self (Hunt and Sampson, 2006, p. 4).

It is this notion of viewing ourselves from a distance and keeping a sense of the familiar context (but always questioning it) that enables reflexivity to avoid stumbling into anxiety and makes it a valid research tool when used in interpretative approaches where the researcher is an active participant of the research.

Examples

Examples of reflexivity can be found in certain ethnographic and action research methodologies which can include classroom-based research (see Chapter 7).

CLASSROOMS AS PLACES OF COMPLEXITY

From the first few lessons that you have taught onwards it is easy to be aware of the complex relationship between your intended learning for your pupils and the reality of the multiple outcomes from your lesson for all your pupils – this has been considered in Chapter 2; classrooms are highly complex places and this is where we suggest you site much of your research.

'Complex systems represent large amounts of information in terms of their organisational structure i.e. the relationships between the elements and therefore do not lend themselves to reductionist analysis' (Radford, 2006, p. 183). Instead of looking at classroom practice in an 'atomistic' way, a 'connectionist' perception 'draws attention to the importance of the interconnectedness of variables' and only makes sense in the context of connections between them (Radford, 2006, p. 178).

Radford challenges practitioner research as it can lead to simplistic assumptions based on a 'linear and causal relationship' between events or situations. He argues that the characteristics of complex systems are easily demonstrated by classroom or school dynamics and as such the use of complexity theory is a means to help understand classrooms. As Radford concludes:

> If schools are to be understood as sites of complexity then the certainties which the reductionist paradigm tries to offer, the expectations of teachers in terms of pupils' learning and control, and the role of research in delivering such certainties, are significantly undermined. Education becomes a much more open enterprise with the emphasis on a more flexible, tentative, imaginative and creative response to the multiple points at which alternative eventualities become possibilities. (Radford, 2006, p. 188)

The implications of this, not just for research but for large-scale, nationally driven policies to 'drive up' Standards, are considerable.

CONCLUSION

This chapter has argued that reflection is synonymous with learning. In order to reflect we must ask questions (either explicitly or implicitly) about issues. These issues are commonly related to improving practice but can be about wider and deeper matters related to the self as a professional, as well as social, economic, political and environmental matters related to theory, research, policy and practice. This involves a consideration of the self and one's beliefs and values, thus enabling the learner to consider their own influence on matters more deeply.

📖 *Recommended further reading*

Bolton, G. (2010) *Reflective Practice*, 3rd edn. London: Sage.
This text will enable you to consider the role of written reflection in your learning. As such it will help you to develop your research through journals and field notes and cement your understandings.

Hopkins, D. (2008) *A Teacher's Guide to Classroom Research*. Buckingham: Open University Press.
This is a concise and up-to-date text written by an acknowledged expert in the field. It takes the reader through the processes associated with classroom research with great clarity.

Moon, J. (1999) *Reflection in Learning and Professional Development*. London: Routledge Falmer.
This text explores different theories that consider reflection as an integral part of learning and professional development enabling you to consider it as a means to understanding practice and also as an emancipatory action.

PART 2

KEY METHODS AND WAYS OF DOING ENQUIRY

5

LOOKING AT CLASSROOMS

In this chapter you will explore:

- Student teachers' conceptions of classrooms
- Personal theories
- Asking 'obvious' questions
- Reflection
- Reflexivity
- Epistemology
- Observing teachers
- Constructing pupils
- Teacher knowledge
- Pedagogies

INTRODUCTION

Classrooms are very busy places with many interactions occurring between teachers, children and other adults in the classroom. In this chapter we will ask you to consider your own preconceptions and personal theories about classrooms and teaching in your own subject areas and/or age phase. It is highly likely that as a student teacher you will have well-defined constructions of classrooms and teaching (John, 1996). These notions or personal theories will have been developed as you moved through school and may well have been reinforced by the messages that you received from other sources such as the media and literature. There is a kind of self-selection process operating here, as the very fact you have embarked on a PGCE course probably means that working with children in school is appealing to you!

As we saw in Chapter 2 many of these personal theories may exist at an implicit level and so may not be readily visible to you, or even to the supervising professionals on a PGCE. In Chapter 2 we drew upon an element of Mezirow's notion of transformative learning, which he suggests is partly about developing the capacity to become aware of one's implicit theories – a disposition we would see as key to student teachers' learning at Masters-level and especially important when considering classrooms.

We have found that student teachers draw on these personal theories to help them make sense of what they see in school.

Examples

Some students may feel that quiet and order is very important in classrooms whereas others may like the organised chaos and babble that exists in other classrooms. Some students assume that classrooms will be organised with tables and chairs in lines facing the front while others may prefer the apparently more loose arrangement of children learning in groups.

Of course we should not assume that 'classrooms' will necessarily be indoor spaces as there are great possibilities for learning in all manner of field work and spaces outside the traditional classroom setting.

Other theories that student teachers will hold may be to do with the nature of children's 'work' and so, for example, when marking children's writing some students may be able to ignore the technical aspects of writing and focus on the meaning-making whereas others may find that they cannot let any technical slips go.

> Some of the knowledge teachers have, like the notion that classrooms are the appropriate place for education to go on in, has its roots in habit, ritual, precedent, custom, opinion or mere impressions. Its rationale must first be recovered from assumption before critical work can begin. (Carr and Kemmis, 1986, p. 41)

In Chapter 4 we introduced the idea of being able to develop a critical distance and an understanding of the preconceptions that you bring to classroom observations as a key quality which is especially important for students who are developing their thinking at Masters-level.

Therefore, when looking at classrooms we urge you to try and take nothing for granted and at the same time try and make explicit the values that you hold dear – a process known as reflexivity which has been introduced in Chapter 4 and will be examined more closely in the next section. When considering the practice that you observe, be prepared to ask the 'obvious' questions that can be hard to ask once you are more settled into the context, as they can then become 'taken for granted' and therefore almost invisible.

The following list gives examples of 'obvious' questions you might ask:

- Why do you set the classroom out as you do?
- Why did you deal with the content in that order?
- Why those learning activities?
- Why do you (or not) set homework?
- Why is homework set at that time in the lesson?

REFLECTION AND REFLEXIVITY

In the previous chapter we introduced the notion of reflexivity which is an awareness of the existing dispositions and attitudes that we bring to situations. Reflexivity takes various forms, such as personal and epistemological. For student teachers, we would see that personal and epistemological reflexivity are especially important.

Epistemology is a branch of philosophy that is concerned with theories of knowledge and is concerned with 'how' we know what we know and also 'what' can we know. One can argue that human experience is mediated historically, culturally and linguistically (Burr, 1995). Therefore, what we know is based on a specific reading of a situation related to our values. In essence, epistemological reflexivity is an understanding of the factors that contribute to our construction of 'our' knowledge.

The following statements demonstrate examples of epistemological preferences:

> I would make sure that all the children have mastered their 1–10 times tables by the end of Year 2.

> I would make sure that all the children have plenty of time to do music in Years 1–6 as I feel it is really important.

> Rugby has to be the major game in Years 7–11.

Personal reflexivity refers to the subjective likes and dislikes that student teachers bring to a PGCE. Below we have given some examples of personal positions that we have heard student teachers take.

- When I was at primary school we had spelling tests. I think they work.
- I went to a single-sex secondary school. I think single-sex education works better.
- I went to a grammar school – it was best for me.

The point we would stress here is that none of the positions outlined above are necessarily 'right' or 'wrong'. Indeed they are all perspectives that find support in sections of the profession. The key is that student teachers, especially those working at Masters-level, have a developing awareness of their own positions and are able to acknowledge how these might affect the way they interpret practice that they see or practise themselves. So, in effect, we see reflexivity as a kind of self-awareness that allows the student teacher to be able to stand back from themselves and even ask themselves the kind of 'obvious' questions quoted previously.

The following excerpt is based on a discussion between a tutor and a PE subject mentor after both had watched a Year 8 basketball lesson and before they spoke to the student teacher:

Tutor: What did you make of the first activity?

Mentor: Well I know that she [the student teacher] is very keen on this 'Games for Understanding approach' but I could not see what the children were getting from that activity. Then again I have had little success with games with that class and I had them all last year! I cannot get away from the warm up, skills and game thing. It seems so logical to me, then again that is all I have ever really known until I became a mentor. We had some very good discussions about this approach ... I am not convinced but I think I am beginning to see the point better now, might even try it in my own lessons one day.

〰 **Reflection**

What personal factors do you hold dear?

In the excerpt above, the mentor is demonstrating high levels of personal reflexivity and also openness to other perspectives, which we see as an important quality for teachers and student teachers to possess as it is a disposition that prevents personal theories becoming fossilised. The process by which personal theories are formed and then recast may be seen as the very essence of learning.

Vignette: Sally's story

'I went to a girl's grammar school and loved every aspect of it. I loved the single-sex aspect and I feel as I am very quiet I might have been overwhelmed in mixed classes. I loved PE, especially the Dance and Gym which I feel are a really

(Continued)

(Continued)

important part of the Secondary PE curriculum. I also loved doing the exam work. GCSE and A-level lessons were great. Since I did my second placement I have come to see that many children don't arrive at lessons with anything like the same frame of mind as me. I came into this thinking that mastery of the technical aspects of netball and understanding how training affects oxygen carrying capacity would be crucial. Now I realise that for many children this is the least appropriate focus, and what I needed to be able to do was to adapt the content in as flexible a manner as possible and be able to engage and motivate children in those activities.'

Reflection

What factors have shaped your knowledge of classrooms?

In the vignette above the student teacher is reflecting on the type of knowledge that she felt would be useful and appropriate and how that changed during her PGCE year which would be an example of epistemological reflexivity.

Questions that might help the student teacher develop an understanding of their own presuppositions are set out below.

- What did you find made for positive learning experiences when you were at school?
- What were the barriers to your learning when you were at school?
- What is it about becoming a teacher that appeals to you?
- What do you hope to get out of teaching?
- What would you expect to see in an effective classroom?

OBSERVING TEACHERS

A problem for learning to teach lies in what we would see as the limits of observation. If I wish to learn to rewire a plug I can observe someone following a procedure and then try and remember the steps and copy them. This is likely to be a useful process given that all plugs tend to be set up in much the same way and that there is no deeper moral purpose to rewiring a plug.

However, when learning to teach we would argue that observation is only a start, as understanding teaching means that we need to know not just what is being done but also why it is being done in that way (Green, 1998). In the following sections we will look at the factors that shape our conceptions of 'good' teaching and also consider issues related to the nature of teacher interactions with pupils.

Constructing teachers

Education is a considerably contested phenomenon and therefore teachers and student teachers are subject to many pressures that will shape them. The issue of teacher observation is complicated by the notion that we can be sure that, like musicians and sportspeople, much of what 'expert' teachers do operates at an intuitive level (Atkinson and Claxton, 2000). This has to be the case as each classroom presents the teacher with what psychologists might refer to as a 'display' that is so complicated that the teacher can only pay attention to a fraction of it at any time, and so the skill becomes giving attention to the aspects of the display that are the most significant, and that will inevitably end up being subjective.

The term 'subjective' can be seen as a negative one but in this sense we would suggest not, as there are many ways to be an effective teacher. Subjectivity provides a breadth of perspective that is potentially enriching, especially as each subjectivity will be underpinned by the values that the teacher holds. In addition, events in classrooms tend to be very dynamic and so not only does the teacher have to attend to the significant factors in the 'display', they also have to make many decisions very quickly.

So, in the same way a driver has to attend to the significant features in the display they see through their windscreen, we would argue that an effective teacher needs to be an expert in a classroom form of signal detection theory. The starting point for signal detection theory is that nearly all reasoning and decision making takes place in the presence of some uncertainty and in a teaching situation we would suggest that what teachers will attend to in the classroom 'display' will be highly subjective. However, we recognise that this is less than helpful to student teachers who need to be able to access the thinking that underpins what teachers do in the classroom and so we would see as important mentors who are able to make their own decision-making processes explicit.

It is worth you taking time to consider what kind of teacher you would like to be as the more explicit you can be about the beliefs and values you bring to classroom observations, the more likely you are to be able to make sense of what you are seeing and even more importantly be in a position to evaluate your own lessons.

In Table 5.1 we have summarised the perspective of three tutors working on ITE courses. As you can see, there are considerable variations, which we would see as some support for the notion that effective teaching is a considerably divergent field. In Chapter 3 we have looked at the limitations of viewing 'teaching' as the filling of empty vessels, and so rather we can look at it as an attempt to share with others what you find personally meaningful (Salmon, 1995), an approach that invites and even celebrates subjectivity and divergence.

TABLE 5.1 Summary of essential knowledge for teachers expressed by three tutors in HE

Three tutors were asked to respond to the question 'What do you see as essential knowledge for teachers?'

Tutor 1	Tutor 2	Tutor 3
• Understanding of how children learn. • Ability to employ pedagogies that are congruent with notions of how children learn. • Having a secure knowledge of subject. • Seeing themselves as responsible for mediating content for learners. • Able and willing to view the learner's world as far as possible. • Able to focus on content of learning and the learners' interaction with it at the same time. • Able to view teaching as a problem-solving activity rather than a performance.	• To know that your practice-the words you use-and your pedagogy are located within a particular political arena, in time and place. Ask yourself, how are teachers in other countries tackling the same content today and how might that differ from what I am doing? • To know that your subject has infinite possibilities for inspirational practice. • To know that your pupils need to know that you know them individually and that you care about them. • To know that learning is messy and chaotic and sometimes takes courage.	• Suitable understanding of relevant subject knowledge and how it can be developed through teaching and learning. • Understanding of the ways that children learn in social contexts and how this is affected by a range of factors. • Know how to adapt practice in order to enable children to engage with the curriculum to develop knowledge. • Have an understanding of how to conduct oneself and communicate with others in a professional manner. • Understand that knowledge is not a fixed commodity and that it is developed in enquiring social contexts.

It is worth considering how teachers may be viewed by children and wider society. It may be that they are seen as people who are 'knowledgeable' and 'finished'. However, we believe this to be problematic and we are drawn to Heidegger's position cited by Rogers and Freiberg (1994, p. 34): 'The teacher must be capable of being more teachable than his apprentices. The teacher is far less assured of his ground than those who learn are of theirs'.

This presents a particular perspective of the teacher who evolves continually through enquiry – as an extended professional who learns from teaching rather than someone who has simply qualified to teach.

〰 **Reflection**

How does your tutor/mentor present themselves to you?
How do the teachers you observe present themselves to their classes?
How would you like to present yourself to the children in your classes?

HOW TEACHERS CONSTRUCT PUPILS

In Chapter 2 we discussed notions of implicit theories and raised the possibility that at some level we often see learning as a process of filling 'empty vessels' rather than one where the learner interacts with the world and actively builds or constructs understandings. This is significant as a construct of how we often see learning, but it follows that this will also have implications for how we see learners. In Reggio Emilia, which is considered to be a beacon of good early years practice, children are constructed as powerful learners rather than mere 'receivers' of knowledge, and are actively encouraged to be active agents in their own learning.

We feel that classroom interactions are shaped by all manner of preconceptions that teachers and pupils hold, which are then reinforced through the interactions that occur in the classroom. Freire (1970) talks about the teacher as a narrator. This, he says, leads to students being required to memorise mechanically the content of the teacher narration and this positions them as empty vessels that exist to be filled by the narration. The result being that the better the teacher fills the vessels, the more effective they may be seen, and the more meekly the vessels allow themselves to be filled, the better students they are. This is a perspective that we see as an impoverished view of the learning process.

In this section where we are asking you to consider how teachers construct pupils, we would ask you to reflect on the issue of learning disabilities or special educational needs (SEN) which Gavine (1988) suggests are less than straightforward. In deciding that a child has a special educational need, the first step is to say that there is a 'need' and therefore there has to be a norm against which this need is compared.

For example, we are familiar with the notions of expectations of children's reading ages. That is to say, a policy might suggest that by a certain age children should be able to demonstrate a minimum level of proficiency in reading as measured by particular criteria in order to get to a normative state in reading. If a child cannot meet those criteria they may be seen to be deficient compared to that norm and therefore have a 'need'.

However there are questions to be asked about how the criteria are set in the first place. To what extent is the minimum level carefully calibrated or is it relatively arbitrary? Is it enough that we provide additional resources to support the child achieve the norm, or should we problematise the norm? If one is thirsty then drink will be required to return to the normative state of not being thirsty.

In relation to SEN, Gavine argues that if we go down a normative line, where, say, the average reading age for a generation of children is defined as x, then inevitably many will fall below that average – does that mean they have a special need, or are merely not as competent at reading at that given moment as others? Careful thought clearly needs to be given to where we set the thresholds and we also need to be careful to try and establish how those criteria have been formulated.

Gavine also makes the point that we need to distinguish between a 'need' and a 'lack'. For example, a person might feel that they 'lack' a mountain bike but it might be harder to say that they have a 'need' for one. Therefore any statement of 'need' contains implicit value judgements about what ought to be the state of affairs as well as what is actually the case.

There is a further issue in that it is clear that the mastery of certain competences is given privilege over others. For example, would we perceive children who find it hard to learn to draw in perspective, tell a C major chord from an E minor chord, or master a cartwheel, as having a special educational need? This notion of labelling children can lead to reification. 'Reification' refers to the concept that when we talk about something intangible the continual references can lead to the intangible becoming a 'thing' in its own right.

Stanovich and Stanovich (1996) suggest that an issue in SEN is that for the vast majority of children who are so labelled it is because of perceived failures in learning to read. This labelling has come into sharp focus again more recently although in a different form. As part of the Excellence in Cities programme, the Government decided to develop high achievers and developed their Gifted and Talented policy. A key idea underpinning this initiative was whether it was a process that sought to develop talented children, or one where the talent in children was to be developed.

We would hope that in considering these issues, you learn to see past the labels, and to see that children are not the sum of their labels. That is not to deny that some children will have learning difficulties, but we encourage you to try and see past that and not let them become defined by these definitions. There is also the point that it can be seen that a key issue is not the learning disability but the manner in which the child deals with it. Below are statements by two adults looking back at their time in school and reflecting on their dyslexia.

Vignette: Sophie's story

'All through primary school I had real problems with reading and writing. I now know that there were many tell-tale signs such as problems with directional language (which persists to this day), I found it hard to make any sense of rhyming words and found it hard to remember nouns. Like many children with dyslexia I just assumed I was stupid. In the first year at secondary school I was fortunate

(Continued)

(Continued)

to get a proper diagnosis and there was help available, but for some reason that makes no sense to me now I chose to reject it and got into a peer group that I can now see was not the best in terms of furthering my education. I can now see I decided to use the diagnosis as an excuse to myself and my teachers not to try and had a miserable time at school mainly due to my own attitude. Now, at the age of 36 I have gone back to Further Education and gained GCSEs and also A levels and now my children are at secondary school I intend to go into Higher Education.'

Vignette: Ben's story

'I am 42 now but can remember all too clearly the agony and the ecstasy of my dyslexia. In the first years at school I loved it and also hated it. The love was just being in school, and with my teachers both of whom I liked, but also the agony of gradually realising that it was all so hard. I seemed to have no idea about anything that required sequencing; I came to see I was so slow at writing and that when I read it felt as if I had not remembered a thing! In Year 3 my teacher spoke to my parents and I was diagnosed as dyslexic. From that day I felt so much better and the help I had made a big difference. I began to work out strategies to help myself and I am now a solicitor! Needless to say I found the whole process of study very hard work and managed it by managing myself and trying to be very creative about how I organised myself. I consider myself a world expert in colour-coded revision aids!'

WHAT KNOWLEDGE DO TEACHERS NEED?

Traditionally teachers have been seen as knowledgeable people, although the nature of this knowledge may be seen to reside in aspects related to cultural cachet and it is certain types of knowledge that define us as teachers. For example is a PE teacher more likely to be seen as someone who knows about the LBW rule and how to repay an oxygen debt or as someone who knows how to help children learn in a physical activity context? As teachers we tend to be defined by our content knowledge related to specific disciplines such as History or Science rather than our capacity to help people learn things.

In the previous section we have demonstrated that the epistemological landscape is culturally hegemonic. That is to say, certain forms of knowledge have privilege and this is essentially a cultural construction. It has been suggested that teachers need seven types of knowledge (Shulman, 1987) (see Table 5.2).

TABLE 5.2   Categories of teacher knowledge (based on Shulman, 1999)

Area of knowledge	Definition
Content knowledge	The specific knowledge related to the subject, e.g. knowledge of History, Mathematics or Science.
General pedagogical knowledge	Refers to broad principles and strategies of classroom management and organisation that transcend subject matter.
Curriculum knowledge	Knowledge of national and local imperatives. Familiarity with issues related to their subject Key Stage. Understanding of contested notions.
Pedagogical content knowledge	Refers to teaching strategies that are viewed as specific to helping children to master certain aspects of the curriculum.
Knowledge of learners	A well-developed understanding of how children learn. A secure understanding of established theories and also a capacity to reflect on practice and adapt practice in relation to classroom events with specific children.
Knowledge of educational contexts	Knowledge of specific groups of children, how schools are governed and financed, character of specific communities and cultures.
Knowledge of educational ends	Knowledge of the various purposes, ends and values of education. Capacity to reflect on and discuss such issues in an exploratory manner.

In the box below we have summarised the responses made by a group of mentors when asked to outline the knowledge that they value in student teachers.

PE mentors working with Graduate Registered Teachers in response to the question: 'What knowledge do you feel student teachers need to leave the course with?'

- Knowledge of outside organisations and clubs
- Knowledge of whole school policies
- Ability to link learning objectives with activities in lessons
- Diversity of pupil need
- Behaviour management
- Understand importance of lines of communication
- Differentiation
- Knowledge of assessment levels
- Able to apply assessment levels

(Continued)

(Continued)

- Subject knowledge in activity areas
- Professional duties – informing parents/carers and other professionals
- Able to be a positive role model
- Teaching styles
- Professional values – knowledge of the wider role of the teacher
- Understand the role of the school sport co-ordinators
- Knowledge of the new national curriculum
- Health and safety – risk assessments/off-site visits
- Knowledge of pupils
- Qualified to drive the minibus.

If we then map the responses by the mentors against Shulman's categories of teacher knowledge, we get the pattern as shown in Table 5.3.

TABLE 5.3   Mapping mentor responses onto Shulman's teacher knowledges

Area of knowledge	Mentor responses
Content knowledge	• Subject knowledge in activity areas
General pedagogical knowledge	• Behaviour management • Differentiation
Curriculum knowledge	• Knowledge of assessment levels • Able to apply assessment levels
Pedagogical content knowledge	• Ability to link learning objectives with activities in lessons • Teaching styles
Knowledge of learners	• Diversity of pupil need • Knowledge of pupils
Knowledge of educational contexts	• Knowledge of outside organisations and clubs • Knowledge of whole school policies • Understand importance of lines of communication
Knowledge of educational ends	• Knowledge of the new national curriculum • Health and safety – risk assessments/off site visits
Not covered by Shulman	• Qualified to drive the minibus • Understand the role of the school sport co-ordinators • Professional duties – informing parents/carers and other professionals • Able to be a positive role model • Professional values – knowledge of the wider role of the teacher.

> ⌇⌇ **Reflection**
>
> What knowledge do you feel the teachers you work with most value in you as
> a student teacher?
> What knowledge do you feel your tutors value most?
> What knowledge do you feel you need to develop? How might this change
> during the year?

WHAT PEDAGOGIES DO TEACHERS EMPLOY?

Pedagogy is a term that refers to the science of teaching, and the equivalent
term for teaching adults is andragogy. It may be argued that until more
recently, the notion of professional training was shunned and that in schools
considered to be the most prestigious, teachers were employed on the basis
of appropriate social origins rather than any academic or pedagogical excellence (Simon, 1988). Therefore it is important to examine the social assumptions underlying the organisation, distribution and evaluation of knowledge
in school (Bernstein, 1988).

Chapters 2 and 3 suggest that the relationship between teaching strategies
and learning is far from straightforward. They also suggest that we tend to
'borrow' strategies sometimes in a relatively unthinking manner. There can
be a tendency to see 'teaching' as a performance that can almost exist in its
own right rather than seeing it as being something that can only be considered in relation to any learning that it might enable.

We are reminded of the Masters student relating the tale of an appraisal
that he had with a senior teacher. At the end of the lesson the headline feedback was that 'his teaching was fine but that the children had not learned
very much'. In a way this is understandable as when you have 30 children
waiting to be taught you have to do something, but the problem can be that
what we tend to do under pressure is to fall back on strategies that we have
seen teachers employ without necessarily being sure what the rationale for
the strategies is, or because we don't have any alternative!

> ⌇⌇ **Reflection**
>
> What pedagogies can you remember as a child in school?
> What teaching strategies has your tutor employed in University sessions so far?
> What pedagogies have you observed in school?

Chapter 3 demonstrated the integrated nature of learning theory, pedagogy and assessment of learning. In considering pedagogy, it is worth drawing upon Fox (1983) who has identified four theories of teaching and then mapped onto that the implications for various elements such as subject matter and the role of the teacher and learner – see Table 5.4.

TABLE 5.4   Theories of teaching (based on Fox, 1983)

	Transfer theory of teaching	Shaping theory of teaching	Travelling theory of teaching	Growing theory of teaching
Verbs commonly used	Convey; impart; implant; give, expound; put over; tell; cover	Develop; mould, demonstrate; produce	Lead; point the way; guide; help; show; direct	Cultivate; encourage; nurture; develop; foster; enable; help; bring out
Subject matter	Commodity to be transferred to the learner	Shaping tools; pattern; blueprint	Terrain to be explored; vantage points	Experience to be incorporated into developing personality
The learner	Container to be filled	Inert material to be shaped	Explorer end point unclear	Developing personality, personal growth; empowered
The teacher	Pump attendant; technician	Skilled craftsperson working on raw material	Experienced and expert travelling companion	Resource provider; gardener
Standard teaching methods	Lectures; reading lists; duplicated notes	Laboratory workshop; practical instruction; exercises with predictable outcomes	Simulations; projects; discussion; exercises with unpredictable outcomes	Experiential methods similar to travelling theory but less structured and more spontaneous
Monitoring progress	Measuring and sampling contents of container	Checking size and shape of product	Comparing notes with travelling companions	Listening to reflections; personal development
Explanations of failure – teachers' view	Leaky vessel; small container	Flawed; faulty raw material	Blinkered vision; lack of stamina; unadventurous	Poor start; inadequately prepared; no will to develop
Explanation of failure – students' view	Poor transfer skills; poor aim	Incompetent craftsperson; poor blueprint	Poor guides; poor equipment; too many restrictions on route	Restricted diet; unsuitable food; incompetent gardener
Attitude to learning	Need simple skills of transfer	Need shaping to British Standard	Need skills of expert guide as well as knowledge of terrain	Need skills of diagnosing needs of individual plant

> 〰️ **Reflection**
>
> Observing teachers in the classroom, where can you locate them within the framework outlined above?

NATURE OF TEACHER INTERACTIONS WITH PUPILS

The place of talk in learning is well established. However it can be hard for teachers to create situations where they can talk to children in terms of their learning rather than in terms of aspects of classroom organisation.

Drawing on the work of Edwards, Mercer (1995) makes the point that we often tend to control talk and actually conspire unwittingly, in most cases, to inhibit learner talk. Mercer proposes the following profile of a child who might be deemed to be a competent class member:

- Listens to the teacher, often for long periods.
- When the teacher stops talking, bids properly for the right time to speak, sometimes when competition for the next term means balancing the risks of not being noticed or seen as too enthusiastic.
- Answers questions to which the answer will be judged to be more or less relevant, useful and correct by a teacher who is seeking not to know something but to know if you know something.
- Puts up with having anyone's answer treated as evidence of a common understanding, so the teacher will often explain something again when you understand it first time or rush on when you are still struggling with what was said before.
- Looks for clues as to what a right answer might be from the way a teacher leads into a question, and evaluates the responses – that last source of clues being often so prolific that even a wild guess may lead the teacher to answer the question for you.
- Asks questions about the administration of the lesson but not usually about its content (certainly never suggests the teacher is wrong).
- Accepts that what you know already about a topic of the lesson is unlikely to be asked for, or even to be accepted as relevant, unless and until it fits into the teacher's frame of reference.

We find that student teachers when reflecting on lessons they have taught, will often talk about children giving 'good' answers. By this they are usually articulating a belief that the questions they ask have 'right' or 'wrong' answers. Asking a child what they understand about a topic and the child responding 'nothing', if a genuine response, could be seen as a 'good' answer, as that allows the teacher to inform their next move. Otherwise the questions in a class may be seen as a form of quiz where 'correct' responses are rewarded, rather than rewarding honest and thoughtful responses and even nurturing children's curiosity by encouraging them to develop their own questions.

Teachers' questions are often used as a means to check understanding with the responses intended to demonstrate what is in the learner's head. However there is a higher purpose which is where the question is used to help the learner build knowledge (Socratic questioning is further expanded on in Chapter 4). In other words the process of considering a question can enable the learner to build knowledge.

Praise is often cited as a positive aspect of teachers' conversations with pupils. Indeed it is often cited as an essential tool in developing crucial characteristics of learners such as self-esteem. While this is something of a cherished belief, Dweck (1999) urges a cautionary note and suggests that far from promoting confidence, praise can also lead to students fearing failure and avoiding risks, or doubting themselves when they fail and coping poorly with setbacks.

Recognising effort is a positive assessment construct, although it should be remembered that this can be highly subjective. This is supported by Biddle and Goudas (Goudas et al., 1994) who concluded that learners like being praised for effort as it is the one thing that is under their control.

〰️ Reflection

What do you notice about the way(s) that teachers give praise?
What do they praise?
How do you feel about receiving praise as a learner?
What sort of praise do you best respond to?
What demands are made of children?

Chapter 2 considered the notion of learning having a general and specific dimension. We also introduced the idea and prevalence of 'empty vessel' conceptions of learning. Over years of observing student teachers' lessons, we have noticed that they tend to be overly concerned with the specific aspects of learning – that is to say the content, rather than looking to see how learners are engaging with content. We have noticed that often student teachers' lessons demand very little of children.

TABLE 5.5 Examples of the demands that learning activities make on learners

	Learning activity	Demands on pupils
	Student teacher shows pictures of sports stadia with very big crowds	
Scenario 1	Children are asked to describe what they see when called on by the teacher.	• Describing • Waiting to be called on by the teacher
Scenario 2	Children are asked to talk in pairs about how they think the performers might feel.	• Children discussing • Children asked to empathise with performers

In Table 5.5 there is a sequence of activities for a student employed with a Year 10 class learning about social facilitation in a GCSE Physical Education classroom lesson. If we think of these activities in terms of the demands made on the pupil, then it may be readily seen that in Scenario 1 there is little demanded of the children whereas in Scenario 2, all children are encouraged to engage with the task.

CONCLUSION

This chapter has introduced you to the complexities behind classroom interactions which can easily remain hidden to student teachers. It has shown how classroom interactions are never neutral and will convey meaning whether the teacher intends to or not, or whether the pupil is aware of it or not.

Recommended further reading

Marton, F. and Tsui, A. (2004) *Classroom Discourse and the Space of Learning*. London: Lawrence Erlbaum Associates.
A very scholarly and clearly written book that assumes language to be central to learning and takes the position that there are certain conditions essential to learning. It also consider the limits of what it is possible to learn and looks in depth at how language not only conveys but creates meaning.

Moore, A. (2000) *Teaching and Learning: Pedagogy, Curriculum and Culture*. London: Routledge.

This book takes a critical look at issues related to models of teaching, and issues related to learning and language and culture. The author also considers issues emerging from educational policy in relation to teaching and learning in a thoughtful and balanced manner.

Pye, J. (1988) *Invisible Children: Who are the Real Losers in School?* Oxford: Oxford University Press.

This significant book looks at the problems we have as teachers, of having classes of so many children that children end up being overlooked or become, in Pye's term, 'invisible'. Pye illustrates his points through the use of strong case study material.

OBSERVING CHILDREN

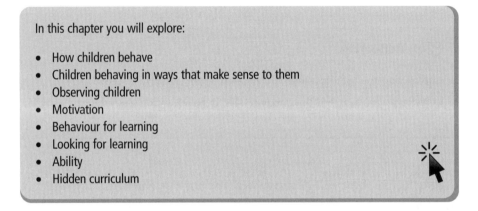

In this chapter you will explore:

- How children behave
- Children behaving in ways that make sense to them
- Observing children
- Motivation
- Behaviour for learning
- Looking for learning
- Ability
- Hidden curriculum

INTRODUCTION

In this chapter we ask you to consider issues related to the kind of behaviours that you might see children adopt in lessons.

HOW CHILDREN BEHAVE IN CLASSROOMS

The issue that probably exercises the minds of all experienced and novice teachers is that of children's behaviour. Our attention tends to get drawn to the immediate demands of teaching a class of children and therefore on the observable behaviours that children may present, rather than considering why children behave in the ways that they do. We may be fairly sure that in general children will behave in ways that make sense to them, even if these behaviours make little immediate sense to us as teachers (Butler and Green, 1998).

Examples

Butler and Green (1998) tell the story of the child who wets her bed on purpose as she has realised that this will mean she does not have to share it with the dog. Similarly, in a school context, this is illustrated by the story of the Secondary school child who turns up to her lesson each Thursday afternoon and is extremely rude to the teacher who then, in line with school policy, sends her to the year head who the child knows is free at that time. The child has a positive relationship with the year head, knows that he is free at that time each week and then spends an enjoyable lesson chatting to him.

Reflection

Considering the non-learning behaviours that you observe in class.

- Why do you feel that the children have behaved in the ways that they did?
- What explanations were the class teachers able to offer?

There are times when we talk about poor behaviour as if it is a permanent defining feature of the child rather than as a condition that they pass through from time to time. In the same way that we might consider ourselves to be a good friend or a good parent but occasionally we pass through a phase when we are not. So in the same way that the state of being a parent or friend is not necessarily a stable condition, the way that children behave has the potential to be changed.

We feel that there is also a tendency for us to talk about 'managing behaviour' which suggests that as teachers we have a degree of control over children, but in reality this is probably an illusion. Claxton (1984) talks about children 'lending' teachers their control rather than 'giving it' away to be managed.

When considering children's behaviour in lessons, we need to think carefully about how we think about motivation to learn. We often speak about children being either 'motivated' or 'unmotivated' as if that were a quality that resides in them rather than a condition that we all pass through from time to time and is dependent on contextual factors. Perhaps a useful way to consider motivation is in terms of a cost–benefit analysis (Claxton, 1996). In other words, if I commit myself to this learning, what are the costs to me and are they outweighed, or not, by the possible benefits? This may well have been a consideration for you before embarking on a PGCE. What do you see as the possible benefits and what are the possible costs to you?

There is also the issue of intrinsic and extrinsic motivation. Claxton (1984) proposes that in the end all motivation is intrinsic and that external factors merely act to apply force to shape intrinsic motivation.

Example

If a Year 11 child is promised a present if they do well in their GCSE exams, that is not extrinsic motivation but the application of an external factor that it is hoped will impact on the child's intrinsic motivation. We talk about low motivation as if it is a cause of lack of engagement whereas it may well be a result of low levels of engagement.

Over the years there has been a tendency for 'behaviour' to be viewed as separate from learning. The idea behind 'behaviour for learning' is that the child's behaviour is viewed in relation to their learning. Therefore teachers are encouraged to see behaviour as a product of the child's cognitive, affective and social perspectives.

Behaviour for Learning is an approach that seeks to emphasise the link between the way in which children and young people learn, and their social knowledge and behaviour. The focus is upon establishing positive relationships across the three elements of self, others and curriculum, as indicated in Figure 6.1. Behaviour for Learning has implications for pupils, teachers, parents and other professionals. Its principles can be applied to all children at any age and not just

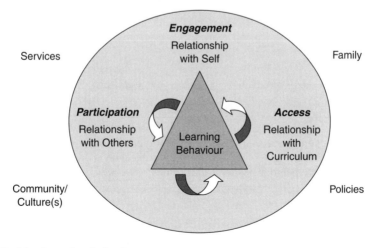

FIGURE 6.1 Learning behaviour

those perceived as being 'difficult to manage'. It applies as much to teachers and their relationship with children as to the children themselves.

PROBLEMS OF NORM REFERENCING?

It is human nature to compare ourselves with others. In busy classrooms children will inevitably compare themselves with others. Too often student teachers will view this as 'normal', but it seems clear that teachers should not be unnecessarily complicit in this. The problem with any kind of norm referenced assessment is summarised neatly by Rowntree (1988) who quotes John Holt's now famous comment about, 'the ignoble satisfaction of feeling one is better than someone else'. We suggest that a more positive focus is to adopt an ipsative, or what Stiggins (1994) calls a 'self referenced', assessment. In this the pupil's achievements are compared only with their previous ones which will reinforce the notion of learning as a trajectory.

LOOKING FOR LEARNING

'When we look for learning what is there to see?' is the question posed by Drummond (1993). Examining learning is a difficult task – as Mercer (1995) points out it only exists as a concept. Learning is a process and is always about learning something, so it is hard to consider learning on its own as it is always linked with what is to be learned.

The issues are also confused for student teachers by the way in which teachers talk about 'learning' as a form of reification (Carpenter, 2008b). Reification is a concept that we came across before in relation to SEN being a process whereby abstractions are regarded or treated as if they have concrete or material existence.

Examples

It might be argued that a concept like gender does not exist, but because it has been an issue that has received considerable attention it then becomes embodied and is spoken about as if it is real and tangible. Another example is taking velocity to be a thing (i.e. a substance or subject in a metaphysical sense) instead of merely being a property that things have, which is what it really is.

The object of learning is a capability that has a general and specific aspect (Marton et al., 2004), the general aspect being the nature of the capability such as remembering or interpreting and the specific aspect being the thing or subject upon which these general acts are carried out. The learner only needs to focus on the specific aspects but the teacher needs to focus on both the general and specific aspects at the same time. In other words, not only does the teacher have to mediate the content, or the specific aspect of learning, they have to attend to the way in which the learners are processing this as they develop in the general aspect.

Example

A Year 6 teacher is working with a class and they are considering the nature of allegories. The teacher uses the parable of the good Samaritan as the context for the lesson.

In this example the specific aspect of learning would be understanding the moral behind the story of the good Samaritan.

The general aspect would be developing the understanding that stories can have more than one layer of meaning.

Reflection

Can you illustrate general and specific aspects of learning in your own subject area?

An important issue to consider is our conceptions of learning. We feel that student teachers often tend to see 'learning' in a relatively narrow manner. That is to say as a process of absorption and reproduction. This is understandable when it can be argued that schooling is essentially about social reproduction, and the high status of examinations tends to reward those who are expert at recall. However, it is important to consider the possibilities of other types of learning than recall. In Table 6.1 we have presented Marton and Booth's summary of types of learning.

TABLE 6.1 Summary of conceptions of learning (based on Marton and Booth, 1997)

Learning as ...	
A. Increasing knowledge	
B. Memorising and reproducing	Learning primarily as reproducing
C. Applying	
D. Understanding	
E. Seeing something in a different way	Learning as primarily seeking meaning
F. Changing as a person	

Classrooms are thought to be places where learning takes place, indeed their very existence is predicated on the basis that children will be in them and learn. However, this is far from a straightforward matter as learning may be summarised as some kind of internal process or the result of the learner interacting with the world in some way. Either way learning is a process and therefore all that is readily visible is performance of some kind, whether it be the production of written work, an artefact such as a painting or a physical performance such as a gymnastic routine. 'However, performance refers to what a student can be observed to do, and learning is merely inferred' (Swann, 1999b, p. 59) (see Table 6.2).

TABLE 6.2 Inferring learning from observable behaviour

What I saw	What learning can be inferred
A child in Year 2 able to place a number of cards in order from the highest number to the lowest number.	That the child has a secure understanding that numbers have value and that they are able to see the relationship between the different values.
A child in Year 6 who in a music lesson is able to beat out 4/4 and 3/4 time with a tambourine.	That a child has learnt to 'hear' and 'feel' different time signatures.
A child in Year 8 who, feeding to themselves, is able to hit a tennis ball on the half volley.	That the child can co-ordinate the feed and hit and that they can make the very precise timing that hitting a ball on the half volley demands.

Looking for learning is even more difficult when it is remembered that essentially it might be seen as about improvement and is therefore best viewed as a trajectory. So, in order for the teacher to be able to note learning they need to know 'what was' and be able to compare it with 'what is now'. This is no mean feat for Secondary teachers who might work with around 20 different classes a week and if each class has 25 children that is a total of approximately 500 children. The situation is easier in Primary education where the teacher tends to stay with their class but then there is the issue of the teacher needing to be able to monitor progress over a number of different curriculum areas. Of course a dilemma with the examples given in Table 6.2 is that we are in effect revealing competence rather than learning. Therefore, it is desirable for the teacher, when assessing learning, to bear in mind the learner's previous state of competence and be able to compare it to the current one.

Example: learning as a trajectory

Context:

- In a Year 5 lesson Sophie and her classmates are considering allegories.
- The teacher reads the children one of Aesop's fables, 'The Thirsty Crow'.

When asked about the story, Sophie is able to say that it is a story about a crow who is very thirsty and finds a heavy pot with some water in the bottom. He finds that he cannot reach the water, he cannot break the pot, he cannot tip the pot and in the end he places pebbles in the pot in order to raise the level of the water so that he can get a drink. Initially this is all Sophie can see in the story. However, as the discussion in the lesson proceeds she can see that it is possible to draw a lesson from this story which is that if we try hard enough we can get what we want.

We can see from this simple example that learning is a trajectory in that at first Sophie could only see the surface features of the story but then develops an appreciation that the story may be interpreted as having an additional dimension.

In terms of ipsative assessment we would say that Sophie has moved from a position of only seeing the surface features to being able to see a simple allegory.

The matter of looking for learning is complicated by the fact that learning tends to be presented in policy and formal assessment criteria as linear and regularly incremental. In Chapter 2 we looked at the power of metaphor and we now suggest that a powerful metaphor for learning is to see it as 'rhyzomic' (Moss, 2004) – that learning is like a rhizome and sprouts out in all directions in an apparently random and chaotic manner.

In a study of PE teachers' implicit theories of learning, Carpenter (2008a) proposes a metaphor based on science: namely that learning is often presented as a vector quality, in other words as having *amplitude* and direction, like velocity, whereas it may be more helpful to see it as a scalar quantity, in other words, as having amplitude but no direction, like mass. If this argument has merit then it can be seen that the paradigms of assessment tend to assume amplitude and direction, whereas the paradigm of learning as scalar is essentially dissimilar, and so there is a kind of dissonance at work where the instrument designed to measure progress in learning may not be fully 'fit for purpose', or that the two are incommensurable.

MATTERS OF ABILITY

Terms such as 'ability' are often applied to describe learners' capabilities. There is a tendency to see a person's ability as a predetermined capacity to acquire a mastery of some kind which can be described in an 'entity' manner (Dweck, 1999). This is a common device and is illustrated in the metaphorical nature of such language as, 'I tried to learn that but there was not enough space in my brain to be able to retain it'.

By contrast researchers such as Sternberg (1998) have developed the idea of learnable intelligence, whereby intelligence is not a fixed capacity. However, we are often subjected to messages that intelligence and all other forms of competence are fixed in some way which is a perception that seems to have little support in more robust research but can underpin some powerful discourses concerning learning.

Don't try to teach pupils who can't learn

Lower-ability students should study the skills they need, not academic subjects they can't handle

Magnus Linklater

Here is a question for Carol Vorderman, as she sets about improving the nation's mathematical skills — a task that she is undertaking for David Cameron. What is the point of trying to train up the 40 per cent of underperforming children from deprived backgrounds in Britain, when there is no evidence that they are capable of making the grade?

If 3.5 million children have left school since 1999 without even a C grade in maths — as Conservative research suggests — could that be because they are being taught academic subjects that they lack the ability to absorb?

And if we really want to raise national standards, would it not be more effective to concentrate on those children who show an inclination to learn?

It is, of course, anathema to the liberal establishment — in which I declare an interest — even to suggest such a thing. For generations, it has been common ground across all parties that ability has nothing to do with social background, and that improving standards is simply a question of widening access to education. By raising the school leaving age, and offering greater opportunities for working-class pupils to go to university, the general level of attainment will steadily increase.

Indeed, the phrase the 'democratic intellect' — a good Scottish concept, which has informed education acts since 1870 — has at its heart the idea that poverty, however ingrained, has nothing to do with ability. Go and see *Slumdog Millionaire* if you want cinematic evidence to prove the point.

Except there is an inconvenient truth that has to be confronted, even — especially — by liberals, if results are to be achieved, and if Ms Vorderman is to come up with something solid, rather than a series of well-meaning initiatives.

It is articulated in his latest book by the social scientist Charles Murray, whose very name has educationists screeching 'heresy!' and who, in his most

(Continued)

(Continued)

controversial work, *The Bell Curve*, suggested that IQ may be determined by genetic differences.

In *Real Education*, he claims that, despite a series of government programmes aimed at raising numeracy and literacy, no real impact can be discerned at the lower end of academic ability.

Murray argues that this is not because of lack of opportunity but lack of the intelligence required to embrace academic subjects, and that this can be measured by how results fall off rapidly as these pupils progress through the school system. They may be able to learn basic arithmetic but cannot cope with anything more challenging. This, he says, is because they have lower abilities.

'When it comes to education, we are phobic about saying that kids are different in their ability to learn the things that schools teach,' he argues.

Half of those who enter the education system are of below-average ability, he reminds us, and less than 20 per cent are qualified to go to university. Therefore, instead of encouraging these children to stay on at school long after they have lost interest, or to go on to further education where they will drop out early, we should relieve them of the normal curriculum and train them in vocational work. Instead of equal opportunity for all, there should be an aspiration to equal dignity.

(The Times, 4 February 2009)

In the extract from Magnus Linklater above, it is clear that Linklater is building an argument that assumes ability is fixed. The phenomenon of seeing ability as fixed is referred to as an 'entity' perspective, whereas if one's ability is seen as malleable and capable of change then this is an 'incremental' perspective. Over the years there have been many instances of successful people looking back at school reports which were damming but which may be seen as the teacher who wrote them having an entity perspective on the particular pupil (see Table 6.3).

TABLE 6.3 Examples of entity and incremental perspectives

Entity perspectives	Incremental perspectives
• 'To be honest you'll never be able to do maths at a decent level.' • 'Of course you can retake your maths O level ... all you lack is ability.' • 'Eric will never get anywhere in life.' (Eric Morecombe's teacher) • 'Certainly on the road to failure.' (John Lennon's teacher) • 'This boy has no ambition.' (Winston Churchill's teacher)	• 'Of course you can try taking Physics A level. Just because you got a grade 'C' at GCSE does not mean you cannot improve.' • 'Yes, please come to Netball Club, I have no doubt that you will improve through playing with stronger players and who knows where that may take you.'

Occasionally, teachers refer to children as having 'over achieved' which probably means that the teacher had less faith in the learner's potential than the learner themselves! However, underlying such statements is an entity perspective.

HIDDEN CURRICULUM

There is a tendency to see the relationship between teaching and learning as a form of straightforward 'cause and effect' – the teacher does something with the aim of producing some kind of change in the learners and then this happens as predicted. However, as we said in the previous section about learning, what tends to happen is that the learner, through interacting with the environment, builds or constructs understandings for themselves.

In addition to this, we can be sure that the learner is learning not only in relation to issues of the content, but will also learn through the processes of the classroom. In other words, learning takes place through the way that the class is organised, the kinds of rules that are set and how they are policed, the nature of the teacher interactions with the pupils, and so on. This phenomenon is commonly referred to as the 'hidden' curriculum.

Another perspective on the hidden curriculum is that posited by Claxton who says:

> The medium of school also transmits false messages about the nature of learning. This dissemination of disinformation is called the 'hidden curriculum'. The way that school works presupposes that learning is painless; that it is limited by ability; that achievement within this limit is determined by effort; that learning requires teaching and that which is not taught will not be valuable. (Claxton, 1984, pp. 237-8)

The following list gives some examples of where the 'hidden curriculum' may be at work:

- Sometimes teachers set up discussions where they are in effect setting up a situation for the children to guess what is in their head. For example, in Year 11 Science, 'Who can tell me what the life span of a house fly is?' invites the children to guess what the number in the teacher's head is. Over time children will learn that in order to please the teacher they need to give 'right' answers.
- In a lesson on creative writing if the children's work is marked with great attention to grammar and punctuation they may get the message that actually 'correct' writing is more valued than creativity and imagination and so in effect the teacher may be undermining the very purpose of the exercise due to their mode of marking.
- Children tend to be very adept at learning how rigorously different teachers apply the rules of the classroom and may well adjust their behaviours accordingly.

CONCLUSION

This chapter has introduced you to the complexities associated with observing children, and in particular the difficulties involved when trying to make judgements about learning. As in Chapter 5, this chapter has uncovered aspects related to learning that may be 'hidden' to the novice classroom observer.

 *Recommended further reading*

Carnell, E. and Lodge, C. (2002) *Supporting Effective Learning*. London: Paul Chapman.
This authored book by two established academics in the field, introduces the reader very succinctly to many issues related to learning in school. Chapters include 'Learning in the classroom', 'Tutors, tutor groups and learning' and 'Learning conversations'.

Drummond, M. (1993) *Assessing Children's Learning*. London: David Fulton.
This book is essentially situated in the Primary phase, but the issues it raises are equally applicable to all age groups. Written in a scholarly yet compassionate style, the author carries out a thorough examination of learning through an assessment lens.

Green, T. (1998) *The Activities of Teaching*. New York: Educators' International Press.
This helpful book closely examines aspects of teaching such as the formation of beliefs, and problems of 'certainty' and its relationship with learning. The writing is rigorous and complex ideas are made accessible through strong examples.

DOING QUALITATIVE RESEARCH

In this chapter you will explore:

- Why we should frame our thinking within a qualitative, interpretative paradigm
- Approaches to interpretative paradigms
- Rigour in qualitative research
- Research methodologies
- Case study
- Ethnography
- Action research

INTRODUCTION

We have explored the ideas of research or enquiry as a part of the identity of a teacher in Chapters 1 and 3. In this chapter we will discuss different approaches to research which you might use in your school-based enquiry. We will discuss various ways to make meaning through your research which will be influenced by the nature of your study, the question(s) you wish to ask, but fundamentally the way that you construct meanings about the world.

In Sebastian Faulks' *Human Traces* (2005), the two key characters (Jacques Rebieres and Thomas Midwinter) are psychiatrists practising in the late 19th and early 20th centuries. United in a quest to understand the causes of mental illness and offer support and treatment for patients, they are, however, very different characters. Their early life experiences were worlds apart and their belief systems developed differently. They are passionate in their quest to understand mental illness and, in each other have found kindred spirits, but nevertheless their approaches to their work differ greatly, causing emotional strain between them. Rebieres and Midwinter are driven by different impulses; the direction of their research is intricately woven into the fabric of their being. They are only ever able to be true to themselves – their world view and therefore their beliefs in their work were formed by their life experiences.

Whilst this is a beautiful and often painful story, what has it got to do with educational enquiry? As a study in enquiry, Rebieres and Midwinter remind us that even though we might be hoping to achieve the same aim – in educational terms, to gain a clearer understanding of issues related to learning and teaching – there is no one method or approach that will provide *the* answer. Your own life experiences, your disposition to certain methods of enquiry, your professional interests, will all shape the methodological approach that will provide you with the answers that you are seeking. It's important to put yourself at the heart of enquiry – that you don't follow methods slavishly, but regard methods as tools to enable you to find answers to the questions you have, in the most ethical and fruitful way possible.

'The first important organizing principle is the paradigm. A paradigm is a set of basic beliefs that provide the principles for understanding the world and, hence, the basic principles underpinning research in the social sciences' (Langdridge, 2007, p. 3). In addition, the paradigm makes assumptions about the 'functions of researchers which, adhered to by a group of researchers, conditions the patterns of their thinking and underpins their research actions' (Bassey, 1999, p. 42). A paradigm can be seen as an overarching view of the world which then determines our approach to a range of research methodologies and methods. Table 7.1 illustrates two examples of paradigms.

TABLE 7.1   Two types of paradigm (based on Langdridge, 2007)

Paradigm	Definition
Positivist paradigm	Tends to be the domain of science and other associated disciplines, e.g. mainstream psychology. There is a belief that there is a real world and that we can gain knowledge about it through the use of 'scientific' methods.
Postpositivist (interpretative) paradigm	Where the real world is still assumed but our knowledge of it is always seen as incomplete, subjective and just an approximation.

All paradigms lead to particular epistemological positions (epistemology is the nature of knowledge). In other words, the nature of the paradigm will determine the nature of the knowledge that is produced by the research.

Your experiences of research may well vary depending on the dominant approaches to research related to your undergraduate subject (see Rajiv in the first vignette overleaf). Hypothesis forming and undertaking a quantitative methodology with a range of associated methods will be familiar to those who have worked within a positivist (natural scientific) paradigm. An alternative paradigm is to see the world in terms of the range of perceptions or interpretations that people have about it and where no particular perceptions have privilege (Burr, 1995). Others of you will have undertaken research where you consider a theme by using a methodology (e.g. a type of literary theory) but will not have needed to overtly consider it as a methodology before, nor placed it within an overarching paradigm.

It is common for students to misinterpret or use interchangeably the terms, 'Method' and 'Methodology'. 'Methodology' identifies 'a general approach to studying research topics', whereas 'method' refers to a 'specific research technique' (Silverman, 1993). Table 7.2 illustrates the differences between these two key terms.

Example

If you were interested in understanding how children interpret the comments you make on their written work you would probably be working within an interpretative paradigm. The kind of methodology you might use might be ethnography and within that the methods you might employ might be lesson observation, semi-structured interviews and a research journal of field notes.

Vignette: Designing your enquiry – identifying your paradigm and methodology

Rajiv has a BSc in Physics and is undertaking a Primary PGCE. During his school placement he became interested in how his pupils make sense of their local natural environment and decided to undertake an enquiry into this as part of his studies.

Rajiv has been used to working within a positivist paradigm, which typically involves hypothesis forming and experimentation through quantitative methodologies which involve statistical methods. Through this process, he assumes that knowledge can be found which will either prove or disprove the hypothesis.

He has come to realise that this sort of approach will not be suitable for his enquiry due to the complexity he has already found with this matter. He has found that the pupils have very different ideas about what the environment is and that this changes over even a short timescale depending on the stimulus. He cannot see a way to quantify their ideas and also is troubled by the size of his sample of pupils and his influence on the pupils' answers.

After discussions with his tutor who suggested working within an interpretative paradigm, Rajiv has decided upon a qualitative methodology which uses grounded

(Continued)

(Continued)

theory ('theory that is grounded in data systematically gathered and analysed' and where there is a 'continuous interplay between analysis and data collection (see Holliday, 2007, p. 16)). He has chosen a series of methods to collect data which will utilise recordings of pupil focus groups, analysis of pupils' drawings and his own reflective diary of the research process.

In summary, Rajiv is using the interpretative paradigm, grounded theory as his methodology and focus groups, pupils' drawings and a reflective diary as his methods.

Education research is often (but not exclusively) associated with social science methodologies within the interpretive paradigm. The interpretive paradigm is often associated with the qualitative paradigm (as opposed to a quantitative one) and we argue that for the purposes of your Masters-level enquiry that this research is best framed within such a paradigm which we will now consider.

◌ **Reflection**

Reflect on a piece of research you conducted. This might be an undergraduate dissertation or piece of educational research for a written assignment.

- What paradigms underpinned your work?
- Were you searching for objective truth (a positivist paradigm), subjective notions of reality (an interpretative paradigm) or neither of these?
- What methodology did you use and how did this relate to the paradigm?
- What methods did you use?
- How might this influence the way you conduct future education research?

WHY FRAME OUR THINKING WITHIN A QUALITATIVE, INTERPRETATIVE PARADIGM?

Your PGCE can be a very pressurised and intensive time in your life. Your research will most likely be short term and small scale with many other demands placed upon you at the same time. It is possible to undertake large-scale research, sometimes framed within a quantitative paradigm, where findings may be generalised. However, given the nature of small-scale enquiry, we will focus upon research which develops specific, in-depth findings based on the focus and site of your research and where generalisation beyond your research is neither desirable nor possible. We will also consider your own influence on your research by the way you are positioned as an integral and recognised component of it. Table 7.2 gives some examples of paradigms, methodologies and methods that you may frame your enquiry within and use as part of your investigation.

TABLE 7.2 Paradigms, methodologies and methods (adapted from Holliday, 2007, p. 16)

Paradigms and perspectives	Methodology	Methods of collecting and analysing data
Natural Qualitative: Postpositivism, realism Reality is still plain to see	**Case Study** Study of a specific 'bounded system' (Stakes, 2005, p. 444), e.g. a teacher, curriculum subject/department or institution	Interviewing Focus groups Observational techniques
Deeper social reality needs qualitative enquiry	**Ethnography** Explores 'the nature of a specific social phenomenon', 'unstructured data', 'a small number of cases', '[interpretation] of the meanings and functions' and 'participant observation'	Interpreting documents Content analysis
Postmodern Qualitative: Critical theory, constructivism, postmodernism, feminism Reality and science are socially constructed	(Atkinson and Hammersley, 1994, p. 248)	
Researchers are part of the research settings	**Participatory Action Research** 'emphasises the political aspects of knowledge production' (Reason, 1994, p. 328) 'involves the individual practitioner	
Investigation must be in reflexive, self-critical, creative dialogue	in continually reflecting on his or her behaviour-in-action' so that 'other members of the community do the same' (Reason, 1994, p. 331)	
Aims to problematise, reveal hidden realities, initiate discussions		

Qualitative research is 'a way of knowing that assumes that the researcher gathers, organizes, and interprets information (usually in words or pictures) with his or her eyes and ears as filters' (Lichtman, 2006, p. 22). The influence of the researcher, therefore, is significant in many of these qualitative paradigms. The key to good qualitative research is that there is a clear line of argument that supports your interpretations.

The important thing in this process is to question all assumptions you tend to make and to remember that not all things are as they may appear (i.e. remember to be critical). It is vital not to jump to easy conclusions in order to quickly complete an assignment! Qualitative researchers tend to (but don't always) immerse themselves in the field and then let the questions or issues emerge, from which the research methodological approach is developed. This seems appropriate for research that will most likely take place in your placement school and whose focus will develop after issues have emerged during your practice and from tutorials and reading that you undertake as part of your PGCE.

In Table 7.3 we consider the activities, underpinning beliefs, steps in developing the research focus and the rigour associated with qualitative research in comparison to quantitative research. It must be pointed out that there are many cases where quantitative approaches are appropriate in education research (e.g. research into the correlation between pupils' SAT level and their CAT score), however, most probably in the case of your research into classroom practices, we feel that qualitative research with its emphasis on situated, deep enquiry into social variables and an evolving approach depending on initial observations/findings will be more appropriate.

TABLE 7.3   Two paradigms of research (taken from Holliday, 2007, p. 6)

Quantitative research	**Qualitative research**
Activities	*Activities*
Counts occurrences across a large population. Uses statistics and replicability to validate generalisation from survey samples and experiments. Attempts to reduce contaminating social variables.	Looks deep into the quality of social life. Locates the study within particular settings which provide opportunities for exploring all possible social variables and set manageable boundaries. Initial foray into the social setting leads to further, more informed exploration as themes and focuses emerge.
Underpinning beliefs	*Underpinning beliefs*
Conviction about what it is important to look for. Confidence in establishing research instruments. Reality is not so problematic if the research instruments are adequate and conclusive results are feasible.	Confidence in an ability to devise research procedures to fit the situation and the nature of the people in it, as they are revealed. Reality contains mysteries to which the researcher must submit, and can do no more than interpret.
Steps	*Steps*
First decide the research focus (e.g. testing a specific hypothesis). Then devise and pilot research instruments (e.g. survey questionnaire or experiment). Then go into the field.	Decide the subject is interesting (e.g. in its own right, or because it represents an area of interest). Go into the field to see what is going on. Allows focus and themes to emerge. Devise research instruments during process (e.g. observation or interview).
Rigour	*Rigour*
Disciplined application of established rules for statistics, experiment and survey design.	Principled development of research strategy to suit the scenario being studied as it is revealed.

Generalisation (the extent to which we can generalise the findings of one piece of research to wider populations) is a fundamental aspect of positivist research and an aim of some other forms of research (see below). In your research, which is likely to be a small-scale enquiry, we urge caution with such approaches. Lincoln and Guba (2000) highlight an essential dilemma: 'generalizations are nomothetic in nature, that is, law-like, but in order to use them – for purposes of prediction and control, say – the generalizations must be applied to particulars. And it is precisely at that point that their probabilistic, relative nature comes into sharpest focus' (2000, p. 33).

Vignette: The nomothetic–idiographic dilemma

Poornima is a Primary PGCE student. Her placement school uses the Primary National Strategy to determine their approach to teaching literacy. After using this strategy with all her pupils (i.e. a generalised or nomothetic approach) for a couple of weeks she reflected upon her assessments of her pupils' progress and noted that a majority of her class seemed to like this strategy and their reading had improved. She identified, however, a minority of pupils who did not seem to improve using this strategy. If she continued using this strategy for all her pupils she would be ignoring idiographic elements in her practice and failing to meet some of her pupils' particular needs at that time. If she continued to use this strategy for the rest of the class, just based on this initial reflection, she would also be ignoring the potential change in the pupils' reaction to the strategy over time.

The application of generalisation to particular instances or people is a significant difficulty for some educational researchers (e.g. see case study methodologies), as generalisations are 'always inductively underdetermined, and they are always temporally and contextually driven' (Lincoln and Guba, 2000, p. 33). In other words, it is difficult to represent the findings that emerge in a particular case in other settings (i.e. a more generalised account) because of their detail and complexity which are bounded by specific time and space.

A significant difference between positivist and interpretative paradigms is the acceptance of particular terms or groups as a unit to focus upon in the enquiry. The former will accept these as units that can be generalised, whereas for the latter, these terms are problematised (see the following vignette).

Vignette: Problematising in the interpretative paradigm

In the first vignette in this chapter, Rajiv found that his pupils consider the 'natural environment' in many different ways resulting in this term having multiple meanings. Thus, any research that uses 'natural environment' without unpacking its multiplicity of meanings will lack depth in this area. The researcher should also consider the term 'pupils'. By problematising this, the researcher questions who exactly Rajiv's pupils are. What is it that marks them out as belonging to this group? Is it about how long he has taught them – in which case are pupils who have been mostly absent still 'his pupils'? By positing these questions and considering responses, the researcher develops a depth of understanding that is not obtained through other approaches.

By problematising these terms they become unquantifiable due to their amorphous nature. Usually in the interpretative paradigm, specific and situated depth of understanding is sought rather than the ability to generalise. We have considered a very simple example above, however it illustrates the power of an interpretative approach in this specific, situated context.

A significant factor in helping determine your interpretation of meaning in the research situation is one of culture. Culture is a popular term, often used to describe aspects of whole regions or nations, professions or ethnic groups. A culture is made up of certain 'values, practices, relationships and identifications' (Walford, 2001, p. 8). 'Within an interpretative paradigm, a more minimal, small, operational notion of culture allows the differentiating characteristics of groups to be discovered rather than presumed. Here culture is an uncountable noun that refers to cohesive behaviour as a basic feature of the human condition' (Holliday, 2007, p. 12).

For your enquiry you will be immersed in a range of cultures. These will be determined by a range of differing factors, for example, your mentor's views, interpretations of, and the school policies themselves (which also represent the culture of a senior management team), the nature of the subject or age phase that you teach, views on the school's catchment area, and so on. From whatever scale you regard culture, the main point to consider is not to presume anything and to suspend initial judgements about the cultures that you find.

APPROACHES TO INTERPRETATIVE PARADIGMS

Postpositivism (see Table 7.1), or naturalism as it is sometimes called, is a more traditional approach to research within the interpretative, qualitative paradigms (see Table 7.2). Like the positivist paradigm it starts from the premise that 'reality' can be found 'out there'. This is demonstrated in qualitative research through the researcher's immersion in the field for a sufficient length of time and through finding 'authenticity by focusing on what local characters say in interview, personal accounts and conversation' (Holliday 2007, p. 18).

Research is undertaken until the findings begin to repeat themselves to the point where the researcher is confident that no further points of relevant interest will be found through further investigation of the particular issue (a point of 'saturation' in grounded theory). It is easy for such approaches, therefore, to produce exhaustive data and accounts from the research field. Certain approaches to case study and ethnography can use a postpositivist paradigm.

In postpositivism there is a strong attempt to reduce the influence of the researcher in the research and its findings. The 'voice' of the researcher, therefore, is minimised. Postmodernists (see Table 7.2) criticise this approach as simplistic in believing that it is possible to minimise observer effect and see a virgin setting 'like it is' without biasing preconceptions or theoretical prejudices (Gubrium and Holstein, 1997, p. vi, cited in Holliday, 2007, p. 19) a process that in phenomenologically based research is referred to as 'bracketing'. So the researcher attempts to 'bracket out' their own preconceptions (Langdridge, 2007).

There is the potential for quantitative elements to be included in such research, although in the case of small-scale research a qualitative approach is most likely to produce robust data.

Postmodernists 'portray people as constructing the social world' and researchers as 'themselves constructing the social world through their interpretations of it' (Hammersley and Atkinson, 1995, p. 11, cited in Holliday, 2007, p. 19). Postpositivists seek to minimise the influence of the researcher and to interpret what they find as objectively as possible. Postmodernists argue that 'every act of "seeing" or "saying" is unavoidably conditioned by cultural, institutional, and interactional contingencies' (Gubrium and Holstein, 1997, p. vi, cited in Holliday, 2007, p. 19), and thus without the researcher constructing meaning through the research process there is nothing – it is all a perception through your interpretations and there are no specific truths to find in the field.

Your response to the postpositivist or postmodernist paradigm will have a strong influence on the way you approach your research. As with all paradigms it is a result of the way you think about the world. On the one hand, you as the researcher are seeking to find your interpretation of the truth which lies there in the field waiting to be discovered. On the other hand, you, the researcher, have a strong influence on the research process and outcomes; the research is a product of your ideologies and behaviours which in turn are influenced by wider cultural settings and your own beliefs. You are not seeking to determine an absolute truth through your research. Your research enables you to develop an in-depth interpretation about the research with the realisation that others will have their own interpretations about the same matter. It is only the research that makes this issue real.

By looking again at Table 7.2 which illustrates the range of approaches that are possible for the qualitative, interpretative researcher it appears from the layout of the table that there are clear distinctions between the paradigms and methodologies. In reality there is a great deal of blurring. For example, it is quite possible for a case study approach to incorporate ethnographic approaches as well as quantitative methods (Holliday, 2007), while qualitative approaches can be considered as a paradigm or methodology.

Whichever paradigm you set your research within, be clear about it, make sure that it informs your methods and that your chosen methods do not conflict with the type of knowledge this paradigm will produce.

RIGOUR IN QUALITATIVE RESEARCH

Whatever paradigm and associated methodology you frame your research within, it is vital that you ensure it is rigorous so that your research findings are valid. Validity refers to 'establishing the truth value of a claim, its authenticity or trustworthiness. This is a matter of rigorous methodological procedure' (McNiff and Whitehead, 2006, p. 157). It is important to consider this in your research design, but it is vital to reflect on your research as it progresses. You will most likely need to adjust your approach to suit the emerging complexities of the research as you learn more about these and the research process in general. Validity differs from reliability which requires a consideration of whether if the research was repeated, it would achieve the same outcomes.

The following points regarding qualitative research apply to establishing the validity within an interpretative paradigm. It is important that within your research you have a clear rationale for the:

- choice of social setting: how it represented the research topic in its role in society (or in school), how feasible and substantial it was (e.g. access, duration, depth, breadth)
- choice of research activities: how they suited the social setting, how they were appropriate to researcher–subject relationships, how they formed a coherent strategy
- choice of research themes and foci: how they emerged, why they are significant, how they are representative of the social setting

- dedication to and thoroughness of field work: how and to what extent the field was engaged (e.g. strategies for 'being there'), how data was recorded and catalogued
- overall need to articulate a judicious balance between opportunism and principle in terms of the methods used for data collection (adapted from Holliday, 2007, p. 9).

RESEARCH METHODOLOGIES

As a Masters-level researcher it is important that you have a clear rationale for your research paradigm, methodology and methods as this will help ensure the knowledge that you produce relates to the kind of knowledge you need in order to consider your research question(s).

Later in the book we will consider typical methods that you may utilise, such as classroom observation, interviews and questionnaires, but before we move on to consider these we need to look at the wider methodologies to which these methods relate. Each methodology has advantages and disadvantages, depending upon the interplay between three conditions: (1) the type of research question; (2) the control an investigator has over actual behavioural events; and (3) the focus on contemporary as opposed to historical phenomena (Yin, 1989, p. 13). The majority of your research, which will be school-based, will have little control over the investigation and will most likely be collecting contemporary data rather than seeking historical dimensions to the research, but the nature of the questions that you pose and what you want to do with the research will have bearings on the approaches that you take. There are many approaches that may be undertaken, however, we consider here three important methodologies in qualitative approaches to educational research: case study, ethnography and action research.

CASE STUDY

A case study is an empirical inquiry that:

- investigates a contemporary phenomenon within its real-life context, especially when the boundaries between phenomenon and context are not clearly evident. (Yin, 2008, p. 18)

Case studies have an important role to play in the type of research you are likely to undertake. Yin notes at least four different applications:

1. To explain the presumed causal links in real-life interventions that are too complex for survey or experimental strategies (i.e. more positivist approaches).
2. To describe the real-life context in which an intervention has occurred.

3. To illustrate certain topics within an evaluation, again in a descriptive mode.
4. To enlighten these situations in which the intervention has no clear, single set of outcomes (Yin, 2008, pp. 19–20).

The case study as a research methodology is used in many settings, in either single or multiple contexts. It is likely for your research enquiry that you will be focusing on either a single school (or a department or other such unit within a school) or possibly undertaking a small multiple case study consisting of two case studies based on research at two of your placement schools.

Quantitative data can, to some extent, be collected as part of case study analysis; however we will focus on the qualitative approach for the reasons given earlier in this chapter and which are explored in the methods discussed in the next chapter.

Yin identifies five aspects of case study research design:

1. the study's questions (probably how and why type questions)
2. its propositions
3. its unit(s) of analysis
4. the logic linking the data to the propositions, and
5. the criteria for interpreting the findings (Yin, 2008, p. 27).

The construction of effective enquiry questions will be considered elsewhere in this text; however, it is important at this stage to consider the nature of the proposition(s) of your research. This is 'what' you should study as determined by your research questions. Yin points out that not every piece of research will have propositions. In these 'explorations' there should still be a purpose to the research which is identified at the starting point of the research.

Example

You might be interested in what children talk about in group work and although this forms a focus for your research you go into this with a very open agenda.

The units of analysis for your case study research may vary considerably. The unit may well be an individual person or perhaps a department or curriculum team in a school. It is possible that these case studies form an overall multiple case study approach for your research project. It is important in such cases to be clear about the propositions of the research, otherwise you may be overwhelmed with a vast array of research data that has very little focus (Yin, 1989). The unit of analysis, may, however, be on a larger scale, say a particular Primary class or year group or Key Stage in a school. 'The definition of the unit of analysis is related to the way the initial research questions have been defined' (Yin, 1989, p. 31). Once the unit of analysis is determined you will also be able to determine what/who falls inside and outside of this unit and therefore be clear about the parameters of your research.

Table 7.4 shows three examples of the development of simple case study approaches with accompanying comments and questions about the propositions and unit of study. It is clear from these short examples that the nature of the research question is crucial in determining the rest of the research design. The need to re-work the question in the light of the initial consideration of the propositions and unit of study is clearly necessary. Try identifying these aspects of research design for yourself and re-work your question to help focus the research.

TABLE 7.4 Developing case study designs

Proposed research question	Propositions (what to study)	Unit of study
How may the Rose review of the primary curriculum influence History teaching? *The focus on History gives direction but at what scale? Is the question too broad and lacking detail?*	The current primary curriculum for History and Rose's proposals as set out in his report. *What and who else? The question does not allude to who will be studied here, e.g. Key Stage 2 teachers' views.*	Year group/whole school/multiple schools? *The question is unhelpful for this and could lead to unfocused research.*
What do Year 7 pupils perceive 'Citizenship' to be?	Year 7 Pupils. *This is clear from the question but you can be more specific, e.g. verbal and written comments, actions, etc.*	A whole year group. *Is the whole year group study feasible? What sort of methods will you utilise to gain these perceptions?*
In what ways (if any) do Year 4 pupils use teacher verbal feedback to improve their writing? *What assumptions are made in the question about causality? Can these be unpacked?*	Pupils' verbal comments about their progress. Observation of teacher feedback. Pupils' written work. Teacher's views on this. *Anything else?*	It is not clear whether this is about one class of Year 2 pupils and their teacher or is it more? *How might this alter the unit of study? Can you improve the research question?*

The final two aspects of case study design concern the predicted methods for data collection that you plan to utilise and the ensuing approaches to analysing it. It is crucial to ensure that these methods enable you to collect data that will allow the propositions of your research and that the criteria for interpreting the findings relate to these (see Chapter 9 for details of methods). Finally it is important that all these approaches tie in with the overarching paradigm that you have framed your research within (see Table 7.5 for two examples).

TABLE 7.5   Example of research using two different paradigms

Research question	In an 8 form entry 11–16 school, when and where do children tend to do their homework?	
Paradigm	Positivist	Interpretative
Methodology	Statistical survey	Multiple case study. One case study per year group (five in total)
Method	Closed questionnaire to 50% sample (approx. 500 pupils)	Open questionnaire asking children to record the times they tend to do their homework. Follow-up group interviews

One approach to case study work is to develop initial theories about your research at the design stage (Yin, 2008). This is a significant difference from other methodologies such as ethnography and grounded theory where theories emerge from the researcher's immersion in the field once the research has begun (Yin, 2008). It is possible, as Holliday (2007) points out, for case studies to utilise ethnographic approaches but in this situation, it is seen more as a method than a methodology.

Generalisation within the case study provokes a range of responses from academics. For your own research we urge you to remain focused on the specifics of your research context and to resist all temptations to generalise your findings.

In summary, the advantages of using case studies are that they:

1. tend to be small-scale works
2. are not artificial like experiments and surveys
3. encourage investigators to work in-depth, to really go beyond superficial research approaches
4. compel researchers to look for meaning and try to construct understandings, to learn what is really going on

5. should remind inquirers of the complexity and variability of the social world
6. can therefore be powerful antidotes to determinisms and overgeneralisation
7. tend to be very human – very person-centred (Knight, 2002, pp. 41–2).

ETHNOGRAPHY

Ethnography is 'an approach to social research based on the first-hand experience of social action within a discrete location, in which the objective is to collect data which will convey the subjective reality of the lived experience of those who inhabit that location' (Pole and Morrison, 2003, p. 16). As a student teacher in school you are ideally placed to carry out such a study.

The definition of ethnography indicates that this is not a methodology for those in a hurry: 'ethnographers tended to study whole cultures and immerse themselves in the topic for extended periods of time' (Lichtman, 2006, p. 41). Although this methodology may not suit every PGCE student teacher, it is beneficial to those of you who are immersed in a placement school for a number of months, during which time you are required to undertake some form of enquiry (see the following vignette).

Vignette: Closely observed children – the diary of a primary classroom

In this diary, Michael Armstrong (1980) studies 'the intellectual growth of the children he teaches. In the intimate relationship of teacher/student he carefully observes, documents, and analyzes the children's learning through their work. Samples of the children's writing, drawing, and pattern work are plentiful and allow the reader to "see" the intellectual growth of the children in the same detail that Armstrong did. In this account, Armstrong chooses to concentrate on "moments of intellectual absorption: those occasions in which the children were engrossed in the subject matter of their activity and evidently concerned with the significance of what they were saying, writing, painting, making, experimenting with, calculating, designing, or inventing." Through this focus on moments of deep engagement in learning, he, at the same time is always evoking in the background of our minds the teaching that engages the children in this way'. (extract from Centre for the Scholarship of Teaching, Michigan State University website)

Although the nature of ethnography varies considerably in its approach and the nature of the knowledge that it seeks, Pole and Morrison propose the following common characteristics of ethnographic methodologies:

1. A focus on a discrete location, event(s) or setting
2. A concern with the full range of social behaviour within the location, event or setting
3. The use of a range of different research methods which may combine qualitative and quantitative approaches but where the emphasis is upon understanding social behaviour from inside the discrete location, event or setting
4. An emphasis on data and analysis which moves from detailed description to the identification of concepts and theories which are grounded in the data collected within the location, event or setting
5. An emphasis on rigorous or thorough research, where the complexities of the discrete event, location or setting are of greater importance than overarching trends or generalisations (Pole and Morrison, 2003, p. 5).

We can begin to consider the important dimensions that your ethnographic research should involve by taking these characteristics and examining them in terms of the key elements of ethnography. Walford (2001) identifies seven key elements of ethnography:

1. A study of culture
2. Multiple methods which produce diverse forms of data
3. Engagement
4. Researcher as instrument
5. Participant accounts have high status
6. Cycle of hypotheses and theory building
7. Intention and outcome (Walford, 2001, p. 7).

'Ethnographers stress that we move within social worlds, and that to understand the behaviour, values and meanings of any given individual (or group), we must take account of some kind of cultural context' and in doing so 'ethnography balances attention to the sometimes minute everyday detail of individual lives with wider social structures' (Walford, 2001, p.7). You will need to determine the breadth of these influencing social structures from a micro level (e.g. the way one teacher approaches a certain task) to a macro level (e.g. the influence of government policy on the profession). See earlier notes on culture to support this.

The need for detailed data and associated analysis reflects the complexity of the real-life world within which the ethnographer is immersed. The ways that you construe the world will have an influence over the interpretations you have of the research setting but 'to reach even a rudimentary understanding of [cultures] requires an openness to looking in many different ways' (Walford, 2001, p. 8). A wide range of appropriate methods producing a similar diversity of data is an important means to develop in-depth understanding of the research setting. Chapter 9 will consider certain methods in detail, however one notable approach to mention here is the compilation of field notes which will record a wide range of observational notes, interviews, spontaneous conversations, overheard comments, notes on documents, sketches, etc. (See the vignette below for an example of field notes.)

Vignette: Example of field notes

'This was the first time I had met "Liz" in this way. I was surprised how nervous she seemed. Even though I assured her, or tried to, that I was interested in her views she seemed to be trying to give me answers I might "like"?

She was very hard to draw out. Many answers were very short and that may be the questions I asked? Even my body language?

When I asked her to describe the new initiatives she really changed. Leant forward and became very animated, but I am not sure that she is basing them on a strong rationale.

The engagement of the researcher through long-term immersion in the research field is an important tenet of ethnography where the researcher 'places a primacy on the importance of situated meaning and contextualized experience as the basis of explaining and understanding social behaviour' (Pole and Morrison, 2003, p. 5). The assumption is that as the researcher becomes more immersed in the research setting, the 'participants are less likely to behave uncharacteristically' (Walford, 2001, p. 9) and that their 'performance' is thus reduced enabling greater insights to be made.

The fourth element of ethonography (see above) of 'researcher as instrument' acknowledges the influence of the researcher on the research process through his or her engagement with, and subjective interpretations of, the research field. This process requires a balance between

'suspending preconceptions and using one's present understandings and beliefs to enquire intelligently ... To achieve such awareness, the ethnographer must constantly review the evolution of his or her ideas ... [and] above all ... must try to articulate the assumptions and values implicit in the research, and what it means to acknowledge the researcher as part of, rather than outside, the research act'. (Walford, 2001, p.9)

You have a big responsibility to try and present the findings such that the participants' views are represented in multiple perspectives (Walford, 2001). As a student teacher in a school who is also undertaking research you will be a researcher-participant. The levels of researcher participation in educational settings will most likely be 'participation as observer' (all are aware that the participant is conducting research) or 'participation in the normal setting' where the participant's research role will be known to only a few key people (e.g. a class teacher when observing a lesson). Further degrees of hiding the researcher's role tend to present greater ethical issues (Pole and Morrison, 2003).

The immersion in the field before theories are built ('emergent design') separates ethnography from case study methodologies. The flexible, open nature of ethnography belies a

> constant commitment to modify hypotheses and theories in the light of further data ... and as new data emerge, existing hypotheses may prove inadequate, the ethnographer's sense of what needs to be looked at and reported on may change and explanation of what is going on may be supplanted by ones which seem to fit better. (Walford, 2001, p. 10)

The need to be adaptable, to suspend judgement in order to follow many lines of enquiry is important in successful ethnographic research (see the following vignette).

Vignette: Changing research strategies

After a few weeks in her middle school, Jetty's initial idea for her research focus was to investigate how teacher-led assessment for learning was used by pupils to understand their learning better. Her initial plan was to use a questionnaire with all 30 staff and a sample of pupils and then to interview four or five teachers and a focus group of pupils based on their responses. As assessment for learning is a common term, she initially thought that the teachers would have a deep and relatively consistent perspective on it linked to the school's assessment policy. However, after overhearing some snatched conversation in the staff room (noted in her research journal) which led her to talk to other staff, she decided that her initial hypothesis and research approach needed changing; there were probably multiple perspective held by staff about this term. She decided she needed to investigate teachers' perceptions of assessment for learning before she could do anything else. She would base most of her research on lesson observation and follow-up post-lesson discussions as well as some informal interviews which would be noted in her research journal. She also thought that, depending on initial findings, her approach may need to be tweaked again.

Finally, in coming to conclusions in your research it is important that you consider the specifics of the situation in which you have been immersed. The data you will have collected will be lengthy, varied and complex with multiple inputs from participants, and your analysis of artefacts and documents will present different 'stories' for you to interpret. Ultimately, you will aim, 'through a judicious blend of empirical experience, systematic activity and appropriate theory … to construct a coherent story that takes the reader into a deeper and richer appreciation of the people who have been studied' (Denscombe, 1995, p. 182, cited in Walford, 2001, p. 11). So the findings should emerge from your generated data with the lines of thought clearly identified (see Table 7.6).

TABLE 7.6 Example of data leading to conclusions

Investigation into the kind of metaphors that teachers use to describe learning

Data extracts	Findings
'That the children can grasp the idea.' 'The children need to be given understanding about …' 'I tell them that at the start so they know it and then …'	That in this study the teachers tend to see learning as a 'transmission'.

So, in summary, ethnography is a research methodology that enables:

1. The collection of detailed data which requires close analysis
2. A comprehensive and contextualised description of the social action within the location, event or setting. Such descriptions are often described as 'rich' or 'thick'
3. The portrayal of an insider's perspective, in which the meaning of the social action for the actors themselves is paramount and takes precedence over, but does not ignore, that of the researcher
4. The construction of an account of the discrete location, event or setting which is grounded in the collected data and which incorporates a conceptual framework that facilitates understanding of social action at both an empirical and theoretical level (Pole and Morrison, 2003, p. 3).

ACTION RESEARCH

Action research is a term with which you may be familiar through your reading or activities regarding classroom-based research. It 'has become something of an evangelical movement designed to change the nature of educational research such that it becomes an integral part of the work of teachers in schools rather than an activity carried out on schools by outsiders' (Walford, 2001, pp. 108–9, quoting Hammersley, 1993).

It builds very much on the ideas of the teacher-researcher discussed in Chapter 3 and is defined as a 'self-reflective, self-critical and critical enquiry undertaken by professionals to improve the rationality and justice of their own practices, their understanding of these practices and the wider contexts of practice' (Lomax, 2002, p. 122).

A key difference between action research and other methodologies is one of intent. It sets out to change the situation being studied (Lomax, 2002, p. 123) and is one form of research that can be undertaken over a relatively short timescale and in small-scale situations, although critics illustrate the reduction in the research validity by doing this.

Lomax suggests the following approaches to action research which stem from her definition of it. Teacher-researchers should be:

- thoughtful and the enquiry be intentional (self-reflection)
- willing to have their ideas challenged (self-critical)
- willing to challenge existing knowledge and practice (critical)
- open-minded and not have prior exceptions of research outcomes
- able to change practice in line with identified values (to improve)
- committed to effective practice (the rationality) (Lomax, 2002, p. 122, cited in Hoult, 2005, p. 162).

Being reflexive in learning to teach opens oneself up to much deeper questioning, with the potential to better understand yourself, your values and beliefs, and the situation you are in. As such, it is very much an inward looking process. However, Lomax, with respect to action research, develops the idea of reflexivity as 'an outward looking dimension [that] puts emphasis on the researcher as a collaborator, actively seeking the validation of their practice and knowledge' (2002, p. 131, cited in Hoult, 2005, p. 163). We have seen in earlier chapters that the need for interpretation and to make meaning of events are crucial to reflection and reflexivity, and therefore also to action research. We should however not see action research purely as a qualitative methodology.

It is important to recognise that you, as the action researcher, are not in a neutral position within this framework for research, a position typical of some of the interpretative paradigms indicated in Table 7.2. The 'I' in the research, rather than an apparently neutral 'researcher' signifies the importance of the researcher's involvement in the process and his/her influence on the outcomes. Thus action research is: 'value laden and morally committed and action researchers perceive themselves as in relation with one another in their social context' (McNiff and Whitehead, 2006, p. 23).

Action research is a valuable methodology for the teacher-researcher. 'Use action research when you want to evaluate whether what you are doing is influencing your own or other people's learning, or whether you need to do something different to ensure that it is' (McNiff and Whitehead, 2006, p. 13).

Given the 'action' based nature of the outcomes of this methodology it is logical that the nature of the questions posed will differ too from those used in the typical social science approach. Table 7.7 taken from McNiff and Whitehead (2006) suggests the following differences.

TABLE 7.7   Social science and action research questions (from McNiff and Whitehead, 2006, p. 8)

Social science questions	Action research questions
What is the relationship between teacher motivation and teacher retention?	How do I influence the quality of teachers' experience in school so that they decide to stay?
Does management style influence worker productivity?	How do I improve my management style to encourage productivity?
Will a different seating arrangement increase audience participation?	How do I encourage greater audience participation through trying out different seating arrangements?

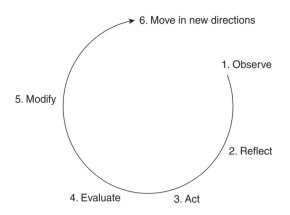

FIGURE 7.1   An action-reflection cycle (from McNiff and Whitehead, 2006, p. 9)

There are a number of models of action research that you may consider in your enquiries. Hopkins (2002) considers a range of these and discusses the relative merits of each. A key dimension of many of these approaches is the cycle or spiral of research (e.g. Kemmis and McTaggart, 1988) such that the research process and then its findings are put into action which itself becomes a focus for future research. Figure 7.1 illustrates a simplified cycle from McNiff and Whitehead (2006).

The spiral approach is not universally approved of and Ebutt (1985) suggests the most appropriate way of considering action research is to 'think of it as comprising of a series of successive cycles, each incorporating the possibility for the feedback of information within and between cycles' (Ebutt, cited in Hopkins, 2002, p. 48) and thus action research is an ongoing process in that it does not stop once findings are analysed and reported, as other research approaches do.

Table 7.8 illustrates a simple action research plan (adapted from McNiff and Whitehead, 2006) with added commentary to illustrate the development of a piece of action research. Although the research is represented in tabular form here it is important to consider the research itself as a cyclical process as discussed above.

TABLE 7.8   Designing a piece of action research (adapted from McNiff and Whitehead, 2006, p.8)

Action research plan components	Example	Comments/Questions
Take stock of what is going on.	Through your usual reflection on your learning you are aware of this and consider your own role within your learning (reflexiveness).	Consider how best you can keep 'taking stock of what is going on' without losing important points. A learning journal will help with this.
Identify a concern.	Your reflection/reflexiveness allows you to question and identify issues for further development/change, e.g. the effectiveness of teacher feedback to aid pupil progression. You identify an alternative approach to teacher feedback and form this into an action research question.	It is important not to see this concern as a negative approach. Use your criticality, as we discussed in Chapter 3.
Think of a possible way forward.	You identify ways to investigate the effectiveness of this teacher feedback. This forms a key part of your research design.	How will you treat this potentially new knowledge? What do you need to do to ensure this is a rigorous research design which is rooted in a suitable paradigm?
Try it out.	You apply the new feedback strategy and review the way forward for the research in the light of this trial.	How did this trial work? Are your research approaches suitable for gathering data in order to consider your research question? Refine these as necessary.

(Continued)

TABLE 7.8 *(Continued)*

Action research plan components	Example	Comments/Questions
Monitor the action by gathering data to show what is happening.	Using the methods you chose earlier, you implement your data-gathering techniques.	Ensure all this is valid and reliable.
Evaluate progress by establishing procedures for making judgements about what is happening.	What has happened so far? Decide how to identify the success of the feedback strategy through action research. What do you think you have found out?	What further questions does this evaluation provoke?
Test the validity of accounts of learning.	Are these findings secure? Why/How? If they are, then you have a secure piece of research on which to consider your new approach to teacher feedback.	What is the nature of this new knowledge that you have developed? Consider how this fits into the research methodology/paradigm.
Modify practice in light of the evaluation.	You decide whether or not to utilise the new feedback strategy or some intermediate adaptation based on your findings.	What further questions will this modification of practice provoke? How could the action research process continue?

A significant potential limitation with action research occurs if the initial research question becomes permanently fixed.

> Reconaissance should involve analysis as well as fact-finding and should constantly recur in the spiral of activities, rather than occurring at the beginning. Implementation of an action step is not always easy and one should not proceed to evaluate the effects of an action until one has monitored the extent to which is has been implemented. (Elliot, 1991, p. 70, cited in Hopkins, 2002)

While action research forms the basis for much teacher-based research there are certain limitations. Hopkins (2002) identified three main concepts about action research. Firstly, he feels that action research, as defined by Kurt Lewin in the 1940s has been misinterpreted and is now a loose term that describes any teacher-based research. Lewinian action research was a functionalist and externally initiated intervention that was prescriptive in practice. This does not describe the teacher-based research characterised by practitioner problem solving.

Secondly, Hopkins identified the potential trap of the research cycle. Research may be constrained by the methodological process indicated by the models. Additionally, the models develop the process of research clearly, but do not define how or what to research at the different points of the cycle.

Finally, Hopkins cites the overuse of action research terms such as 'problem' and 'improve' as though action research is always a deficit model of professional development (Hopkins, 2002, p. 51). 'There is a need for teacher-researchers to be positive about practice' (Hoult, 2005, p. 163).

Action research is a popular methodology with teacher-researchers. However, it is important (as with all methodologies) to ensure that this approach is applied rigorously with an appropriately developed and refined research design and incorporating a series of methods that enable a valid and reliable piece of research to be undertaken.

At best it is a potentially transformative research methodology for teachers to understand and influence their work through the formation of theories that are put into practice to improve learning and, as such, action research can be viewed 'as a methodology for real-world social change' (McNiff and Whitehead, 2006, p. 12).

CONCLUSION

In this chapter we have reviewed the importance of considering the overarching paradigm for your research. This is determined by the ways you think about and construe meaning but also by the nature of the research question. A qualitative, interpretative paradigm is suggested as probably the most appropriate paradigm to consider for your school-based research. The differences between paradigms, methodologies and methods have been outlined and the importance of ensuring that they are congruent with each other identified. It is vital that you consider the validity of your research and ensure it is reliable. Three methodologies were considered and their uses for education research were explored.

📖 *Recommended further reading*

Holliday, A. (2007) *Doing and Writing Qualitative Research*, 2nd edn. London: Sage. The book explores qualitative research fully, considering the range of complexities that this research develops, including approaches to research, writer voice, appropriate data, claim-making and writing.

McNiff, J. and Whitehead, J. (2006) *All You Need to Know About Action Research*. London: Sage.

This text considers the nature and appropriate use of action research. It takes the reader through ways of developing action planning, data collection and testing and critiquing knowledge as well as writing.

Pole, C. and Morrison, M. (2003) *Ethnography for Education*. Maidenhead: Open University Press.
This text thoroughly outlines the nature of ethnographic methodology and its uses in educational research, as well as approaches you can take to undertake such research.

Yin, R. (2008) *Case Study Research*, 4th edn. Thousand Oaks, CA: Sage.
This text provides a detailed outline of case study methodology and covers the whole process of research design, data collection, analysis and writing.

8 READING AND WRITING CRITICALLY

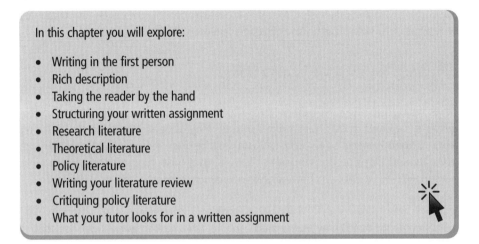

In this chapter you will explore:

- Writing in the first person
- Rich description
- Taking the reader by the hand
- Structuring your written assignment
- Research literature
- Theoretical literature
- Policy literature
- Writing your literature review
- Critiquing policy literature
- What your tutor looks for in a written assignment

INTRODUCTION

This chapter will support your Masters-level writing. We put words under the microscope and consider the ways in which accomplished writers use language. We draw attention to features of text and offer you models that might be useful in your own academic writing.

We begin by considering different writing styles in order to draw your attention to appropriate styles for academic assignments. We then consider ways to structure an assignment and support you in crafting dynamic introductions, in developing criticality in the literature review and interrogating policy texts. Finally, we invite four experienced colleagues to tell you what they look for in an M-level assignment, what disappoints, what they like to see and what advice they give to their students about 'good writing'.

During your PGCE year, you will be on an incredibly steep learning curve, developing and enhancing your understanding of learning and teaching and enriching your subject knowledge. You will be socialised into the cultures of the schools in which you are learning to practise, and be introduced to the political landscape of education. Additionally, you will no doubt be acutely aware of the assignments you are required to submit. In particular, you will have heard and read about the need for criticality in your writing at Masters-level.

Before we explore criticality in writing and what that means for your assignments, it is useful to immerse yourself in the power of words and to explore the skill and craft of accomplished writers. Much can be learned by carefully examining the ways in which accomplished authors communicate their ideas. We have selected extracts from a range of novels below that will be useful in developing your approach to your writing.

WRITING IN THE FIRST PERSON

Texts written in the first person provide the reader with direct access to the writer's feelings, thoughts and emotions. We have selected three extracts, from Robert Harris' *The Ghost*, Kate Atkinsons' *Behind the Scenes at the Museum* and Daphne du Maurier's *Rebecca*, that have been written in the first person. We have chosen the opening passages from each text:

The moment I heard how McAra died I should have walked away. I can see that now. I should have said, 'Rick, I'm sorry, this isn't for me, I don't like the sound of it,' finished my drink and left. But he was such a good storyteller, Rick — I often thought he should have been the writer and I the literary agent — that once he'd started talking there was never any question I wouldn't listen, and by the time he had finished, I was hooked.

The Ghost, Robert Harris

I exist! I am conceived to the chimes of midnight on the hall clock on the mantelpiece in the room across the hall. The clock once belonged to my great-grandmother (a woman called Alice) and its tired chime counts me into the world. I'm begun on the first stroke and finished on the last when my father rolls off my mother and is plunged into a dreamless sleep, thanks to the five pints of John Smith's Best Bitter he has drunk in the Punch Bowl with his friends, Walter and Bernard Belling. At the moment at which I moved from nothingness into being my mother was pretending to be asleep — as she often does at such moments. My father, however, is made of stern stuff and he didn't let that put him off.

Behind the Scenes at the Museum, Kate Atkinson

Last night I dreamt I went to Manderley again. It seemed to me I stood by the iron gate leading to the drive, and for a while I could not enter, for the way was barred to me. There was a padlock and chain upon the gate. I called in my dream to the lodge-keeper, and had no answer, and peering closer through the rusted spokes of the gate I saw that the lodge was uninhabited.

Rebecca, Daphne du Maurier

When an author uses the first person, the reader is taken immediately into the world of the character. In the extract from *The Ghost* above, Robert Harris plunges the reader instantly into the narrator's reflections and troubles. Similarly, Kate Atkinson's use of the first person has the effect of ensuring that the reader makes that first graphic journey with the character. We are given intimate insight into the personality of each character – there is no 'middle man' providing the reader with their opinion of someone – we make our minds up as a direct result of the use of the first person. It is intimate and insightful. In Daphne du Maurier's *Rebecca*, the exquisite dream-like quality of the opening passage takes us into the world of the character – we instantly feel a sense of sadness, abandonment, isolation.

The use of the first person in academic writing is often debated and strong views are held on both sides of the argument. From our point of view, the writing you undertake in this social science assignment might have different 'voices' running throughout – and it is useful to think now about where the use of the first person might be a powerful tool to enable you to communicate your ideas.

Reflection

Your voice is important – where will you use the first person in your written assignment?

RICH DESCRIPTION

Whilst criticality in Masters-level writing is essential, rich description can also have an important place. Read these beautifully crafted descriptions below. As before, we have selected opening passages from texts.

Imagine a ruin so strange it must never have happened. First, picture the forest. I want you to be its conscience, the eyes in the trees. The trees are columns of slick, brindled bark like muscular animals overgrown beyond all reason. Every space is

(Continued)

(Continued)

filled with life: delicate, poisonous frogs war-painted like skeletons, clutched in copulation, secreting their precious eggs onto dripping leaves. Vines strangling their own kin in the everlasting wrestle for sunlight. The breathing of monkeys.

The Poisonwood Bible, Barbara Kingsolver

It was inevitable: the scent of bitter almonds always reminded him of the fate of unrequited love. Dr Juvenal Urbino noticed it as soon as he entered the still darkened house where he had hurried on an urgent call to attend a case that for him had lost all urgency many years before. The Antillean refugee Jeremiah de Saint-Amour, disabled war veteran, photographer of children, and his most sympathetic opponent in chess, had escaped the torments of memory with the aromatic fumes of gold cyanide.

Love in the Time of Cholera, Gabriel Garcia Marquez

Okonkwo was well known throughout the nine villages and even beyond. His fame rested on solid personal achievements. As a young man of eighteen he had brought honour to his village by throwing Amalzine the Cat. Amalzine was the great wrestler who for seven years was unbeaten, from Umuofia to Mbaino. He was called the Cat because his back would never touch the earth. It was this man who Okonkwo threw in a fight which the old man agreed was one of the fiercest since the founder of their town engaged a spirit of the wild for seven days and seven nights.

Things Fall Apart, Chinua Achebe

In the space of approximately 100 words, and with the use of simile, metaphor and powerful imagery, each of the authors above has introduced the reader to their unique world. In *The Poisonwood Bible*, the reader is at once introduced to the mysterious ruin amongst teaming, brutal life. In *Love in the Time of Cholera*, Marquez sets a deeply mournful tone and introduces the reader to two characters, details of their lives, their relationship and something of their personalities. Chinua Achebe, in *Things Fall Apart*, sets the landscape of the story, characters, cultural concepts of honour, customs and the history of the place.

Activity

Using no more than 100 words, craft a rich description of your school or setting. This might be useful as part of your introduction.

TAKING THE READER BY THE HAND: INTRODUCING A DILEMMA OR PHENOMENON

Stories usually develop around a dilemma, a phenomenon or a journey. Characters are faced with choices and consequences of their actions. The author's task is to take the reader by the hand, at an early stage in the writing, and introduce the dilemma or issue. This locates the reader in time, and in the culture and customs of the characters. The extracts we have chosen are, again, all opening passages.

When Sultan Khan thought the time had come to find himself a new wife, no one wanted to help him. First he approached his mother.

'You will have to do with the one you have,' she said.

Then he went to his oldest sister. 'I'm fond of your first wife,' she said. His other sisters replied in the same vein.

'It's shaming for Sharfina,' said his aunt.

Sultan needed help. A suitor cannot himself ask for a girl's hand. It is an Afghan custom that one of the women of the family conveys the proposal and gives the girl the once-over to assure herself that she is capable, well brought up and suitable wife-material. But none of Sultan's close relations wanted to have anything to do with this offer of marriage.

The Bookseller of Kabul, Asne Seierstad

It was 7 minutes after midnight. The dog was lying on the grass in the middle of the lawn in front of Mrs Shear's house. Its eyes were closed. It looked as if it was running on its side, the way dogs run when they think they are chasing a cat in a dream. But the dog was not running or asleep. It was dead. There was a garden fork sticking out of the dog. The points of the fork must have gone all the way through the dog and into the ground because the fork had not fallen over. I decided that the dog was probably killed with the fork because I could not see any other wounds in the dog and I do not think you would stick a garden fork into a dog if it had died for some other reason, like cancer for example, or a road accident. But I could not be certain about this.

The Curious Incident of the Dog in the Night-Time, Mark Haddon

---

The impulse for your focus in your academic writing is likely to be something that fascinates you, that you feel you need to know more about, or even something that troubles you. You will need to take the reader by the hand, early on in your assignment, and introduce them to the context – to the issue that is interesting or troubling. While this process is helpful to your reader it also serves to help you define the issues for yourself. You will notice that the extracts above, whilst conveying rich information, providing a setting, characters and dilemmas, have done so in between 100 and 150 words.

 Activity

Using no more than 100 words, set out the impulses that drive your interest in this assignment. What is it that has caused you to want to explore this issue further? Why is this work so important to you?

STRUCTURING YOUR WRITTEN ASSIGNMENT

PGCE tutors will have designed the assessment opportunities on your PGCE to offer you a range of modes through which you can provide evidence of your learning, your understanding and your criticality. Your written assignment may be an analysis of policy, a report on a piece of action research or a critique of the literature, a case study, a reflective log, or any number of blends of the above! Most written assignments, however, require an introduction, and this next section considers the key elements needed in an introduction.

The introduction

Your introduction may need to cover all or some of the following elements:

- the policy context
- the background
- your key question(s) or dilemma
- the setting
- the method(s) you have employed
- the aim of the research.

You should also aim to convince your reader of the importance of your study – what we call the 'so-whatness' of the work.

The following extracts are examples of the choices that authors have made in terms of structuring their introductions. All articles are from refereed journals and all are opening passages. You will see that the authors have introduced their writing with a focus on either the policy context within which the research takes place, a dilemma or the aims of the piece. In the section below we provide you with extracts, commentaries and writing activities to support you in drafting your introduction. We suggest that you aim to keep your word count down – elegant writing requires simplicity of expression, using as few words as possible.

The policy context

Policy context 1

'The Steer Committee report emphasizes that "the quality of learning, teaching and behaviour in schools are inseparable issues" and that "the support of parents is essential for the maintenance of good behaviour". The report also recognizes the difficulties of developing effective solutions to the different forms of difficult behaviour in schools (Department for Education and Skills [DfES], 2005a, p. 2)'. (Hayden, 2009, p. 205)

Hayden quotes from a policy document in the opening sentence of this introduction. She brings to the reader's attention the key emphasis of the policy document and, as a secondary point, highlights the recognition in the document of the problems inherent in finding solutions.

Activity

Set the policy context of your assignment in no more than 50 words, using a powerful quote from the document to set the scene.

Policy context 2

'We begin this article by drawing attention to a recent policy emphasis on social and emotional education, in which a value for self-awareness and closely related concepts is embedded. The "Birth to Three Matters Framework" (Sure Start, 2005) recommends the development of "the strong self" as a key goal incorporating four elements: "me, myself and I", "being acknowledged and affirmed", "developing self-assurance" and "a sense of belonging"'. (Warin and Muldoon, 2009, p. 289)

Warin and Muldoon, in a similar fashion to Hayden, open their Introduction with reference to a key policy document. Unlike Hayden, however, they do not quote directly from the policy document, but rather, introduce the reader to key concepts from within the document.

Activity

In no more than 50 words, craft the opening sentences of your introduction with direct reference to key themes.

The dilemma

Dilemma 1

'This article is an exploration of the problematic transition from GCSE to AS-level mathematics. This has always been a difficult transition and one that troubled me during the eight years that I taught A-level mathematics'. (Mendick, 2008, p. 711)

In this introduction, Mendick has articulated the dilemma through personal experience, writing in the first person. She has used fewer than 35 words to set this scene.

 Activity

Articulate your dilemma or troubling issue, using the first person, in no more than 35 words.

Dilemma 2

'Over 100 million children worldwide go without primary schooling. In almost all respects, the challenge of universal primary education (UPE) (http://portal.unesco.org.education/) is greatest in sub-Saharan Africa (SSA). Four out of every ten primary-age children do not go to school (UNESCO, 2005) and only a small proportion of those who do attend school reach a basic level of skills'. (Leach, 2008, p. 783)

This introduction sets a global scene. Jenny Leach draws on research by an internationally recognised body to support her claims. She has not used the first person, but rather, has set the context in terms of numbers of children, information on UPE and where the greatest problem is, plus she has provided reference to UNESCO.

Activity

Articulate your dilemma in the context of a national or international context.

The aim

Aim

'The aim of this article is to examine the link between gender, school contexts and academic self-concept. Do girls rate their abilities in mathematics and science more highly if they are in a girls-only school? And do boys rate their abilities in English and modern languages more highly if they are in a boys-only school? The impacts of parental social class and education and selective schooling on self-concept are also examined'. (Sullivan, 2009, p. 259)

Sullivan has opened the article by telling the reader instantly what the aim of the article is. You will notice that she has also asked key questions that will be addressed in the research.

Activity

Write the aim(s) of your assignment in one sentence. Raise key questions using no more than 50 words.

ENGAGING WITH THE LITERATURE

A critical engagement with the literature is a requirement of Masters-level writing. The first question, though, is what is meant by 'the literature'? Poulson and Wallace (2004) suggest that there are four types of literature:

- Theoretical literature
- Research literature
- Policy literature
- Practice literature.

You may very well engage with all four types of literature during your PGCE, and for differing reasons. Most teachers will have texts on their bookshelves that offer exciting ideas for practice – perhaps a book on themes for assemblies, starting points for drama or craft books. Whilst these books will form part of your armoury (and you will no doubt have favourites that you cherish over the years), they are probably not the types of literature that you will use in your Masters-level assignments. What we are left with, then, is literature relating to theory, to research and to education policy.

In the same way that you will develop favourite 'practice' books, we hope that you will develop 'favourite' authors of theoretical literature and research literature – writers who seem to write exactly what you are thinking and whose ideas resonate with your own. Hofstede (1991) refers to such influential people as 'heroes'. You may already have discovered heroes from the literature on your PGCE – and no doubt your tutors will have guided you to their heroes. Take a critical look at the reading lists you have been given, both for professional studies and subject studies.

Activity

Ask your tutors who their heroes and heroines are …
   If you look back to the authors we have referenced and whose ideas we have engaged with in Part 1 of this book, you will easily be able to identify many of our heroes.

Research literature

Research literature relating to education is that which is written by academics or those in education-related contexts. Research literature presents empirical research in research journals. Refereed journals are those which send articles out to reviewers for comments and approval before they are published. Your tutors will direct you to appropriate research journals related to aspects of professional studies and subject studies. You will no doubt be directed to specific articles on book lists. Articles in refereed journals are usually structured using the following format:

- Abstract
- Introduction
- Literature review
- Methods/methodology
- Data analysis
- Conclusions.

You will notice that all the extracts we used in the section above on writing your introduction are from refereed journals – they have all engaged in empirical research. Conclusions in research journals 'sometimes make recommendations for improving policy and practice' (Poulson and Wallace, 2004, p. 21).

Theoretical literature

Theoretical literature is written by academics or researchers and presents conceptual systems that they 'apply ... to understand an aspect of the social world, and sometimes advocate improvement in practice' (Poulson and Wallace, 2004, p. 21). Research literature is often drawn upon to develop conceptual systems which seek to offer ways of reading or understanding the social world. You will notice that in Part 1 of this book we drew heavily upon theoretical literature.

Policy literature

Policy literature is developed by policy makers. Education policy can be understood as that which is written or spoken by policy makers, that is, those in government or aspiring to government. Policy texts articulate clearly defined ideological perspectives. They assert authority, position the past, present key policy platforms and are written in persuasive language. Policy texts can be spoken as well as written – ministers speaking during an interview will always be 'on message' as it were, and as such, their words represent the policy position of their respective political party.

WRITING YOUR LITERATURE REVIEW

The aim of the literature review is to synthesise and critique that which is known and published from policy literature, theoretical literature and research literature. You have ownership of your literature review. You decide on the types of literature – the balance of policy documents, theoretical literature and research literature. In this way you craft and shape the review – your voice is heard in the synthesis and critique of the texts.

The poorest literature reviews are those which merely present a shopping list of authors:

Jones (2004) reports that ... Smith (2001) tells us that ... Hammond (1997) wrote that ... Hunter (2000) noted that ...

In critiquing the literature you should aim to interrogate the texts you have chosen to use, rather than simply listing them. When reading and taking notes, many of us do use the 'shopping list' method of compiling information, knowledge building and sorting out our thinking. The question is, how do we move from the shopping list to a rich critique of the literature?

We advise our PGCE students to try to avoid beginning any paragraph (and any sentence if possible) with the name of the author whose work they are critiquing. Rather, aim to explore the *key issue* or *dimension* that the author offers to the context. You should reference the author's name at the end of the sentence. In this way, you foreground the rich thinking that will hopefully provide a new dimension to the context you are exploring. The following extract models this perfectly.

> The extent to which fathers are involved in their children's early development has been the subject of debate. Some contend that fathers' involvement in housework and child care is lacking (Hochschild, 1989; Thompson and Walker, 1989; Shelton, 1990) and that fathers tend to avoid such responsibilities (Walkerdine and Lucey, 1989); much of this literature is influenced by feminist theories. Some have argued that women may be reluctant for their partners to become more involved in family work and child care, fearing that they may lose their traditional power over home activities (Polatnik, 1974; Lamb, 1997; Bonney et al., 1999). Others contend that fathers' involvement in children's development is increasing, focusing on the changing nature of fatherhood and the 'new father' image (Lamb et al., 1987; Lewis and O'Brien, 1987) which emerged during the 1980s. (Morgan et al., 2009, p. 167)

If we now take each sentence from the extract above, we can analyse the way the dimensions within the literature have been introduced to the reader and a critical stance is developed (see Table 8.1). In analysing writing in this way you will enhance your own writing skills.

The extract above has been written in an elegant yet informative style. The reader is introduced, in no more than four sentences, to a wealth of research and the multi-dimensional context within which this research has taken place.

Activity

Go to the research journals. Browse through the literature review sections in a range of articles – try the analysis modelled above to really get to the heart of what the author(s) is/are doing in their writing.

TABLE 8.1 Analysing criticality

Sentence	Analysis
The extent to which fathers are involved in their children's early development has been the subject of debate.	This sentence highlights the central issue.
Some contend that fathers' involvement in housework and child care is lacking (Hochschild, 1989; Thompson and Walker, 1989; Shelton, 1990) and that fathers tend to avoid such responsibilities (Walkerdine and Lucey, 1989); much of this literature is influenced by feminist theories.	This sentence is in three parts. The first part of the sentence takes the issue highlighted in the previous sentence and offers one dimension to involvement in early development – that of lack of involvement in housework and child care. This section is then referenced in its own right. The second part of the sentence offers another dimension to this theme – that of avoidance on the part of fathers. Again, this is referenced to the specific authors who undertook this research. The third part of this sentence follows the semi-colon. It informs us that much of the literature in this field is influenced by feminist theories. In just one sentence the reader has been introduced to a range of research that develops dimensions to the overall research area of fathers' involvement in early child care – that of involvement and avoidance. The reader is also informed that this field is influenced by feminist literature. Note: this sentence begins with the phrase 'some contend that'.
Some have argued that women may be reluctant for their partners to become more involved in family work and child care, fearing that they may lose their traditional power over home activities (Polatnik, 1974; Lamb, 1997; Bonney et al., 1999).	A new dimension to this issue is offered in this third sentence; that of the reluctance of women to involve their partners, and, again, this is referenced fully at the end of the sentence. Note: this sentence begins with the phrase 'some have argued that'.
Others contend that fathers' involvement in children's development is increasing, focusing on the changing nature of fatherhood and the 'new father' image (Lamb et al.,1987; Lewis and O'Brien, 1987) which emerged in the 1980s.	Yet another dimension is added in this fourth sentence – that of the 'new father'. Again, the references are offered at the end of the sentence. Note: this sentence begins with the phrase 'others contend that'.
	This paragraph has added layers of thinking around one key issue. The authors' voice is heard throughout the paragraph and all references are given should the reader wish to develop their reading further.

CRITIQUING POLICY LITERATURE

Education policy literature will be written from an ideological stand-point. In interrogating education policy texts, you will be revealing the ways in which policy texts 'position' or 'construct' the past, parents, teachers and learners. Policy texts will also assert authority and provide a vision, followed by the means to achieve that vision (Poulson and Wallace, 2004).

We have chosen *Higher Standards, Better Schools For All: More Choice for Parents and Pupils* (DfES, 2005b) to model the ways in which you might interrogate the text (see Table 8.2).

TABLE 8.2 Analysis of policy text

Theme	Extract	Commentary
Policy texts position the past.	'We are at an historic turning point: we now have an education system that is largely good, after eight years of investment and reform, which has overcome many of the chronic inherited problems of the past'	The (former) Prime Minister Tony Blair refers to the past (before a Labour government) as a time that has left a legacy of 'chronic inherited problems'.
Policy texts present the here and now as a time of 'best' practice.	'Now, with the best teaching force and the best school leadership ever …'	Policy texts will always present the achievements of the party in the most positive light.
Policy texts present the transformational achievements of the party.	'After 1997, this government extended such accountability … … Under-performing schools were challenged … …The government sought to re-energise comprehensive education … …These reforms have been supported by an unprecedented level of investment …'	The language used to describe transformational change is energetic and dynamic.
Policy texts position parents.	'… put parents at the centre of our thinking giving them greater choice and active engagement in their child's learning and how schools are run …	Parents have become key policy themes – at the heart of government thinking.

(Continued)

TABLE 8.2   *(Continued)*

Theme	Extract	Commentary
	We will ensure that: • parents receive regular, meaningful reports during the school … • parents have the chance to form Parent Councils … • parents have better local complaints procedures … • parents have access to more and clearer information about local schools … • parents are able to set up new schools supported by a dedicated capital pot'	
Policy texts present a vision, followed by the means to achieve it (Poulson and Wallace, 2004).	'… we are poised to become world class if we have the courage and vision to reform and invest further and put the parent and pupil at the centre of the system …' (Tony Blair).	The vision is articulated as having world-class status. The means to achieve this is presented as a process of reform and investment, with parents and pupils at the centre of the system. All this, Tony Blair writes, will take 'courage'.

There is more, of course. Policy texts position teachers, learners, knowledge and skills.

Teaching and learning exist within a policy landscape. Policy documents, it can be argued, operate not only at the macro-level, but at the micro-level, in the interactions between you and your pupils. The 1988 Education Reform Act introduced new terminology to the classroom – 'National Curriculum', 'core subjects', 'foundation subjects'. The Literacy and Numeracy Strategies of the late 1990s introduced more new terminology ('Literacy Hour', 'Numeracy Hour', 'Word, Text and Sentence Level' work) and a new pedagogy in the form of the literacy hour.

Policy texts influence the way we think and talk about teaching and learning – from terminology around assessment to our relationships with parents. We feel strongly that you should have a sound understanding of the policy arena within which you practise. Understanding how to interrogate policy texts will enable you to write policy texts for your school at a later stage.

WHAT DOES YOUR TUTOR LOOK FOR IN A WRITTEN ASSIGNMENT?

We invited four experienced tutors to e-mail us with their thoughts on what they look for in an M-level 'traditional' written assignment (always accepting that the marking criteria is a given). Our four tutors were asked to think about the following dimensions to marking:

- What first impressions 'speak' to you?
- What do you particularly like to see in an M-level written assignment?
- What things (if any) disappoint you when you first look at a written assignment?
- What advice do you give your students when they are about to embark upon a written assignment?

Here is what they told us.

First impressions

Tutor 1

> ... a title that grabs me helps — also subheadings that are more interesting and indicative than 'literature search', 'methodology', etc.
>
> I should be able to tell from the first paragraph what this piece of work IS and what it is ABOUT (and I would have the learning outcomes in mind).
>
> ... presented and organised well (headings, paragraphs) ...
>
> ... a glance at a few pages will tell me whether there are enough references and whether they are correctly cited and what ground the assignment covers — I would be wary of lots of old references, repetition of the same references, loads of web references and nothing else. I go to the end and look at the reference list too.

Tutor 2

> My first impressions probably come in this order — they are built around what I would like to see, what I expect of an M-level student and what I hope they've been taught to do:
>
> - A 'sense' of commitment to the work
> - Literature and research-rich work
> - Awareness of reader
> - Strong voice

- Fluent academic style and tone
- Presentation — paragraphing, spelling, punctuation ...

Tutor 3

To gain a first impression — the first thing I always do is look at the reference list/bibliography. Why? To see the range of sources and to see how it is presented — this often gives a good 'signpost' with regard to the quality of the work (but it's not infallible of course).

Tutor 4

Can I read it? Does it take me 10 minutes to get it out of the folder? Has the student provided a mark sheet? If they haven't bothered to do the very simple things, like a spell check, then it suggests they can't be bothered with the over-all assignment.

Things I like to see

Tutor 1

- Clear arguments
- Passion, engagement and authenticity
- Someone who takes nothing for granted and questions everything
- Valuable insights for the reader, demonstrates learning for the student
- A sense of wrestling with something to reach a standpoint (theory, practice, ideas, methodology)
- Good use of a range of appropriate references woven into the argument
- Style — fluent? Engaging? Authentic? Authoritative?
- Innovation — does it use interesting techniques of enquiry or presentation or have a new take on things?
- Really well organised with page numbers (if appropriate), subheadings, cross-referencing, illustrations and examples

A good assignment should be a real page-turner. If the author has found it exciting to write then it should be exciting to read.

Tutor 2

The things I like to see are the same as the things I first look for:

- A 'sense' of commitment to the work
- Literature and research-rich work
- Awareness of reader
- Strong voice

- Fluent academic style and tone
- Presentation — paragraphing, spelling, punctuation ...

Tutor 3

Things I like to see: structure is important — a good introduction that sets the context and tells me what the work is going to cover (important for any writing) and headings that help to signpost on the way.

Tutor 4

The best thing of all, at any level is to read an essay where it is clear that the student has been engaged with an idea, or a text or an argument ... anything that indicates that they are interested in something. Even if I disagree with what they're saying it's so unusual to detect passion that you can't help but feel warm towards the writer.

Things that disappoint

Tutor 1

- Formulaic approach
- Rushed/sloppy presentation and grammar (poor use of apostrophes — bug-bear) and lack of proofreading
- Lack of checking, e.g. blank pages, repeated paragraphs, misspelt words
- Lack of respect for referencing conventions, e.g. putting authors wrong way round, leaving out co-author, misspelling names (Rudduck is often spelt Ruddock, etc.), inconsistencies in references list at end with punctuation, italics etc.
- Sweeping statements such as 'a high noise level indicates that the class is not being well-managed'
- Cliches (especially steep learning curves)
- Clumsy colloquialisms, e.g. 'Ofsteded'
- Use of one text all the way through
- Cherry picking of quotations bolted on to text to confirm argument so that author's voice is lost
- Lack of recognition of the self — no 'I' in the writing

... and questionnaire after questionnaire after questionnaire after questionnaire after questionnaire ...

Tutor 2

I imagine we all have pet hates but I'm always disappointed to see:

- Complacency, assumptions made
- A lack of personal involvement/investment in the work

- Pretension and use of 3rd person — 'one is ....', 'it could be thought ...'
- Absence of any sense of self/voice in a study
- Aggressive writing, attacking the subject and sweeping away opposition
- Clumsy writing
- Distracting punctuation, sentence structure, grammatical errors.

Tutor 3

Things that disappoint: sloppy editing — easy marks thrown away; poor referencing not acceptable at PG/M level; loads of tables or diagrams that add little to the critical arguments; extensive appendices — ditto; incorrect use of the apostrophe and numerous split infinitives (I'm beginning to sound hard to please but this is M-level!); sandbagging (lots of references to shore up an inadequate argument); and conflation!

Tutor 4

Boring essays — even essays where the referencing is impeccable, the bibliography perfect and the analysis concise ... sometimes they read like they've been produced by a machine.

Advice our four tutors give students as they begin the writing process

Tutor 1

You can easily work too hard and you can start too late. You can carry on reading and planning and making notes forever. This easily becomes a substitute for actually starting the writing. The writing itself will help to clarify the ideas. You develop criticality by constructing arguments and presenting them formally in writing. Therefore don't put it off and don't be surprised by how long it takes. It is no good handing in a first draft.

Find your own style and voice — it isn't an exercise in stringing everyone else's voices together.

Get used to the criteria and use the feedback so you end up tutoring yourself.

Get feedback early. This doesn't always need to be from your tutor — what about peer feedback? Get used to sharing your writing and learning from it, not keeping it to yourself.

Imagine a reader who has never met you or seen your setting and has no prior knowledge.

Check, check and check again. Silly mistakes can easily creep in if you rush.

Learn your weaknesses and do something about them — if grammar, spelling and sentence structure are a problem then get help. Actually LEARN how to use the apostrophe, which to use out of their/there and which version of practise/practice to use (all examples from a recent batch of work).

And finally, BACK UP continually.

Tutor 2

Advice prior to the study about *writing* rather than content would be to:

Write about areas, a field, an element that you're really interested in and care about … choose titles, focus with care — then you can write with commitment and passion.

Read widely and openly to begin to gather a sense of your place in the field, then focus more specifically.

Keep referring back to the literature.

Never make a broad claim without supporting evidence.

Develop a sense of reader/audience.

Use the first paragraph or section to take your reader by the hand, welcome them into your world of words and show them where the parameters are and tell them clearly where you intend your focus to be. Lay out the rest so that they know what to expect …

Use your conclusion wisely — to draw together themes, to draw implications from your work towards practice and further research but, importantly, to shout loudly your findings — however small in the scale of national and international work, your findings count — towards your thinking, your practice and your future work and they may also have broader impact.

So, a gentle introduction but a noisy conclusion.

Tutor 3

Have an introductory paragraph which signposts the content of the assignment. Set the scene so that a non-expert would understand the context for guidance practice. Be sure you make links between the different sections of your essay. Be focused and avoid a scattergun approach. Use the conclusion to pull together your arguments and remember to reflect on the question set (this can often be forgotten as we progress in our discussion in an essay). There should be no new material in the conclusion. Do not throw away easy marks by poor referencing or poor re-reading/editing of your work.

Tutor 4

Imagine you are having a conversation with the author of one of the texts you are writing about. Your essay should be a record of that conversation/argument. This means that before you start writing you need to have a sense of what you agree with and what you disagree with.

CONCLUSION

In this chapter we have put words under the microscope – we have considered the way accomplished writers use language to powerful effect. We have supported you in structuring your writing – in thinking about ways to structure sentences to develop a rich, informed and critical perspective.

 *Recommended further reading*

Lodge, D. (1993) *The Art of Fiction*. London: Penguin Books.
This is a beautifully crafted book in which the author takes extracts from literature and considers them through themes. If you are new to writing – and thinking about your writing – or indeed an English Literature specialist, this book will open your eyes to the ways in which writers harness the written word.

Poulson, L. and Wallace, M. (eds) (2004) *Learning to Read Critically in Teaching and Learning*. London: Sage.
This text will support you in developing critical reading for self-critical writing. It offers structures for thinking, for reading and for writing.

DOING FIELD WORK: INTERVIEWS AND QUESTIONNAIRES

In this chapter you will explore:

- Starting points
- Interviews
- Relational space
- Involvement and detachment
- Confidentiality
- Anonymity
- Sample selection
- Gaining access to the research site
- Interviewing groups and young children
- Questionnaires
- Data analysis

INTRODUCTION

You will probably find qualitative methods of enquiry the most useful during your PGCE year – the time to engage in research, and your resources, will be limited and if you want to undertake empirical research, then your time on teaching placement will need to be well organised. Qualitative research will enable you to focus upon and begin to 'read' the messy reality of classroom life, the social complexities of schools and the personal perspectives of pupils and adults. By using qualitative methods you will not have to set up laboratory-style experiments, but rather, you will be approaching this 'real world research' with an open mind and be aware of the deeply complex nature of learning and learning contexts (developed in Chapter 2). Learning is, after all, a human endeavour involving intellectual, psychological, physical and emotional engagement, all of which are important for teachers to acknowledge.

As a qualitative researcher with a simultaneously developing identity as a teacher, you will probably be interested in how pupils and teachers behave in given contexts and how pupils and teachers talk and feel about their behaviours. We are thinking here about perspectives, about engagement, and the affective domain of learning, all of which can be accessed using qualitative methods.

Consider the examples below.

Example

You notice that one particular teacher has effective behaviour management strategies and pupils respond positively in this teacher's company. There is much here that you would like to emulate, but it all seems very complex and intertwined with this teacher's personality.

What could you do to further explore this from the perspective of the teacher, the pupils and the school behaviour policy?

Example

You are responsible for marking pupils' work on teaching placement. How can you find out what would best help pupils to reflect on, and enhance their learning through your comments?

What information and whose perspectives would be most useful to you in this endeavour?

Example

As a teacher, and student teacher, you will be required to make personalised provision for those you teach (including support for those pupils with English as an Additional Language, Special Educational Needs, diversity, equality and inclusion).

How do the teachers in your current placement school approach this requirement and what could you do to find out about the experiences and perspectives of pupils?

Example

On placement, you notice that some pupils consistently fail to submit their homework.

What could you do to find out more with the intention of supporting these pupils?

In considering these examples you will probably have identified the need to talk to pupils and teachers, gather further information from pupils and teachers, watch what happens in classrooms and schools and do some further reading. From a research perspective, these activities can be classified as:

- Interview (structured, unstructured or semi-structured)
- Questionnaire
- Observation
- Analysis of policy documentation (national, Local Authority wide or school-based)
- Engagement with the literature including theoretical and empirical studies.

These activities are encompassed within a paradigm known as qualitative research. This way of undertaking research promotes a systematic approach to real-world enquiry that will probably be useful to you when working at M-level, during the PGCE year. This chapter will take you through the steps you should follow when undertaking qualitative enquiry, and challenge you to ask and answer appropriate questions throughout the whole process to ensure your work is *systematic*, *ethical*, *critical* and *achievable*.

STARTING POINTS

The starting point for your enquiry is likely to be an issue you have encountered on placement, something you are *interested* in, an *experience* in school, a *conversation* with a teacher, pupil or other professional in school, or something that has interested you from your own *observations*. In this sense, your impulse should be *inquisitiveness* – you won't be setting out to *prove* something, but rather to investigate, illuminate issues, reflect upon your findings and consider the implications for your practice. The 'so-what-ness' of your study and findings should be a key element of and the starting point in the design of your enquiry.

As a teacher-researcher, you should be driven by the impulse to constantly ask questions:

- Why is this pupil doing so well?
- Why is this pupil struggling?
- What are the factors contributing to this pupil's motivation?
- How can I motivate this pupil who is seemingly disengaged?
- What implications does this new policy initiative have for me and my practice?
- How will I introduce this new subject area?
- Do I need to gain support from another experienced teacher with this issue?

Once you have broadly identified the area you are interested in researching, your next step should be to ask, and answer, the following questions.

Question 1: What am I trying to find out?

Using bullet points, list all the things that occur to you about this issue. There may be many different 'voices' that you need to tune in to – differing perspectives on what is happening.

These bullet points will form the basis of your research at a later stage.

Question 2: Why is this issue so important?

Try to write a paragraph outlining the 'so-what-ness' of your study: how persuasive can you be?

Try to justify your study – convince the reader of the importance of this work. This paragraph could form the basis of your introduction at a later stage.

Question 3: Do I need to talk to people to find answers to the questions I am asking?

Using the list of questions you have drawn up in Question 1, identify where you will need to talk to people, and begin to think about which people. The range of voices may be extensive at this stage and you will probably have to select the most relevant in order to make your study manageable in the time and word space available to you. That said, you can craft a rich introduction to your assignment setting out the range of voices from which you have selected your sample. There will be voices directly relevant to your study, and voices that are more distant yet which still have a bearing on your enquiry. You may even wish to follow this study up at a later stage after the PGCE year, on your Masters degree.

Question 4: Which methods will be most useful to me in this enquiry?

Using the list of bullet points from Question 1 above, map out the most useful method against each of the questions you have asked.

Crucially, you have limited time and resources available to you this year.

So ... is this study achievable? (Question 5)

Clough and Nutbrown (2007) suggest the 'Goldilocks test', which might be useful at this stage in your thinking:

Is the study too big, bearing in mind the time constraints you are working to?
Is the study too small – have you mapped out the issues sufficiently?
Is this too sensitive an issue for enquiry as a PGCE student?

This approach to research is known as *inductive enquiry* – that is, where you formulate a theory after you have undertaken the research. This way of working is probably most useful to you during your initial teacher education – it will enable you to enter the 'research site' with an open mind and sharpen your skills of observation and criticality. As you develop a deeper understanding of areas that interest you on your M-level journey, you might wish to engage in *deductive enquiry*. That is, where you develop a hypothesis *from* theory. At this stage though, your aim is unlikely to be to test a scientifically constructed theory, but to 'construct interpretive accounts which grasp the intelligibility and coherence of social action by revealing the meaning it has to those who perform it' (Carr, 1998, p. 78).

INTERVIEWS

If you decide that interviewing people is essential in your research, you will need to consider the following questions:

- Who will I interview?
- Why have I chosen these participants?
- How will I gain permission to interview them?
- Where will the interviews take place?
- What will we discuss in the interview?
- What other organisational issues should I consider?

Each of these issues is explored in detail below. Before you set about organising your interviews, it's important to consider yourself, your role and your influence, in this endeavour. It will also be important for you to address confidentiality and anonymity during the interview process, and these issues are considered below.

Relational space

Interviews are normally private interactions between two people, the interviewer and the interviewee. You will probably be interviewing a pupil, teacher, parent, governor or other professional in the school. During the interview you will ask questions and you will hopefully talk comfortably to each other, explore issues and clarify things. You'll probably find yourself saying things like:

can I just go back to something you said earlier

would you mind saying a bit more about that ...

so, do you mean ...

what makes you think that?

In this way you will listen to their narrative, their way of telling the world and events as they see them. Remember that language is the tool we use to shape and articulate our thinking: your interviewee may be hesitant, may need to say something a number of times, in different ways, as their ideas take shape through speech. Through language, your interviewee will be opening a window to their orientation to the world – their cognitive processes, their emotions and their values.

It is likely that you will use a semi-structured interview design – this affords opportunity for both you and the interviewee to explore issues as they arise whilst following a broad list of questions (the structured interview affords the interviewer the greatest amount of control, but allows the least opportunity for the participant to elaborate or engage in a shared endeavour). As you engage with the interviewee in discussion, the narrative will become a shared understanding of events, as together you 'create and construct narrative versions of the social world' (Miller and Glassner, 1997, p. 99). This reciprocal interaction creates what is known as relational space.

By relational space we mean the zone created between you and the interviewee in which you can both explore ideas, consider different ways of seeing the world and exchange information. The balance of active listening, probing a little further with questions and respectfully seeking clarification is central to good communication in an interview. You will need to create a sense of empathy, without compromising your neutrality in the interview.

Clearly, you will need to be conscious of the fact that by sharing information, your interviewee may also share their hopes and possibly concerns. This exchange will require you to be professional yet reciprocal, non-hierarchical as far as possible, and respectful at all times; a complex balance that creates a space for creative reconstruction of understandings, not simply the transmittal of knowledge from the interviewer to the interviewee.

You and the person or persons you interview, will generate knowledge and construct reality between you (Walford, 2001). In this way, your data is *generated*, not simply collected. And it's during these conversations that meaning is socially constructed. Crucially, you are always and necessarily part of the result: 'we are always part of what we research' (Atkinson and Hammersley, 1998, p. 111).

In essence, what you are dealing with here are perceptions of reality; you are trying, throughout the course of the interview, to see the world through someone else's eyes, perhaps a teaching assistant's view, perhaps stepping into a child's plimsolls: it might involve humour, anxiety, sadness, anger. In this sense, the interview can become a rich experience for both you and the person(s) you are interviewing; a sensory navigation that will involve the interviewee in cognition and the co-creation of a narrative.

As you engage in the knowledge-building process throughout the course of the interview, your interviewee may rely on memory to explore and describe, to reflect and argue. Your interviewee will be constructing and reconstructing their perceptions of reality, setting out the landscape of their experiences with you. In return, you will need to be responsive and personable. Your objective should be to create space that enables your interviewee(s) to feel that their identity is respected, to explore their ideas with you, to be listened to and to feel that the space is a safe and confidential one.

This way of learning (researching) about other people's thoughts and ideas, principles, hopes and concerns is founded upon constructivist beliefs. We use the term constructivism to mean the way in which knowledge and perception evolve through multiple exchanges, experience and reflection:

> The construction, or better, the composition, of knowledge does not take place in a progressive or linear way, but as a developing network, based on a dynamic interweaving of interconnected elements. Perception, action, and reflection become the fundamental strategies for individual cognition, and individual knowledge is constructed, deconstructed and consolidated as a result of exchange and relations with others. (Ceppi and Zini, 2001, p. 21)

In this meaning-making context, you are likely to engage in deep discussion with someone you may never have met before. As you explore issues together, the interviewee will be making judgements about you – about whether they like you, whether they should have agreed to this interview and whether they are finding the experience rewarding. Their experience is largely down to your skill in putting them at their ease. There are many famous interviewers on radio and television that are worth observing and listening to – interviewers who are skilful in the art of relaxing their interviewee and adept at asking searching questions. Striking a balance between a chat show host and a Radio 4 *Today* interviewer will probably hit the right tone! Of course, whilst you can do much to put your interviewee at ease, there are some variables that you can do little to effect.

So, consider yourself as others might see you. Who are you? How will the interviewee respond to you in terms of the following classifications:

- Age
- Gender
- Dress code
- Body language
- Researcher identity
- Trainee teacher identity
- Postgraduate student identity.

If we consider 'age', you may find that you are significantly younger and clearly less experienced than those you interview. It's important to be aware of your feelings, and also the possible feelings of those you interview. Whilst you may be feeling quite vulnerable and inexperienced, the person being interviewed may be feeling quite uncertain themselves – you may be seen as someone who is up to date with initiatives and theories in education, or as someone who is an outsider making judgements about practice in a particular school. The power-play dynamics of any interview is something you should consider in advance.

Involvement and detachment

Although you are slightly removed from the context you are researching by virtue of the fact that you are a student at the school, you will have become part of the culture you are attempting to understand and illuminate. As such, you will need to seek to make the 'known' strange, to view the phenomena with a degree of detachment and objectivity. As Holliday writes, 'a major tenet of qualitative research is that all scenarios, even the most familiar, should be seen as strange, with layers of mystery that are always beyond the control of the researcher, which need always to be discovered' (Holiday, 2002, p. 4). The interview will enable the sensitive researcher to delve into the 'layers of mystery' (Holiday, 2002, p. 4) that can inhibit a clear understanding of even well-known contexts.

The process of 'radical looking' is the 'means by which the research process makes the familiar strange and gaps in knowledge are revealed' (Clough and Nutbrown, 2007, p. 24). As you immerse yourself in your interviews, you will move from simply 'hearing' what your participants say to 'radical listening', where your attention is drawn to the positions the various voices in your study take (Clough and Nutbrown, 2007, p. 25). This will become more apparent as you move into data analysis, but try to begin to think about the various positions your participants are taking in relation to your questions.

Confidentiality

It is essential that you ensure confidentiality during interviews. Your interviewees will be sharing their opinions with you, opinions which they may never have voiced in school before. They may disclose personal information, or become distressed when talking through difficult professional situations. In this respect, your mantle of 'researcher' is crucial – you should listen carefully to them but avoid joining in and do not offer opinions of your own.

On the other hand, your interviewees may disclose information about colleagues in school – again, do not be tempted to join in, but rather, guide your interviewee back to the questions. As a researcher you will be faced with all sorts of ethical dilemmas during the interview, some of which may affect the dynamics of the interaction. A key consideration for you, when listening to an interviewee's answers, and asking questions to elucidate as much information as possible, is how far you should allow the interviewee to think you agree with them (Walford, 2001, p. 136).

Whilst endeavouring to appear engaged and sympathetic, you should strive to keep obvious personal opinions to yourself. In this way you will conduct yourself ethically, and if you remain in the school on teaching experience, you will not have compromised your professionalism.

Anonymity

When you get to the stage of analysing your data and writing up your findings, it will be important to ensure that your participants are anonymous in the assignment you submit for assessment. With this in mind, it is probably wise to give your interviewees pseudonyms early on, so that you get used to them and don't get confused.

Likewise, you should endeavour to keep your school(s) anonymous. It is perfectly acceptable to describe the school(s) involved in your study in terms of the broad geographical location, number on roll, number of Free School Meals, if this is appropriate to your study. You may have used certain criteria to select your school in the first place, in which case this information will provide an important portrait for the reader. Depending on the assignment you are writing, this rich description of the school(s) in your study may form part of your introduction.

Sample selection

You will probably focus your empirical research in your placement school – with limited time and resources available to you this choice is entirely justifiable, and is known as a 'convenience sample'. If this is the case then you will need to select a sample for your study. If you are on a block teaching experience, you are likely to be very busy and your teaching placement is the obvious setting. Clearly, if your enquiry focuses upon subject teaching then pupils with whom you are already working are an obvious sample. You may wish to organise to work with another group of pupils within the school that you wouldn't normally come into contact with. If this is the case, ask your class teacher or mentor for support with this. Indeed, your class teacher and mentor will hopefully be engaged in supporting you through this study.

Consider the example below:

Example

You are interested in finding out what children in Reception class understand about the concept of 'measure', the language they use and if there are common misconceptions. You have organised an outdoor activity.

Will you observe children engaged in the activity?
If so, why is observation a useful tool to you in this context?
Which children will you observe?
Why these children?

Will you talk to any children?
If so, why is talking to children useful to your learning?
Which children will you talk to?
Why these children?

Will you interview any adults?
If so, why is interviewing adults useful to your research?
Which adults?
Why these adults?

The selection of pupils needs some careful consideration, and you will be wise to build your sample with the support of your class teacher and mentor. The same applies to the selection of parents if you are considering interviewing them. Your class teacher and mentor will know the pupils and parents well and will be in a good position to advise you.

The following variables will help you refine your sample selection:

- Gender: it might be appropriate to your study to ensure you have a gender balance in your sample.
- Key Stage consideration: a sample from different Key Stages may be helpful to your study.
- Ability: a range of ability might illuminate issues for you.

It may be that you intend to select schools for your enquiry, in which case you will need to select a sample and provide justification for your choices. The following variables will help you to make a selection:

- Catchment area: location in terms of inner-city school, large town school, village school.
- Free School Meals (FSM): the number of pupils entitled to FSM is a social indicator.
- Size of school.
- Type of school: academy, technology college, comprehensive, high school, grammar school.
- Church Aided: faith schools.

Gaining access to the research site

Once you have decided upon your sample, you will need to begin the process of gaining access to the research site. Gaining access to the research site means being given permission to interview staff and/or pupils and/or parents or other professionals in school. This will possibly involve writing a letter (or sending an e-mail) to the Head Teacher and/or Chair of the Governing Body and/or parents, depending on the nature of your intended study.

You should never send letters home to parents or pupils without the approval of your class teacher, mentor and/or Head Teacher. The letter you write is the first point of contact with your prospective participants, and as such, needs to be carefully crafted. The question is, just how much information should you put in your letter? Clearly you don't want to write pages of detailed information about your assignment, but you do want to provide enough information to ensure approval is granted without further questions being asked. It is probably judicious to be brief in the letter and offer a detailed conversation with those who want it.

So, what should you write in the letter? It is wise to explain that you are a student teacher and give the name of your institution. You should explain what you are interested in and why their particular views and opinions (or that of their children) are so important to your study. It will be important here to ensure confidentiality and anonymity in the assignment. It is also a good idea to explain that if they do agree to the interview, you will provide a set of questions in advance of the interview in order that the interviewees are comfortable and not anxious about the kinds of questions they are going to be asked.

You will want to add credibility to your request and this can be done by using the logo of your institution on your paper, if you are sending hard copies. Remember also that if you want replies by post, you should send stamped addressed envelopes with your letter. Alternatively, and probably far more sensible given your inevitable time constraints, is for you to ask to be e-mailed or phoned with replies to your invitation, or, where appropriate, that potential participants call in to see you in school.

Proceeding with your interviews: physical space

An important consideration is the location of the interviews. The characteristics of the location and the atmosphere will influence the experience for both you and the interviewee. Interviews should be conducted in a comfortable, private fashion (Holstein and Gubrium, 1997, p. 118) – you are, after all, expecting your interviewee to tune in to their values and personal experiences and share these with you.

What sort of space will enable you and your interviewees to accomplish this? It will probably be important to work within the architecture of your interviewees' experiences, within the physical environment that shapes their professional lives, opinions and beliefs. With this in mind, you should organise the location of your interviews well in advance – don't leave it until the last minute and expect your class teacher or mentor to find you a room! Remember that timetabling is complicated in schools and most rooms are used throughout lunchtimes, so do be careful to arrange the use of a room in advance.

Your second consideration, and one that should go into the letter when requesting an interview, is the length of time you expect the interview to take. Do try to be reasonable with time. Give yourself enough time to enable your interviewee to relax, but resist the temptation to keep them in the interview room for too long – they are giving of their time freely and helping you with your enquiry. If you are interviewing during lunchtime, make sure you are aware of the time – neither you nor the interviewee(s) will want to be late back to class.

Interviewing the youngest children

Educational research increasingly draws upon the voices of young children (Lewis and Lindsay, 2000). In fact, Cathy Nutbrown (Clough and Nutbrown, 2007) reminds us that young children can, and indeed should, be regarded as *participants in research* rather than *subjects of research.* Nutbrown goes as far as to argue that this is a matter of right. Interviewing young children presents some challenges, but with careful planning and attention to detail this should be rewarding and fruitful for both you and the participants. Students sometimes express concerns about interviewing young children. Here are some comments from students preparing to interview young children for their final MA dissertation:

> I'm not sure that they'll be able to understand my questions.
>
> They can't read so I can't show them the questions beforehand — is that ok?
>
> How will I know that they're telling the truth — they'll probably just say things to please me.

The concerns above all focus on the student and the integrity of the study. Other concerns focused upon the young child:

> How will I know if they are frightened?
>
> Will they say if they want to stop?
>
> What will I do if they get upset or tell me something very personal?

Most of these concerns can be alleviated with careful preparation. The first steps involve gaining permission to interview the child(ren) – you will need to seek the permission of parents, but it is wise to do this after consultation with your class teacher or mentor. Parents may wish to have details of the questions, of the length of the interview and where it will take place, so have this information ready. Parents may also wish to know what their child/ren said in interview – talk this through with your class teacher or mentor. You should consider where you will interview – choose a place where the child is comfortable and at ease, a place that is familiar to them. At the start of the interview, there are protocols you should follow that will ensure the child is informed and positive:

- Talk to the child about the interview – make sure the child is happy to take part. You should not proceed if the child is reticent or unwilling.
- Ensure the child understands that they do not have to take part – they have choice.
- Explain that they can ask you to stop should they feel tired or unhappy.

In terms of designing the questions, the same considerations apply to interviewing young children as to anyone else. A semi-structured interview schedule is likely to be the most useful to you, and with this in mind you should phrase the questions in such a way as to ensure the child(ren) will understand them. Take care in your use of language and be prepared to explain the question or phrase it differently should the need arise.

The structure of the interview will follow the pattern of interviews with older young people and adults – open the interview with an easy question that will put the child at ease. Ensure that your questions are structured in such a way as to invite rich comment and try to avoid closed questions. You may wish to ask the child for clarification or follow up something interesting they have said – this is a natural part of the semi-structured interview.

You have many choices about the way you conduct your questioning and the way you interact with the child. Don't be tempted to jump in quickly and answer for the child – try to stay silent and allow the child time to think about your question and answer in their own way. You can repeat the question should you need to, or re-phrase it. You might want to pick up something the child said – in this case you can repeat their words back to them and ask them to talk about it a bit more.

The aim here is to adopt a style that will enable the child to feel in control and confident. It is, after all, their voice that you are interested in. Make sure you give the child the opportunity to talk about other related things before finishing the interview. It is wise to pilot your interview – that way you will be able to alter your language should the need arise or rephrase questions.

Group interviews

Group interviews provide participants with the opportunity to engage in debate. This might be incredibly valuable to you in your research. The dynamics of a group (if managed well) will create a space where hypothesis can be suggested, viewpoints challenged or affirmed and new ideas developed.

The group interview will enable you to capture dynamic and complex meaning making. The important thing to remember when setting up a group interview is that it should not be a turn-taking exercise. To insist on turn taking – whilst making it easy for you to identify the speaker – will inhibit impulsive and lively debate. The group interview will provide a wonderful opportunity for new thinking, for capturing embryonic ideas or strong opinions. It also has the potential to be an efficient means of data generation for a busy researcher.

There are factors that you should be aware of, though. The group interview has the potential to exclude quieter members of the group, or those who are less dominant. It could also give rise to a situation where undecided participants side with more dominant participants rather than articulating uncertainty or hesitancy. Bear this in mind.

The number of participants in a group interview should vary between four and six. Four is probably the optimum number – the greater the number, the less likely it is that everyone in the group will engage. Managing a group interview is likely to differ from the way in which you conduct a one-to-one interview, which will involve turn-taking between you and the interviewee.

In a group situation, you might find that you are silent for a period of time whilst the group debates an issue. You may wish to intervene to ask for clarification (or to probe further), or to bring the debate back on course. You may have to be assertive in this, perhaps changing tack and intervening with a new question. This will involve you listening, being very attentive to the debate, and deciding whether you need to follow up a new line of thought or get back to your interview schedule. Whilst all this is going on, you may also be taking field notes. Do remember to round off the interview by inviting the group to offer any further thoughts.

QUESTIONNAIRES

You may decide that you need a broad sweep of information from a specific, clearly identified sample group. This might be a whole class of pupils, or a significant number of parents or teachers in school. You may need standardised information (data) at an early stage of your research to gain a clear picture, without delving into personal opinions and values straightaway. If this is the case, then you will probably want to design a questionnaire to gather the information you seek.

The key to gathering useful information is to know exactly what it is you wish to find out. Questionnaires can provide a panoramic view that you may well use to enable you to select specific participants to interview at a later stage, but you do need to be very clear about what it is you are interested in finding out. Hand in hand with this requirement is the art of questionnaire design – good design is absolutely central if you hope to achieve a good response rate, and will enable you to analyse your data swiftly and accurately. Additionally, it is important to construct your questionnaire around a simple coding system that will enable you to read the data efficiently across any number of responses.

If interviews are 'special forms of conversation constructed in situ' with the need to keep interaction 'strictly in check' (Holstein and Gubrium, 1997, p. 113), then questionnaires are special forms of conversation with a remote audience. The problem you may very well face is not so much keeping in check the information offered, as gaining enough information for the questionnaire to be useful and informative. The respondent will still have an image of a person to whom they are responding when completing your questionnaire, and all the issues explored above in relation to interviews are, to varying degrees, still in play here. Your respondents are people with histories, stories to tell, experiences and lives located geographically and psychologically.

It is important that we issue you with a health warning at this stage – you have limited time on your PGCE in which to engage in your enquiry. If you do decide that a questionnaire is essential to your study, make sure you consider carefully the number of questionnaires you intend to issue. We will consider data analysis at a later stage in this chapter, but do make sure, from the outset, that you set yourself an achievable goal in terms of numbers of questionnaires issued.

Your sample

Write a paragraph in response to each of the bullet points below. This will form part of your rationale for the use of questionnaires in your written assignment.

- Why is a questionnaire useful to this study?
- Who will you invite to complete this questionnaire?
- Why are their views important to your study?

Your questions

You now need to consider the content and design of the questionnaire, and these two considerations go hand in hand (see Table 9.1).

TABLE 9.1 Questionnaire design possibilities

Types of questions	Content of questions	Format
Factual questions	What type of factual information might be useful to you in your study: Age? Gender? Number of years in post? Number of years qualified? Number of years in the school? Subject specialism?	In what format will you present these questions? Here are some possible examples: male female Number of years qualified: 1–5 6–10 11–15 16–20 More than 20

(Continued)

TABLE 9.1   *(Continued)*

Types of questions	Content of questions	Format
Closed-ended questions	Closed-ended questions provide the respondent with categories of answers from which they choose a response. These are very quick to complete and quick for you to analyse. You do need to be sure, though, that you provide a range of responses likely to meet the needs of all respondents. It can be terribly frustrating, from a respondent's point of view, to be faced with a questionnaire that doesn't allow them to answer in the way that they would wish.	Do you think that homework: | Can be of benefit to pupils	Can never be beneficial to pupils	Not sure
---	---	---	 *(please circle)*
Open-ended questions	Open-ended questions provide the respondent with the opportunity to write from a very personal perspective. This is where you will have an opportunity to gauge opinion and belief. Respondents may even provide you with new information that you had not previously thought about. However, open-ended questions are time-consuming to analyse.	How do you feel about homework?

A blend of factual, open-ended and closed-ended questions will provide you with a snapshot of specific answers and richness of opinion from your respondents. You will probably need to spend a little time considering the format of your questionnaire: a Likert rating scale will provide respondents with the opportunity to make value judgements, where the quantifiers can indicate a level of feeling (see Table 9.2).

TABLE 9.2   Example of Likert rating scale

Please consider the importance of the following types of homework:										
	of little importance					of significant importance				
Reading	0	1	2	3	4	5	6	7	8	9	10
Learning times tables	0	1	2	3	4	5	6	7	8	9	10
Researching from the internet	0	1	2	3	4	5	6	7	8	9	10

You will need also to be mindful of the experience from your respondents' point of view: an Inverted Funnel Sequence is probably the best design structure, where simple questions come first, followed by more thought-provoking questions. This way you lead the respondent into your questionnaire.

As far as your questions are concerned, you should seek to avoid ambiguity and jargon at all costs. Take care to be sensitive when wording your questions, and ask others to look at them for you. Do look carefully at your instructions as well – make sure they are crystal clear. There is little point in constructing good questions if your respondents don't know how to complete your questionnaire!

You should code each question and sub-question so that you can read and analyse across questionnaires – this will enable you to, for example, compare all responses to question 3.2 from 15 questionnaires. Careful coding will enable you to be efficient and accurate in your analysis. In addition to coding the questions, you might wish to give each questionnaire a serial number – this will enable your respondents to remain anonymous whilst proving you with information on identity.

Administering the questionnaire

If you are intending to invite a class to complete your questionnaire, you will no doubt do this in lesson time, which will probably afford you a 100% return. There are, however, ethical considerations here: have you assured anonymity to your pupils? Can they really feel confident that their questionnaire is anonymous if you are in the room? It is probably wise to talk this through with your class teacher, mentor and tutor.

If, on the other hand, you are asking teachers or parents or other adults to complete your questionnaire, you need to consider the following procedures:

- How will I approach them in the first instance?
- Will I write a covering letter to accompany my questionnaire?
- How will I get the questionnaire to them?
- How long will I give them to complete the questionnaire?
- How will they know how long I have given them?
- What will they do with it when they have completed it?
- What will I do if people don't complete it?
- Will I ask for personal details (name)?
- Will I assure confidentiality and anonymity?

When you have completed your questionnaire design, you should pilot it if at all possible. Before you ask someone else to look at it, though, make sure you have addressed the following points, and that your questionnaire is:

- accessible to your respondents: are there any language considerations you need to be aware of?
- well constructed with simple questions at the beginning
- simple to follow: are your instructions clear?
- unambiguous in its language
- interesting: will the respondent enjoy completing it?

DATA ANALYSIS

Interviews

Transcription
You should endeavour to transcribe your interviews as soon as possible after the event. It's worth investing time in transcribing the interviews yourself rather than asking someone to do this for you. As you transcribe, you should note the hesitancies, the 'umms' and 'ahs' of your participant. If they were silent for a period of time show this on your transcript. The humour, nods, silences and personal perspectives of your respondents have to be captured and organised effectively and appropriately on paper. In a sense, this is a technical process that provides you with the raw material to capture interesting and possibly surprising things from the data. Do remember to keep your transcriptions anonymous.

Summary comments
Straight after each interview try to make a few comments that will bring the interview back to life for you when you begin your analysis at a later stage. List your thoughts about the location and length of the interview and if you need to alter anything for next time. Reflect on your questions – were they appropriate or did you find yourself spending time rephrasing questions? Were there any surprises? How did your participants respond to you and, if you conducted a group interview, how did they respond to each other?

Sorting your data
Once you have transcribed your interviews, you have a corpus of qualitative data which is ready to be analysed. Table 9.3 outlines the key stages in sorting your data.

By following this staged process you will engage in a critical analysis of your data by:

- hearing what your data has to say
- asking questions of your data from your research questions
- asking questions of your data using key themes from the literature.

TABLE 9.3 The key stages in sorting your data

Step 1	Immersion in your data	The first step should be to read your transcriptions a number of times. This process of immersion in your data is important – you may feel worried that you have little useful information at this stage, but you will be surprised at how much information you have once you start the analysis. Immersion in the data will be helped by reading the interview summaries you made straight after each interview.
Step 2	Data reduction	You need to make your data manageable. In order to further immerse yourself in the transcripts, it is useful at this stage to list key context words, or words that are significant to your participant. This will enable you to 'dip your toes' into the data and give you a sense of some possible themes that might emerge. Once you have listed key context words for each individual transcript, you may find it useful to look across transcripts to see if patterns or themes emerge. Start to code or group these patterns as they will form the basis of analysis in your writing.
Step 3	Hearing what your data has to say	Riley (1990) talks about 'hearing what your data has to say'. Are there any metaphors that are used in the transcripts? (Chapter 2 explores the use of metaphor, language and learning). If you do find metaphors, list them. This will begin to take you from 'empirical data to a conceptual level' (Miles and Huberman, 1994, p. 74). What else is your data telling you? Are there emotive phrases emerging? Again, look across your transcripts to find patterns or emerging themes and code these.
Step 4	Asking questions of your data	In order to critically analyse your data you should ask questions. What was your key research question? Are there responses that address this question? Were there sub-questions? Are there responses that address these sub-questions? What were the key issues from your literature review? In what ways does your data illuminate these issues? Are there dimensions from the literature review that are affirmed or challenged by your participants? In this way you will begin to plumb the depths of your transcripts. Once you have systematically done this for each transcript, look across transcripts for themes and code these.
Step 5	Theme your data	By now you will have lists of key context words from each transcript and some possible themes or patterns across the key context words (Step 2). You will have lists of metaphors from each transcript and patterns from across your transcripts (Step 3). You will also have asked questions of your data using your research questions and the key themes from the literature review. These themes should form the basis of your data analysis writing. You can quote from your transcripts, and weave themes from the literature review into your analysis.

Computing software is available at your University for data analysis if you have sent out a large number of questionnaires. There is a time factor that you should consider in terms of inputting your raw data into the software package – with little time available to you this is likely to be unrealistic on the PGCE. A more manageable approach is probably to simply count each coded response and capture this numerical information. This is called a **frequency count** and will provide you with basic numerical information. Should you wish to use your data to look for richer connections between variables you will begin to engage in **bivariate** or **multivariate** analysis.

When beginning your qualitative analysis you should report all response rates and therefore, all non-responses. It is important to provide an honest picture of response rates. You may wish to consider why the non-response rate (and indeed the response rate) was as it was – what factors contributed to this rate and what you might learn from this.

As you begin to look through the returned questionnaires you may find that some have been only partially completed. This again is important to record and perhaps to consider if there was anything ambiguous about the questions that were incomplete – is there a pattern emerging or not?

You may wish to capture your findings in bar-chart form, with a commentary that provides critical analysis. In terms of the open-ended questions in the questionnaire, you may wish to include quotes from the questionnaires, and again, provide a critical analysis of these in terms of the literature review and your research questions. Are there surprises? Are there themes?

Data analysis consists of a number of systematic procedures that you should follow:

- Immersion in the data – reading your transcripts a number of times
- Cleaning or reducing the data – making lists of high frequency and key context words
- Listening to what the data is telling you – are there metaphors? Are there surprises?
- Asking questions of the data in line with themes from the literature and your research questions
- Finding themes and coding them systematically.

It's important to be honest in your data analysis – a 100% response rate for a questionnaire is unusual unless you have a captive audience. Similarly, it's unlikely that every questionnaire will be completed perfectly. Be honest and report this in your writing-up – it's all part of the research process. Ask yourself why this might be and include your thoughts in the writing. Similarly, you might find that things don't go smoothly in the interviews – write this up and reflect on the process.

You will have realised by now that in some ways you are fracturing the data – by bringing themes to the data you are homing in on specific aspects of the data that speak to you. You will also have realised that by reflecting back to the themes and issues raised in your literature review, you can use these in the data analysis to provide a rich and reflective commentary.

CONCLUSION

In this chapter you have been taken, step-by-step, through some of the key issues you should consider when planning your interviews and question-naires. You have also been supported in analysing your data.

Recommended further reading

Clough, P. and Nutbrown, C. (2007) *A Student's Guide to Methodology.* London: Sage. This text deals with methodological issues in accessible yet detailed form. There are par-ticularly useful ideas in relation to 'radical listening' and 'radical looking'.

Miles, M. and Huberman, M. (1994) *Qualitative Data Analysis: An Expanded Source Book.* London: Sage.
This book takes you through issues related to analysing qualitative data. It provides lots of examples and is clearly written. The diagrammatic approach is particularly helpful.

Robson, C. (2002) *Real World Research.* Oxford: Blackwell.
A very popular book among academics, students and practitioners alike. The thing we like about this book is that nothing is taken for granted and there are step-by-step com-ments that will be useful to you.

PART 3

PROFESSIONAL DEVELOPMENT AND MOVING FROM STUDENT TO TEACHER

WORKING WITH
OTHER PROFESSIONALS

In this chapter you will explore:

- Working with teaching assistants
- The pastoral manager
- Professionalism beyond the classroom
- Liaising with SENCOs and other professionals
- Issues related to multi-agency working
- Policy analysis of ECM

INTRODUCTION

In this chapter we ask you to consider the roles of other professionals and adults that you may be required to work with in school. We explore the genesis of the role of the teaching assistant and consider ways of initiating rich practice in order to develop complementary practices and team work. We also consider the role of the pastoral manager and issues relating to care, emotions in learning and the curriculum. The panoramic policy initiative of Every Child Matters (ECM) has given rise to Workforce Reform, Extended Schools and Services and new pressures on SENCOs.

With this policy initiative as a backdrop we then take you through issues relating to the work of the SENCO, and ask you to think critically about Extended Schools and Services. Workforce Reform is considered, followed by an exploration of multi-agency practices. Finally we offer a model of critical policy analysis by interrogating the aims of ECM in order to support you in your future decoding and enacting of policy.

WORKING WITH TEACHING ASSISTANTS

The number of teaching assistants, formerly known as classroom assistants, has grown a good deal in recent times. In the last decade the number of teachers in

England has risen by around 10% – from 399,000 in 1998 to 440,000 in June 2008. During the same period the number of teaching assistants has risen by almost 200% from 61,000 to 177,000 (*BBC News*, June 2008). This represents a significant growth in numbers of adults working in classrooms.

The reasons for this increase are twofold. Firstly, in recent times there has been a move towards including pupils with special educational needs in mainstream schools. This has inevitably led to a greater need for additional support in classrooms, a role often provided by teaching assistants. Secondly, in the attempt to raise standards in schools and address issues of teacher workload there has been a move to redefine the role of teaching assistants.

A National Agreement 'Raising Standards and Tackling Workloads' between the Government, local authority employers and school workforce unions was established in January 2003. The Agreement had a number of key features, which included contractual changes for teachers and a progressive reduction in teachers' overall hours, which have inevitably led to further changes in support staff roles. The Agreement was structured according to a three-phase remodelling process.

Phase 1 (September 2003): 24 general clerical tasks were identified that should be undertaken by staff other than qualified teachers. The 24 tasks comprised:

- Collecting money
- Chasing absences: teachers will need to inform the relevant member of staff when students are absent from their class or from school
- Bulk photocopying
- Copy typing
- Producing standard letters: teachers may be required to contribute as appropriate in formulating the content of standard letters
- Producing class lists: teachers may be required to be involved as appropriate in allocating students to a particular class
- Record keeping and filing: teachers may be required to contribute to the content of records
- Classroom display: teachers will make professional decisions in determining what material is displayed in and around their classroom
- Analysing attendance figures: it is for teachers to make use of the outcome of analysis
- Processing exam results: teachers will need to use the analysis of exam results
- Collating pupil reports
- Work experience: teachers may be required to support pupils on work experience (including through advice and visits)
- Administering examinations: teachers have a professional responsibility for identifying appropriate examinations for their pupils

- Administering teacher cover
- ICT trouble shooting and minor repairs
- Commissioning new ICT equipment
- Ordering supplies and equipment: teachers may be involved in identifying needs
- Stocktaking
- Cataloguing, preparing, issuing and maintaining equipment and materials
- Minuting meetings: teachers may be required to communicate action points from meetings
- Coordinating and submitting bids: teachers may be required to make a professional input into the content of bids
- Seeking and giving personnel advice
- Managing pupil data: teachers will need to make use of the analysis of pupil data
- Inputting pupil data: teachers will need to make the initial entry of pupil data into school management systems (TeacherNet, 2009 – see www.teachernet.gov.uk/whole school/remodelling/cuttingburdens/keysteps/).

Phase 2 (September 2004): cover arrangements for non-contact time were to be in place by September 2004 including new limits on cover for absent teachers.

Phase 3 (September 2005): 10% planning, preparation and assessment time (PPA time) was to be in place by September 2005. Dedicated time for Headship and invigilation was to be in place by 2005.

The use of Higher Level Teaching Assistants (HLTAs) to cover PPA time has again caused an increase in numbers as well as some considerable debate around whether using unqualified teachers to cover PPA time is acceptable. Generally, schools cover PPA time with a blend of HLTAs and part-time qualified teachers.

〰 **Reflection**

Do you think it is acceptable for HLTAs to be in charge of a class to cover PPA time?

Teaching assistants were originally employed in special schools. This role has its origins in the Warnock Report of 1978. Before the Warnock Report, pupils with varying degrees of need were labelled according to one specific need. This categorisation assumed that pupils had only one need – labels and language positioned and constructed pupils according to that one identified need. The Warnock Report highlighted the fact that pupils are likely to have a variety of medical, social, educational or psychological needs. Indeed, a child's 'needs' will naturally change as they develop. Thus, the provision of 'need' should be kept under constant review, and not thought of in terms of an exclusively medical model.

The Warnock Report caused those in education to re-think the concept of 'need' – from something that was originally thought of as a static state, to something ever changing and relevant to pupils in mainstreams schools as well as pupils in special schools or units. Just a few years after the Warnock Report, the 1981 Education Act effected groundbreaking change in terms of special education provision where, for the first time, pupils from special schools or units began to be integrated into mainstream schools. This integration resulted in Local Authorities employing increasing numbers of non-teaching assistants (or 'classroom assistants' as they were then known) and placing them in mainstream schools to support pupils in accessing the curriculum. The 1981 Education Act introduced the concept of 'integration' into the educational system and with this concept came increased numbers of adults other than teachers into mainstream classrooms.

Just a few years later in 1988, the Education Reform Act introduced two fundamental changes into schools in England: the National Curriculum and the concept and practice of 'Local Management'. The introduction of Local Management altered the balance of power between Local Authorities, schools and their respective communities. Whereas in 1981 Local Authorities employed classroom assistants and placed them in schools, after 1988 recruitment fell to the school Governing Body. The responsibility of managing the entire school budget fell to the Governing Body and Head Teacher who, for the first time, had to make decisions relating to the financial position of their schools. Delegated finance enabled schools to consider their specific context and prioritise accordingly, and it was within this context that the numbers of TAs in mainstream schools began to grow substantially.

During a review of non-teaching staff in schools by Her Majesty's Inspectorate in 1992, it was found that some secondary schools were phasing out a third Deputy Head post to employ more non-teaching staff (1992, para. 2). The freedom of choice bestowed upon Governing Bodies and Head Teachers in terms of budgets caused a rethink in terms of the most effective means of supporting pupils' learning. The huge growth in numbers of classroom assistants came about then as a result of new curriculum demands and new opportunities in school finance.

In terms of teacher professionalism, this era represents the beginning of the current complex state within which you will practise. The 1988 Education Reform Act provided the opportunity for schools to make localised financial decisions and in this way the teacher in the classroom, in theory, had a 'voice'. That is, specific need could be considered by the

Head Teacher and Governing Body of the school and budgets allocated accordingly. In this way, classroom assistants were being increasingly employed in schools. The questions being asked at that time related to the professional role of the teacher and the ways in which classroom assistant and class teacher could best work to the benefit of pupils. This question is still asked today.

This can represent a challenge for you as you begin your teaching career: in addition to addressing your focus on supporting pupils to learn there is the prospect of working with other adults in the class and being in a situation where, even though you are the 'teacher', you may well be working with a teaching assistant who is older than you and who also knows the class a good deal better. Wilson and Bedford (2008) concluded that working with teaching assistants should be a feature of all initial teacher education programmes. They also suggested that there was a case for joint training of teachers and their teaching assistants to develop team-working skills and the need to share good practice from Primary and special schools across into the Secondary sector. The organisation of the Secondary curriculum around subject special- ist teachers means that teaching assistants will end up supporting the child they are allotted to in a variety of classrooms, each with their own expecta- tions, and so the development of team work, such a feature of good practice in Primary schools, is less likely.

The key to good team work with the teaching assistant in your classroom is to get to know them well:

- Read their job description: this will support you in understanding what their role should be.
- There is a range of qualifications that TAs can take. Are they a Higher Level Teaching Assistant? What does that mean in terms of their skills and practice in the classroom?
- Find out from them what, if any, professional development courses they have taken. You may very well be working with a TA who has undertaken extensive study in, for example, supporting pupils with dyslexia. It is to everyone's benefit if you can maximise this expertise.
- Invite your TA to talk through with you how they see their role. It's wise to talk to each other at the start about the perceived role. You may change certain practices over time, but getting off to a good start is important.

In addition to getting to know your teaching assistant personally and in terms of their job description, grade and expertise, you should seek to find out about localised practice in your school in terms of how teaching assis- tants work. This is often an issue with regards to time. Teaching assistants may be paid from, say, 9am to 12.30pm. If this is the case then there is little point in you hoping that you will have time to discuss plans in detail before school. Similarly, you will want feedback from your teaching assistant after the lesson – how will you manage this if they leave at the end of the lesson? Consider the following time constraints:

- What time does the teaching assistant start work?
- What time do they finish?
- How can you work together to plan beforehand and find feedback time afterwards?

You will find that gathering information on the teaching assistant's job description, expertise and working conditions in terms of time constraints will put you in a stronger position to then begin to think about ways in which you will jointly support pupil learning in your classroom. By now, you will have developed a good understanding of issues and theories related to 'learning' and your own opinions in terms of 'good' interactions between pupils and adults in the classroom. At this stage it is worth revisiting your principles in relation to pupil–adult interactions in the classroom, bearing in mind that teaching assistants are likely to be working with pupils in small groups or one-to-one situations.

Effective learning – the pupil

- What are the optimum conditions necessary for effective learning to take place?
- What is the place of exploration and meaning-making in learning?
- What is the place of language development in learning?
- What do we know about self-esteem and emotions in relation to learning?
- What is the place of scaffolding in pupils' learning?
- What do we know about the Zone of Proximal Development in pupils' learning?

Supporting effective learning – the teaching assistant

- How will the teaching assistant facilitate pupils' exploration and meaning-making?
- In what ways can pupils' language development be enhanced by the teaching assistant?
- How much adult (TA) talk should there be in relation to pupil talk?
- How will the teaching assistant enhance pupils' self-esteem through their approach and practice?
- How might the teaching assistant scaffold learning?
- In what ways might the teaching assistant – and other pupils – support learning that is on the cusp of understanding?

Hopefully your relationship with the teaching assistant in your class will develop into one of trust and professionalism. By focusing on the learning needs of the pupil first, you should find that the 'tasks' you wish the teaching assistant to undertake will be obvious and many. In this way the 'management' of the teaching assistant becomes less of an issue, as you will both be focused upon pupil learning. The questions above should support you in establishing your principles in relation to learning. In addition to working with pupils, the teaching assistant will be in a position to record information that may be invaluable to you in relation to pupils. Your teaching assistant can become a second set of eyes and ears in a busy classroom.

〰 Reflection

How have you seen teachers working with teaching assistants in your school?
How have you collaborated with teaching assistants so far?
What paperwork/learning opportunities will you develop that will enable the TA to capture information that will help you to further plan pupils' work?

In their recently published work on teacher pressure, Galton and Macbeath (2008) reported that teachers offered the following list in answer to the kinds of support they felt they needed:

- Assistance with lower-ability groups
- Behavioural support
- Time to plan together with other staff
- Support with special needs and/or able and talented
- Planning courses
- Assistance with ICT usage in class
- Help in developing new teaching materials
- Help in preparing resources and organising field work
- Smaller classes
- Varying approaches and working with different learning styles (Galton and Macbeath, 2008, p. 50).

〰 Reflection

In considering each of the items above, which ones might you gain support for from the teaching assistant?

THE PASTORAL MANAGER

The tradition in schools in the UK has been for schools to organise their responsibilities to children under the divisions of 'pastoral' and 'curriculum'. Concern for the child's well-being is normally seen as a 'pastoral' responsibility, while the acquisition of culturally valuable knowledge is seen as a 'curriculum' issue.

By culture we do not necessarily mean 'high culture' but those aspects that are seen to have value by the school and which in Secondary schools tend to be what is laid down in exam specifications. The term 'pastoral care' tends to be institutionalised in Secondary schools through posts of responsibility such as Year Heads or Heads of House (Best, 2007). However, this role can be subverted and, in practice, in Secondary schools, can become a system of 'behaviour management'. Since Workforce Reform, there has been a 'structural division' (Galton and Macbeath, 2008, p. 53) between the curriculum and pastoral care.

The introduction of pastoral managers has seen a shift in the overall responsibility of the teacher – the caring aspects of the role now fall to the pastoral manager whilst the teacher has responsibility for learning. Pastoral managers are not required to be qualified teachers – they may have formerly been teaching assistants. This practice of separating 'learning' from 'behaviour' or 'emotional care' resonates with the issues raised in Chapter 1 around Modernism and the segregation of tasks to achieve perceived 'efficiency'.

In Primary schools where the class teacher tends to be the predominant mode of organisation, there is no overt 'pastoral system' as such, but there is a long-standing culture of care for children and the roles of 'pastoral' and 'curriculum' are not divided – rather they are enacted by the class teacher simultaneously. In a sense we would see this as a better way of thinking about the roles of the teacher: to separate 'learning' from emotional well-being seems illogical and even dehumanising.

〰 Reflection

Reflect on your time as a pupil in school: how do you remember your teachers enacting a 'pastoral' and a 'curriculum' role?
How do you see the 'curriculum' and 'pastoral care' enacted in your school?
At this point how do you think about yourself in terms of assuming 'pastoral' and 'curriculum' responsibilities?

It is worth pausing at this point to consider more deeply what we mean by 'curriculum'. Do we see the 'curriculum' as the material that is in the folders in the curriculum office and represents the content that has to be 'transferred' to the children or is the curriculum what the child experiences from the moment they pass through the school gates until they leave at the end of school, or something else again? The first perspective seems aligned with more impoverished views of how learning happens (from, perhaps, a behavioural perspective), whereas the second embraces what the child experiences in terms of the whole-school experience (a more all-encompassing and constructivist perspective).

In thinking more about curriculum, Moore (2000) suggests that policy impacts on teaching and learning in two principle ways. The first is concerned with the nature of the curriculum as presented in National Curriculum documents and exam specifications. The second concerns issues of enforced or 'encouraged' forms of teaching which may include such matters as class size, classroom organisation and appropriate methodologies. To these we may add the nature of the summative assessment procedures as we can be sure that from the learner's perspective the assessment defines the curriculum (Ramsden, 2003).

PROFESSIONALISM BEYOND THE CLASSROOM – LIAISING WITH SENCOS AND OTHER PROFESSIONALS

At the heart of these roles is the principle that all children need to be able to access the National Curriculum. This access will be strongly influenced by individuals', curriculum teams' and whole-schools' approaches to inclusion.

Inclusion is described as the connection of two processes: 'It is the process of increasing the participation of students in the cultures and curriculum of mainstream schools and communities; it is the process of reducing the exclusion of students from mainstream cultures and curricula' (Booth, 1996, p. 91). Booth suggests that we should view inclusion as a process rather than a fixed commodity. It has been suggested that the process requires us to have inclusive values that then stimulate inclusive polices that in turn will give rise to inclusive practices. As soon as we enact inclusive policies, the process of increasing participation begins (Booth and Ainscow, 2002). Thus, the more inclusion is placed at the heart of a school's thinking and practice, the more likely it is that issues about inclusion will be at the heart of that school's planning and resourcing.

Although the senior management team in your school will ultimately determine school policy, colleagues such as your Special Educational Needs Coordinator (SENCO) will probably have a strong influence over the school's approach to inclusion.

Inclusion in schools is demonstrated by:

- valuing all students and staff equally
- increasing the participation of students in, and reducing their exclusion from, the cultures, curriculum and communities of local schools
- restructuring the cultures, policies and practices in schools so that they respond to the diversity of students; reducing the barriers to learning and participation for all students
- learning from attempts to overcome barriers to participation
- viewing the differences between students as resources
- acknowledging the rights of students to an education in their locality
- improving schools for staff as well as for students
- emphasising the role of students in building community and developing values as well as increasing achievement
- fostering mutually sustaining relationships between schools and communities
- recognising that inclusion in education is one aspect of inclusion in society
(Booth and Ainscow, 2002, p. 3).

〰️ **Reflection**

Look at your school policies on inclusion or special educational needs, including those that relate to gifted and talented pupils:

- How do these policies relate to the ways in which inclusion is enacted in your placement school?
- Consider practices from your placement school in the light of Booth and Ainscow's guidelines above.
- Discuss your own practice regarding inclusion with the SENCO (or other colleagues).

Booth (1996) argues that inclusion is a process rather than a point of arrival. If this is the case then the two discourses identified in Table 10.1, although viewed from very different ideological stances, could be used as descriptors of extremes within a continuum, in order to review the curriculum and your approach to it. This may take the form of seeing failure through two lenses: that of the pupil and that of the curriculum. It also offers two ways of viewing the role of the teacher: that of subject specialist or as specialist in pedagogy. Skidmore's model (2004) (see Table 10.1) is based on the pedagogical discourse of inclusion and deviance (i.e. a difference from the 'norm').

Booth's assertion that inclusion is never reached serves as a useful starting point for school policy review and for teachers' development (Hoult, 2005, p. 110).

TABLE 10.1   Discourse of deviance and inclusion (from Skidmore (2004) cited in Hoult (2005))

Dimension	Discourse of deviance	Discourse of inclusion
Educatability of students	Hierarchy of cognitive ability in which pupils are placed.	All students have an open-ended potential for learning.
Explanation of educational failure	Source of difficulty in learning lies in students' deficits of ability.	Source of this difficulty lies in insufficiently responsive presentation of the curriculum.
School response	Support for learning should seek to remediate the weaknesses of individual students.	Support for learning should seek to reform curriculum and develop pedagogy across the school.
Theory of teaching	Expertise in teaching centres on the possession of specialist subject knowledge.	Expertise in teaching centres on engaging the active participation of all students in the learning process.
Curriculum model	An alternative curriculum should be provided for the less able.	A common curriculum should be provided for the students.

〰️   **Reflection**

Consider the 'curriculum' at your placement school. You may wish to refer to schemes of work or teaching, learning and assessment policies and practice in order to do this:

- How do the teachers at your school talk about the 'curriculum'?
- How is the curriculum adapted in order for it to be inclusive?
- Based on your understanding of pupils' learning, what aspects of the curriculum are particularly challenging to access?
- Reflect on a dilemma you have faced in school with regard to curriculum access. Consider this in relation to Skidmore's model. What do you notice?

ISSUES RELATED TO MULTI AGENCY WORKING – WHAT DOES RESEARCH TELL US?

Following the Laming Report on the Victoria Climbié Inquiry (Laming, 2003), there was a clear social and political imperative to improve child protection.

This led to the publication of the Children Act (2004) and the development of the Government's Every Child Matters (ECM) policy.

In this book we have conveyed the importance of criticality and analysis, and so in this section we will consider three major implications for educational policy and practice in order to highlight the key issues and to look at the underlying dilemmas and tensions that exist. It may readily be seen that ECM has three important implications for educational policy and practice:

- Extended Schools
- Workforce Reform
- Multi-agency work.

Extended Schools

The principle underpinning Extended Schools is that schools are located at the heart of communities and are therefore well placed to enable the implementation of ECM. The core offer should consist of:

- A varied range of activities, including study support, and sport and music clubs, combined with childcare in Primary schools
- Parenting and family support
- Swift and easy access to targeted and specialist services
- Community access to facilities including adult and family learning, ICT and sports grounds.

It is the intention that schools will provide a range of services beyond the school day to help meet the needs of children and their families.

While all this seems logical and supportive there are problems with such an initiative, not least that it might become little more than 'adult education plus' (Roche and Tucker, 2007). For such an initiative to work, structural changes have to be allied to how communities view schools. This also has implications for how professionals construct their identities. As might be expected, the way that indiviual schools have developed the extended nature of their schools has varied a good deal. Wilkin et al. (2003) reviewed 160 schools early in the initiative and found that some were using the model to enhance curriculum provision and related opportunities while others were looking more at community learning and leisure facilities. This is not surprising as, inevitably, a process similar to Chinese whispers occurs as policy moves from formation to implementation with, at each stage, the meaning interpreted and reinterpreted by different groups placing different emphases upon various aspects of the policy.

Perhaps the biggest hurdle may prove to be changing the culture of some schools (Roche and Tucker, 2007), as the very nature of the initiative will challenge the traditional position of many schools.

> 〰 **Reflection**
>
> What have you experienced in the way of Extended Schools and Services?
> What might be the functions of a school within a community?

Workforce Reform

With any new initiative there is a clear need for the 'workforce' to be in a position to make the policy work. At the heart of the agenda set out by ECM is the recognition that professionals will require new skills in six broad areas of expertise (DfES, 2005a):

- Development of effective communication skills
- An understanding of child development
- Promoting children's welfare
- Supporting transitions
- Multi-agency working
- Sharing of information.

We argue that there is also a need for teachers to have a 'disposition' to develop these new skills. The word 'reform' means the 'improvement or amendment of what is wrong, corrupt, unsatisfactory' (Online dictionary, accessed 16 June 2009). With the need to develop new skills there is an almost built-in assumption that the existing skills are now in some way redundant, which is clearly a potentially disabling message to give a professional. You might like to consider how deliberately policy makers would have employed a term such as 'reform' of the workforce.

Multi-agency work

At the heart of Every Child Matters is the notion that schools become the hub for professionals working together to provide services for children.

> 〰 **Reflection**
>
> In what ways have you seen Every Child Matters enacted in school?
> What opportunities does Every Child Matters offer? Think of this from multiple perspectives.
> What are the perceived barriers to working in a multi-agency way?

A key issue with such an initiative is that each of the professionals will have evolved their practice in very different ways. There are issues about the nature of engagement, terminology and practice. In a study of how 10 members of a multi-agency team construct their professional identities, Hymans (2008) raised a number of questions and issues:

- Should professional identity develop as the team evolves or be laid down when it is established?
- There was an understanding that being part of a homogenous team meant being together in the same team but having different skills.
- The best way forward might be to develop in a multi-agency team rather than a homogenous team.

Multi-agency working has its genesis in special education, and special schools in particular, where expert teams work intensively with the pupil. While it may be seen that multi-agency working is a principle underpinning Every Child Matters, it is, in many cases, embryonic in mainstream schools. Barnes (2008), in a study involving 30 SENCOs and nine parents, concludes that while multi-agency working was seen as a 'good thing', no specific set of protocols was identified as the most suitable way forward.

At the heart of Every Child Matters is the well-being of the child or young person. Working from the diagram below, map all those who come into contact with the child or young person in school over the period of one school year.

Using this information, plot against each person how often they interact with the pupil over the school year.

Looking at this information:

- Who is coordinating the interactions?
- What is being done with the information?
- Are there opportunities for the range of professionals to work together?
- What part does the SENCO play in this?
- What is the role of the class teacher?
- Are parents involved?
- If yes, in what ways?
- Are parents informed?
- If yes, in what ways?

As multi-agency work develops in mainstream schools, you will be increasingly required to work with other professionals for the benefit for your pupils. It is important to understand the practices that are embedded within your school in relation to multi-disciplinary practice. A starting point will be your mentor and SENCO. The questions outlined above will support you in developing an early overall picture of multi-agency practices in your school.

POLICY ANALYSIS OF ECM

In Table 10.2 we have modelled the kind of close analysis that we see as important in developing a deep understanding of policy and becoming educated consumers of educational policy. As this is a chapter on working with other professionals we have used the aims of ECM as a context for consideration.

 **Reflection**

Reflect upon the experiences you have had in school to date:

- Who are the professionals with whom you have worked?
- Which professionals are located within your school?
- Which professionals visit your school at given times to work with pupils?
- What do they do and who determines the work they undertake?
- What part do parents play?

TABLE 10.2 Analysis of the aims of Every Child Matters

Aims of Every Child Matters	Analysis
Every Child Matters is a new approach to the well-being of children and young people from birth to age 19.	The title of Every Child Matters is interesting as it is impossible to argue against it. We could not sustain an argument for suggesting that every child did not matter. Was there a time when every child did not matter? Policy titles and phrases are often chosen for this very reason – they make perfect sense and are difficult to argue against. The wording in policy texts is never naïve – a policy position has been taken. The American policy initiative 'No Child Left Behind' is the blueprint for Every Child Matters. Where then does the impetus for policy development come from, and who is responsible for 'creating' education policy?
The Government's aim is for every child, whatever their background or their circumstances, to have the support they need to: • be healthy • stay safe • enjoy and achieve • make a positive contribution • achieve economic well-being.	This statement is clearly reinforcing the Government's commitment to inclusive strategies but it might be seen that it is also a recognition that inequalities exist, in spite of the concept of 'equality of education' being a key feature of the Labour Government's strategy as far back as the 1970s, when the comprehensive system was introduced. When considering the aims of policy it is always worth considering what is written, but also what is not. Watson (2006) reminds us that there are no specific references to children's spirituality in ECM. Is there anything else that you would like to see in the aims of this panoramic policy initiative? The first three bullet points (be healthy, stay safe, enjoy and achieve) are relevant and immediate to the pupil. They are in the here-and-now, as it were. Achieving economic well-being and making a positive contribution however, are clearly intentions for the future, based on the model of the good citizen – should education that concerns itself with schooling the youngest children have economic well-being as an aim? 'Making a positive contribution', the fourth bullet point, is interesting. In what ways might this be interpreted? What might the school do to facilitate this aim?
This means that the organisations involved with providing services to children – from hospitals and schools, to police and voluntary groups – will be teaming up in new ways, sharing	The language of policy tends to be couched in consumerist terms like 'providing services' rather than providing 'care', e.g. health 'service' or health 'care'. Schools have been positioned as businesses since the 1988 Education Reform Act,

TABLE 10.2 *(Continued)*

Aims of Every Child Matters	Analysis
information and working together, to protect children and young people from harm and to help them achieve what they want in life. Children and young people will have far more say about issues that affect them as individuals and collectively.	open to the peaks and troughs of the free market. As such, parents are positioned as customers and pupils as consumers. Every Child Matters is a 'new' approach. Is there an assumption that 'new' is automatically better? 'Children and young people will have more say' – this policy initiative positions children and young people at the heart of, not only this policy text, but of future practice. Pupil voice is pivotal in this policy text. In this way, Every Child Matters resonates with other key policy texts in placing the pupil at the heart of the text.
Over the next few years, every Local Authority (LA) will be working with its partners, through children's trusts, to find out what works best for children and young people in its area and act on it. They will need to involve children and young people in this process, and when inspectors assess how local areas are doing, they will listen especially to the views of children and young people themselves.	An implication here is that this will be based on 'on the ground' research. What happens if the people that are surveyed are not in a position to make an informed choice? This raises issues around the multi-layered nature of policy texts and competing intentions. This section of the text determines that there will be inspectors assessing how local areas are doing. However, if local authorities are true to the principles of pupil voice and act upon the suggestions and advice of young people, it will be problematic to inspect 'quality'. This highlights the complex nature of policy making – the centralised Modernist approach of inspection fails to dovetail with personalisation and responsive providers.
In March 2005, the first Children's Commissioner for England was appointed, to give children and young people a voice in Government and in public life. The commissioner will pay particular attention to gathering and putting forward the views of the most vulnerable children and young people in society, and will promote their involvement in the work of organisations whose decisions and actions affect them.	This is saying that there will be high levels of consultation and that any actions will be at the behest of the recipients. What impact has this initiative had? Where are children's and young people's voices heard and when are they reported back to other young people?
In addition, the Children's Fund was launched in November 2000 to tackle disadvantage among children and young people. The programme aims to identify at an early stage children and young people at risk of social exclusion, and to make sure they receive the help and support they need to achieve their potential.	'Reaching' potential is an enticing idea but very hard to 'get hold of' as it suggests unlimited opportunities in unlimited contexts.

CONCLUSION

In this chapter we have explored some of the issues you will encounter in your NQT year as you begin to work with other professionals in school. We have sought to help you understand current practice in schools by considering the antecedence of para-professionals in the classroom and issues related to pastoral care and multi-agency working.

 Recommended further reading

Grove, M. (2004) 'The Three R's of Pastoral Care: Relationships, Respect and Responsibility', *Pastoral Care in Education*, June: 34–7.
This paper highlights the paucity of research and literature in the field of pastoral care, bringing attention to what the author believes to be the central tenets of pastoral care. The author argues that there is a vacuum between pastoral care needs and the theoretical and practical knowledge of how to fill that void.

Hryniewicz, L. (2004) *Teaching Assistants: The Complete Handbook*. Ely: Adamson.
This book covers issues related to teaching assistants in a very systematic and thorough manner. It will be of significant value to you in your NQT year.

Soan, S. (2006) 'Are the Needs of Children and Young People with Social, Emotional and Behavioural Needs Being Served within a Multi-Agency Framework?', *Support for Learning*, 21(4): 210–15.
This paper draws on two case studies to illuminate issues around multi-agency working. The article highlights both positive and negative dimensions to multi-agency practice.

DEVELOPING PROFESSIONALLY AT MASTERS-LEVEL

In this chapter you will explore:

- Continuing professional development
- Continuing professional development today
- Considering teacher identities
- Career trajectories
- Continuing and completing your Masters degree
- Final thoughts on Masters-level study in education

INTRODUCTION

In this chapter we support you in considering your professional development needs and interests. We contextualise the landscape of CPD so that you are in a position to make informed decisions relating to your career progression. You will probably be wondering what kinds of support you will be offered in your NQT induction year and we map out the possibilities for you. Finally we consider the Masters-level journey that you have embarked upon – we encourage you to continue and complete your Masters degree thereby emerging as an extended professional and expert in your field.

In the past, professional development was a consideration for teachers who had been in the profession for a number of years. There was a time when a teacher had to have qualified for a minimum of three years before being considered to undertake a part-time Masters degree. Things have changed. The introduction of Masters-level work into the PGCE year provides a bridge between initial teacher education and professional development. The choices you make in your early career will possibly be informed by your Masters-level journey to date, but they might be more strongly influenced by the needs of the school or department within which you find yourself. This chapter will support you in developing an understanding of your developmental needs and the options available to you. The chapter begins, though, with a consideration of the changing CPD landscape.

CONTINUING PROFESSIONAL DEVELOPMENT(CPD)

Evolution of teacher learning

The days when a qualified teacher was seen as the 'finished article' have long since passed. Professional development today is regarded as an intrinsic aspect of professional identity. This was not always the case; in the past, teachers were able to choose CPD that was of personal interest to them and so was essentially led by them.

The catalyst for the change from *personal-led* CPD to what might be termed *systems-led CPD* was, arguably, the 1988 Education Reform Act. In Chapter 1 we saw that since the Educational Reform Act (1988) the policy landscape of education has changed a good deal. This inevitably had a significant impact on teacher professional development because it became necessary for teachers to learn how to implement initiatives and therefore there was a shift from CPD that was initiated by the individual to CPD that was led by the demands of systems. Initiatives including centrally determined assessment and standards measures gave rise to a situation where professional development for teachers was essential if teachers were to deliver the new policy initiatives. In this way, CPD was seen as pivotal in raising standards and as a driver for school improvement.

The period 1988–2001 saw the development of centralised CPD initiatives. High-profile training programmes were developed to support the implementation of policy reforms in numeracy and literacy in 1998, namely the National Numeracy and National Literacy Strategies (DfEE, 1998). Launched in 1998, they arguably represent the apex of government intervention at the level of subject knowledge, pedagogy and 'training'. Literacy and numeracy consultants were employed to train teachers across England – ensuring that policy was understood and therefore accurately driven into practice *via* CPD.

Whole-school developmental needs in relation to externally determined initiatives began to emerge in 2001, with the publication of a national strategy for CPD. *Learning and Teaching: A Strategy for Professional Development* (DfEE, 2001) presented a suggested framework for CPD. Located within the wider context of 'standards' and 'accountability' one purpose of this policy was that school deficiencies (identified by Ofsted) were to be addressed via CPD, that is, via *systems-led* CPD. As a result of this, professional development expectation was closely aligned to performance and school improvement.

In 2005, the then Secretary of State, Ruth Kelly, began the process of developing a structured CPD trajectory for teachers (DfES, 2005b). This she called the 'New Professionalism', arguing that this would bring 'coherence' to the previous patchwork of teacher CPD opportunities. This New Professionalism is closely associated with the Training and Development Agency for Schools and is, arguably, positioned as a key lever in the reform agenda, the vehicle through which teacher re-professionalisation might be realised.

The Training and Development Agency for Schools (TDA; established in 2005 with a remit to include the strategic direction and delivery of CPD for qualified teachers) has worked with social partners including HEIs to develop a Masters in Teaching and Learning (MTL), which aims to 'raise standards, narrow the achievement gap and give children a better chance' (DCSF, 2008, p. 12). It also aims to 'develop and improve teaching quality' (DCSF, 2008, p. 12). This, in turn, is directly linked with the economy: 'Our ambitions for our society and our economy are high, because the challenges we face as a country are high' (DCSF, 2008, p. 1).

Up until this point the former Teacher Training Agency had engaged mostly with those involved in initial teacher education and professional development, but the MTL marks a change in direction, where ITT and CPD are bridged through M-level engagement. Many HEIs will offer an M-level NQT course which will enable you to build upon your M-level PGCE credits, but the MTL marks a new direction for the TDA. This contemporary context in England has a focus upon strengthened performance management and the Professional Standards Framework.

In this way it could be argued that *teacher agency* in relation to CPD choice has been eroded – school needs and national policy initiatives are likely to dominate the CPD choices you are offered as a teacher in school. The important point for you is to know what your CPD options are and to not necessarily be confined to what is most obviously on offer. Indeed, probably the most fundamental questions for you to ask at this stage are: 'what kind of teacher do I want to be?' and, therefore, 'what is my professional development for?'

CONTINUING PROFESSIONAL DEVELOPMENT TODAY

The Department for Children, Schools and Families (DCSF) defines current CPD thus: 'CPD consists of reflective activities that are designed to improve an individual's professional attributes, knowledge, understanding and skills. It supports individual needs and improves professional practice' (www.tda. gov.uk/teachers/continuingprofessionaldevelopment/epd.aspx).

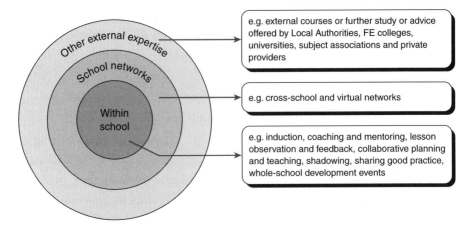

FIGURE 11.1 CPD activities

It is worth noting that in the statement above the DCSF has aligned itself to the professional standards for teachers and so can be seen to be articulating a systems-led approach to CPD. The TDA has provided guidelines, shown in Figure 11.1, which can be found at: www.tda.gov.uk/teachers/continuing professionaldevelopment/what_is_ cpd.aspx

Examples of what the TDA considers to be good CPD practice can be seen at: www.tda.gov.uk/teachers/continuingprofessionaldevelopment/cpd_in_ practice.aspx

However, there are many possible sources of CPD.

Modes of CPD

For a long time CPD was seen as synonymous with off-site courses. The notion of CPD as having to be a 'course', rather than professional development that is ongoing and located in the professional context of the school, determined by colleagues, is interesting. Courses delivered off-site were indeed synonymous with CPD, however this is to see CPD in a narrow way and we would argue that there are in fact a range of activities that may be seen as CPD (see Table 11.1).

Craft (2000) refers to the activities listed in Table 11.1 as 'CPD activities'. In fact we see these as modes of possible CPD. The question you might like to consider is which of these modes would suit different types of professional development activity. In considering the range of CPD activities summarised by Craft in Table 11.1, it is worth reflecting on the status that may be given to different activities, the benefits of each and the possible problems (see Table 11.2).

TABLE 11.1 Examples of CPD activities (based on Craft, 2000)

- Action research
- Distance-learning materials
- School-based and off-site courses of various lengths
- Job shadowing and rotation
- School cluster projects
- Teacher placement or exchange
- Experiential assignments
- Collaborative learning
- Self-directed study related to awards such as an MA or PhD
- Receiving and giving on the job coaching
- Peer networks
- Membership of a working group
- Personal reflection
- ICT mediated learning through e-mail discussions or self study using multi-media resources.

TABLE 11.2 Analysis of CPD activities

Professional development activity	Possible advantages	Possible issues
Action research	Deep interaction with your pupils and opportunity to work with colleagues.	It is important to step outside of one's practice from time to time. Focus upon direct classroom practice should be balanced with other forms of professional learning.
Distance-learning materials	Can be studied at a time and place to suit you and can link you to a community beyond school.	Can be an isolating experience if interaction is not built in.
School-based and off-site courses of various lengths	Time during the school day is invaluable – you are not exhausted at the end of the day and this raises the status of professional development.	In school, CPD means that you are still probably thinking in school mode – you might get distracted or called away.
School cluster projects	An excellent way to develop your network of colleagues and discover the cultures and practices of other schools.	Does not allow you to step away from your immediate location.
Self-directed study related to awards such as an MA or PhD	Sustained study enables you to focus deeply upon issues that are important to you – you develop as an expert in a given field.	Sustaining a level of commitment needs support and interest from your school.
Receiving and giving on the job coaching	Working in a collegial fashion is rewarding.	Norms and routines can be self-perpetuating (McCulloch et al., 2000).

Rationale for teacher learning – in what ways will you carry on with your learning?

The CPD that you are likely to be offered will probably be negotiated between you and the school and is most likely to be related to policy initiatives and/or the school development plan. Questions have long been asked about the nature of professional development on offer to teachers: should you undertake development that will enable you to fulfil the technical aspects of the requirements of the professional or should you undertake learning that will develop your creativity, feed your curiosity and enrich your subject knowledge?

We acknowledge that there is no easy answer and that decisions will differ according to the context within which you find yourself, the needs of your school and your own particular interests. You may also have an eye on promotion and be looking to develop a particular career trajectory.

〜〜 **Reflection**

In thinking of your own CPD needs, consider the questions below. For each one think about where support might come from:

- What are your specific CPD needs at this stage in relation to your practice?
- What are your interests in terms of subject knowledge?
- What are your interests in terms of pedagogy?
- What are your thoughts about your career trajectory and what might be helpful at this stage?

The development you choose will have a fundamental affect on your professional identity.

CONSIDERING TEACHER IDENTITIES

The notion of thinking about ourselves in terms of 'identity' is an implicitly social concept (Burr, 1995). Professional identity may be defined as a combination of who and what we are and the meanings that we attach to ourselves and our work (Day, 2004). In earlier sections we have stressed the importance of knowing yourself. This is known as reflexivity. It may be argued that in order to develop an identity as a teacher it is vital that we have an understanding of ourselves and how we see the value of our subjects.

There are many pressures on teachers, and also student teachers, to become particular sorts of teachers. However there are many ways that one can be as a teacher and you do have a choice. We feel strongly that the way we construct our identity is very important, although it may not be a regular part of everyday discussions where the pressing demands of attending to tasks tends to dominate. A valuable way to consider teacher identity is provided by Sachs (2001) and is summarised in Table 11.3.

TABLE 11.3   Teacher identities (based on Sachs, 2001)

Entrepreneurial identity	Activist identity
• Individualistic • Competitive • Controlling and regulative • Externally defined, seeking approval from outside sources such as Ofsted	• The open flow of ideas, regardless of their popularity, that enables people to be as fully informed as possible • Faith in the individual and collective capacity of people to create possibilities for resolving problems • The use of critical reflection and analysis to evaluate ideas, problems and policies • Concern for the welfare of others and the 'common good' • Concern for the dignity and rights of individuals and minorities • An understanding that democracy is not so much an 'ideal' to be persuaded as an 'idealised' set of values that we must live and that guide our life as people • The organisation of social institutions to promote and extend the democratic way of life.

As we can see in Table 11.3, Sachs considers identities to lie at opposing ends of a continuum. She summarises the 'entrepreneurial' identityas essentially an individual one where the teacher seeks approval from outside sources. This identity tends to be competitive and, it might be argued, sees teaching as about power rather than service.

Consider the vignettes below.

Vignette: Brian's story

I left school immediately after having taken my A levels and went to study business and economics at a university in the north of England. I ended up with a first-class degree and then went straight on to take a PGCE at a university in London. While on school placements I was struck by how poor the organisation

(Continued)

(Continued)

in both the departments I was placed with seemed to be. While I was surprised by this, in a way I was also heartened by this as I felt that I would be able to do a better job. During the PGCE year I managed to get a job at a school in Bristol and took up my appointment in the July of my PGCE year. My post involved me teaching at a school with specialist status in Business and Enterprise. The Business Studies department consisted of me, the HOD and four other teachers, only one of whom worked in the department full time.

In the January of my NQT year the head of department fell pregnant and from the Easter I was in effect acting head of department. I managed to make a few changes especially to the recording of assessment and managed to institute a few policies on issues such as homework, and the following December, following a successful performance management meeting, when the HOD decided to work part time after the birth of her child, the Head Teacher, who had been very appreciative of my efforts since I had started in the school, offered me the job full time. In the first term we had an Ofsted inspection and to my delight the department managed to get an honourable mention in the full report and a glowing report from the inspector. Needless to say this showed me in a good light and now in my fourth year in the job I am an assistant head at another school in Bristol with responsibility for working with the deputy responsible for assessment. The school have promised that they will support me through NPQH and I am hoping to be in a position to apply for deputy headships in the near future.

Vignette: Teresa's story

I went to school in the West Country and then studied History at a university in the Midlands. When I had finished my degree I wanted a break from education and so I got a job teaching English in Zurich and then Madrid. I spent six months at both schools and then resigned and travelled to Australia and New Zealand. When I came back to England I had no job and was not sure what to do and so I worked as a TA in a school in London where an old friend from university was a teacher. While at the school I became fascinated with the children and also kind of appalled at how low their educational standards were, in my perception! I also came to realise that their home circumstances were in many cases very challenging to say the least and I realised that I wanted to work in such a school as a teacher to try and make things better. After a while I decided to apply for PGCE and ended up back in the Midlands learning to be a primary teacher.

At my first school placement I found I loved working in the school that had very low educational achievement but again in a context where the children often came from fractured homes. At the end of that year I got a job in a school in a metropolitan area in the north-west of England. I found that the teachers at the school were very committed to the children and I love working with them on various projects. I have also found that I get such satisfaction from helping children to see that there are things in school that they can grapple with and succeed in. I am now in my fifth year at the school and although in a state of what feels like permanent exhaustion I cannot imagine being anywhere else for a while. When I look back I am really proud of the way I have been able to develop my teaching and feel really excited about the prospect of learning a lot more in the future.

If we apply Sachs' 'entrepreneurial' and activist identities in the two brief overviews above, we can see that essentially Brian is articulating an entrepreneurial identity as he is focused on pleasing external bodies such as Ofsted and the Head Teacher, and it might be argued he is more concerned with power. On the other hand Teresa is more concerned with helping the children and developing herself as a teacher and sees the job as more about service.

A weakness of Sachs' model might be seen to lie in the rather stark dualism it presents between the entrepreneurial and the activist identities, and it may well be that at different times in our careers we adopt more of one set of characteristics than the other.

〰 **Reflection**

In the light of Sachs' professional identities:

- Where would you like to see yourself within the 'entrepreneurial' and 'activist' identities?
- Where do you place yourself within the 'entrepreneurial' and 'activist' identities?
- Thinking about the teachers you see and work with, where would you place them within 'entrepreneurial' and 'activist' identities?

CAREER TRAJECTORIES

What can you expect in your induction year?

In the past, teachers qualified to teach arrived at a school where induction would not go much further than being given a set of keys, a register and a timetable. However, over the years there has been a gradual increase in support for teachers new to the profession. The advent of the career entry and development profile has been intended to enable a smooth transition between PGCE and the NQT year. You can gain further information at www.tda.gov.uk/teachers/induction/cedp.aspx

As you enter your NQT year, you will be supported at many levels, in terms of time and personal mentoring from within the school and from a Local Authority perspective through the Induction Programme. You may also find that HEIs now work in partnership with Local Authorities to offer the NQT induction programme at Masters-level (Kerry and Shelton-Mayes, 1995) (see Table 11.4).

TABLE 11.4 Summary of multi-support systems for NQTs (based on Kinder and Earley, 1995)

Local Education Authority Induction Programme	Adviser visits	Mentoring in school	Conditions of service
• Allows NQTs to meet new teachers in the area	• Visits from the adviser	• NQT is mentored by an experienced teacher who is given the time to enable them to carry out the role	• Start in the previous July • Decreased contact time • No cover or work as a form tutor • Extra release time • School induction programme • Observation visits

Career routes within teaching

In the past the career trajectories for teachers were very straightforward but limited. One qualified to teach and subsequently stayed in the classroom or followed management career trajectory. In Primary schools this usually meant becoming a subject coordinator and then moving on to be a deputy head and then perhaps headship. In secondary schools teachers progressed through the pastoral system or became heads of department and then progressed to deputy headships and headship. In recent years the educational landscape has been in a state of constant flux, and the increasing demands made on teachers by policies and systems of accountability might seem either daunting or appealing (or both). This has implications for middle managers' identities. Indeed, Thomas and Linstead (2002) conclude that we should not ask 'what has become of middle managers?' but rather, 'how are middle managers becoming?'

In the longer term for those of you interested in becoming Head Teachers there is now the National College for School Leadership (NCSL) which provides the National Professional Qualification for Headship (NPQH). The NPQH is seen as the NCSL's flagship provision for headship, and from April 2009 all first-time Head Teachers will be required to be NPQH graduates.

The role of the Advanced Skills Teacher (AST) was introduced in 1998 with the intention of rewarding excellent teachers who wanted to stay working in classrooms rather than following traditional routes to promotion which tended to reside solely within management. The role of the AST was seen as a form of advisory teacher, which involved them working with colleagues in their school and other schools to develop good practice.

CONTINUING AND COMPLETING YOUR MASTERS DEGREE

In this section we have included two case studies of teachers who have taken Masters courses later in their careers and for whom it has been a transformative experience.

Vignette: Ellen's story

Having completed a PGCE in secondary English I was appointed at an 11–18 comprehensive school which was situated in an area of socio-economic disadvantage. This was precisely the type of situation I wanted to work in at the start of my career.

At the school I was one of eight established English specialists. From the outset I wanted to enable all children to access a wide variety of works including those from the traditional canon. What I found was that if I was able to engage the children and make the learning relevant to them they were motivated. However, I found that a number of children seemed to struggle no matter what I tried. I also became increasingly aware that my approaches and ambitions for the children differed greatly from the head of department and the majority of the other teachers in the department.

(Continued)

(Continued)

At this point I felt helpless but then in the regular meetings I had with my induction tutor I became aware of CPD opportunities outside of English education. Around this time I saw that it was possible to take an MA in education at a local university. In my second year I was appointed as head of post-16 English and as part of this promotion I negotiated part funding of an MA in education.

Once on the MA I was able to meet teachers from a range of establishments with a variety of backgrounds and this allowed me to develop my thinking in a range of areas through discussion, reading and tutorials, and I found this to be helpful in developing my practice through understanding more deeply what I was doing and why. I feel this understanding and my heightened ability and confidence to ask questions about policy and practice will sustain my interests through the next stages of my career.

Vignette: Ross's story

When I was at school I had the chance to do a week's work experience and when my first choice fell through I ended up in a primary school. I found I loved it and from that week nurtured the idea that I might want to be a teacher in the future.

After leaving school I went to study Sport and Exercise Science at a university in the south-west. While there I did some voluntary work in another primary school to see if I still wanted to follow a career in teaching. I found that little had changed and after graduating I secured a place on a PGCE. I thoroughly enjoyed the PGCE although found that as a male in a predominantly female world I was a bit of a novelty. I then took up a post in the north-east and enjoyed the job very much.

Over the next 10 years I moved schools twice more and ended up as a deputy head. All along I had enjoyed the work and I got the idea that people felt I was good at it, but increasingly I came to feel I did not really understand much about how children learnt. In particular I enjoyed working as a mentor to PGCE students and after speaking to a tutor from the university during a school visit I enrolled on a Masters course at the local university.

Attending the course ended up being very significant as I found I was able to stand back from my own practice and the reading enabled me to develop better understandings. One of the things I came to realise was that the learning I did on the course gave me the tools to analyse things so much better than I had been able to before. Before there had been some things that really frustrated me and I kind of knew intuitively that they were flawed but I was unable to develop any strong counterarguments. It also allowed me to develop a much more explicit theoretical underpinning to classroom practice that previously I had intuitively felt was sound but had not been able to advance a clear rationale for why this might be.

⟨⟨⟩ **Reflection**

What did you notice about the stories told by Ellen and Ross?

What is your personal career trajectory to date?

How have you found yourself training to teach?

Who have been the influential people in bringing you to this point in your career?

Who are your heroes and heroines?

While we cannot generalise from two case studies, it is clear that in these case studies, Masters study has been an enriching experience.

CONCLUSION

Final thoughts on Masters-level study – what is in it for you?

As we saw in Chapter 2, motivation to learn can be viewed as a cost–benefit analysis. In other words what is in this for me and will any costs incurred be worth it? In the past there have been discussions as to the extent to which learning to teach is an apprenticeship or some other form of professional training.

Related to this there have also been arguments over whether learning to be a teacher is a matter of 'training' or 'education'. We may see education as a matter of developing knowledge and powers of reasoning and judgement – something which is, therefore, essentially divergent. Training on the other hand may be defined in a more convergent way – as a process of induction into a discipline. It has been argued that no episode of teaching is value free (Pring, 2000) and if this is the case then it is vital that teachers are able to see both the explicit and implicit messages that are conveyed to the learner.

Over recent years there has been an emphasis on a skills agenda and perhaps in a profession such as education there needs to be a shift towards values? These issues are hotly contested in the profession and we would argue that studying at M-level fosters a disposition not to hold and articulate a particular position, but to feel comfortable in being able to identify and weigh up the key issues, and even to expose inconsistencies and contradictions.

Recommended further reading

Claxton, G., Atkinson, T., Osborn, M. and Wallace, M. (eds) (1996) *Liberating the Learner: Lessons for Professional Development in Education*. London: Routledge.
This is a multi-authored book which includes contributions by some of the leading, thinkers in professional learning. Themes for chapters include theories of learning, assessment, mentoring and professional doctorates, and there are also case studies.

Craft, A. (2000) *Continuing Professional Development: A Practical Guide for Teachers and Schools*. London: Routledge Falmer/Open University.
This book provides a good overview of issues related to the 'why' and 'how' of CPD. The author also examines methods of evaluating professional development and considers issues related to planning CPD.

Sachs, J. (2003) *The Activist Teaching Profession (Professional Learning)*. Buckingham: Open University Press.
This book provides a critical perspective on teacher professionalism today. Sachs explores the ways in which teachers are in danger of becoming 'designer' products rather than autonomous professionals.

BIBLIOGRAPHY

Achebe, C. (1958) *Things Fall Apart.* London: Heinemann.

Armstrong, M. (1980) *Closely Observed Children.* London: Writers and Readers.

Athey, C. (1990) *Extending Thought in Young Children.* London: Paul Chapman.

Atkinson, K. (1997) *Behind the Scenes at the Museum.* London: Black Swan.

Atkinson, P. and Hammersley, M. (1998) 'Ethnographic and Participant Observation', in N. Denzin and Y. Lincoln (eds) *Handbook of Qualitative Research.* Thousand Oaks, CA: Sage.

Atkinson, T. and Claxton, G. (2000) *The Intuitive Practitioner: On the Value of not Always Knowing what One is Doing.* Buckingham: Open University Press.

Bailey, R. (2000) *Education in the Open Society: Karl Popper and Schooling.* Aldershot: Ashgate.

Ball, S.J. (1999) 'Labour, Learning and the Economy: a Policy Sociology Perspective', *Cambridge Journal of Education,* 29(2): 195–207.

Ball, S.J. (2008) *The Education Debate.* Bristol: The Policy Press.

Balls, E. (2009) Schools White Paper Statement, 30 June 2009. Available at www.dcsf. gov.uk/21stcenturyschoolssystem/

Bandura, A. (1969) *Social Learning and Personality Development.* London: Holt, Rinehart and Winston.

Barnes, P. (2008) 'Multi-Agency Working: What are the Perspectives of SENCOs and Parents Regarding its Development and Implementation?', *British Journal of Special Education,* 35(4): 230–40.

Barnett, R. (1994) *The Limits of Competence.* Buckingham: Society for Research into Higher Education (SRHE)/Open University Press.

Bassey, M. (1999) *Case Study Research in Educational Settings.* Buckingham: Open University Press.

Bennett, N. and Dunne, E. (1994) 'How Children Learn: Implications for Practice', in B. Moon and A. Shelton-Mayes (eds) *Teaching and Learning in the Secondary School.* London: Routledge.

Bereiter, C. and Scardamalia, M. (1998) 'Rethinking Learning', in D. Olson and N. Torrance (eds) *The Handbook of Education and Human Development.* Oxford: Blackwell. pp. 485–513.

Bernstein, B. (1975) *Class, Codes and Control.* London: Routledge and Kegan Paul.

Bernstein, B. (1988) 'Education Cannot Compensate for Society', in R. Dale, R. Fergusson and A. Robinson (eds) *Frameworks for Teaching: Readings for the Intending Secondary Teacher.* London: Hodder and Stoughton. pp. 377–99.

Best, R. (2007) 'The Whole Child Matters: The Challenge of *Every Child Matters* for Pastoral Care', *Education* 35(3): 249–59.

Black, P., Harrison, C., Lee, C., Marshall, B. and Wiliam, D. (2003) *Assessment for Learning: Putting it into Practice.* Maidenhead: Open University Press.

Blair, T. (2005) *Higher Standards, Better Schools for All.* London: DfES.

Blakemore, J. and Frith, U. (2006) *The Learning Brain: Lessons for Education.* Oxford: Blackwell.

Bolton, G. (2010) *Reflective Practice: Writing and Professional Development*, 3rd edn. London: Sage.

Booth, T. (1996) 'Inclusion and Exclusion Policy in England: Who Controls the Agenda?' in D. Armstrong et al. (eds) *Inclusive Education: Contexts and Comparative Perspectives.* London: David Fulton. pp. 78–98.

Booth, T. and Ainscow, M. (2002) *Index for Inclusion: Developing Learning and Participation in Schools.* Bristol: CSIE.

Boud, D., Keogh, R. and Walker, D. (1985a) 'What is Reflection in Learning?', in D. Boud, R. Keogh and D. Walker (eds) *Reflection: Turning Experience into Learning.* London: Kogan Page. pp. 7–17.

Boud, D., Keogh, R. and Walker, D. (1985b) 'Promoting Reflection in Learning: a Model?' in D. Boud, R. Keogh and D. Walker (eds) *Reflection: Turning Experience into Learning.* London: Kogan Page. pp. 18–40.

Brew, A. (2006) *Research and Teaching: Beyond the Divide.* Basingstoke: Palgrave Macmillan.

Broadfoot, P., Osborn, M., Planel, C. and Sharpe, K. (2000) *Promoting Quality in Learning: Does England have the Answer? Findings from the Quest Project.* London: Cassell.

Brookfield, S. (1983) *Adult Learning, Adult Education and the Community.* Milton Keynes: Open University Press.

Brookfield, S. (1987) *Developing Critical Thinkers: Challenging Adults to Explore Alternative Ways of Thinking and Acting.* New York: Teachers College Press.

Brookfield, S. (1995) *Becoming a Critically Reflective Teacher.* San Francisco: Jossey-Bass.

Bruner, J. (1986) *Actual Minds, Possible Worlds.* London: Harvard University Press.

Bruner, J. (1999) 'Folk Pedagogies', in J. Leach and B. Moon (eds) *Learners and Pedagogy.* London: Paul Chapman. pp. 4–20.

Burr, V. (1995) *An Introduction to Social Constructionism.* London: Routledge.

Butler, R. and Green, D. (1998) *The Child Within: The Exploration of Personal Construct Theory with Young People.* Oxford: Butterworth and Heinemann.

Carnell, E. and Lodge, C. (2002) *Supporting Effective Learning.* London: Paul Chapman.

Carpenter, C. (2008a) 'Investigating PE Teachers' Implicit Theories of Learning in Descriptions of Exemplary Lessons: a Case Study Set in a Specialist Sports College', paper presented at Athens Institute of Educational Research.

Carpenter, C. (2008b) 'Investigating PE Teachers' Implicit Theories of Learning: a Case Study Set in a Specialist Sports College', paper presented at British Educational Research Association, Herriot Watt University.

Carr, D. (2000) *Making Sense of Education.* London: Routledge Falmer.

Carr, W. (1998) *For Education: Towards Critical Education Enquiry.* Buckingham: Open University Press.

Carr, W. and Kemmis, S. (1986) *Becoming Critical: Education, Knowledge and Action Research.* London: Routledge Falmer.

Ceppi, G. and Zini, M. (eds) (2001) *Children, Spaces, Relations: Metaproject for an Environment for Young Children.* Milan: Domus Academy Research Centre.

Clark, R.E. and Squire, L.R. (1998) 'Classical Conditioning and Brain Systems: the Role of Awareness', *Science*, 280: 77–81.

Claxton, G. (1984) *Live and Learn: An Introduction to the Psychology of Growth and Change in Everyday Life.* Milton Keynes: Open University Press.

Claxton, G. (1996) 'Implicit Theories of Learning', in G. Claxton, T. Atkinson, M. Osborn and M. Wallace (eds) *Liberating the Learner: Lessons for Professional Development in Education.* London: Routledge. pp. 45–58.

Claxton, G. (1998) *Hare Brain, Tortoise Mind: Why Intelligence Increases when you Think Less.* London: Fourth Estate.

Claxton, G. (1999) *Wise Up: Learning to Live the Learning Life.* Stafford: Network Educational Press.

Claxton, G. (2007) 'Expanding Young People's Capacity to Learn', *British Journal of Educational Studies,* 55(2): 115–34.

Clough, P. and Nutbrown, C. (2007) *A Student's Guide to Methodology: Justifying Enquiry.* London: Sage.

Conan Doyle, A. (1887/2006) *A Study in Scarlet.* London: Headline Publishing.

Craft, A. (2000) *Continuing Professional Development: A Practical Guide for Teachers and Schools.* London: Routledge Falmer/Open University.

Darling-Hammond, L., Brandsford, J., LePage, P., Hammerness, K. and Duffy, H. (2005) *Preparing Teachers for a Changing World: What Teachers Should Learn and Be Able to Do.* San Francisco: Jossey-Bass.

Day, C. (2004) *A Passion for Teaching.* London: Routledge Falmer.

Denscombe, M. (1995) 'Teachers as an Audience for Research: the Acceptability of Ethnographic Approaches to Classroom Research', *Teachers and Teaching: Theory and Practice,* 1(1): 173–91.

Department for Children, Schools and Families (DCSF) (2007) *Report of the 'Teaching and Learning in 2020' Review Group.* London: HMSO.

Department for Children, Schools and Families (DCSF) (2008) *Being the Best for Our Children.* London: HMSO.

Department for Children, Schools and Families (DCSF) (2009) White Paper, *21st Century Schools System.* London: HMSO.

Department for Education and Employment (DfEE) (1992) *Curriculum Organisation and Classroom Practice in Primary School.* London: HMSO.

Department for Education and Employment (DfEE) (1997) White Paper, *Excellence in Schools.* London: HMSO.

Department for Education and Employment (DfEE) (1998) Green Paper, *Teachers Meeting the Challenge of Change.* London: HMSO.

Department for Education and Employment (DfEE) (2001) *Learning and Teaching: a Strategy for Professional Development.* London: HMSO.

Department for Education and Skills (DfEE) (2001) White Paper, *Schools Achieving Success.* London: HMSO.

Department for Education and Skills (DfES) (2003) National Agreement, *Raising Standards and Tackling Workloads.* London: HMSO.

Department for Education and Skills (DfES) (2004) *The Children Act.* London: HMSO.

Department for Education and Skills (DfES) (2005a) *Every Child Matters.* London: HMSO.

Department for Education and Skills (DfES) (2005b) *Higher Standards, Better Schools for All.* London: HMSO.

Department for Education and Skills (DfES) (2007) *2020 Vision: Report of the Teaching and Learning in 2020 Review Group.* Crown Copyright.

Department of Education and Science (DES) (1979) *A Framework for the School Curriculum.* London: HMSO.

Department of Education and Science (DES) (1988) *Education Reform Act.* London: HMSO.

Dewey, J. (1933) *How Do We Think?* Boston, MA: D.C. Heath and Co.

Drummond, M. (1993) *Assessing Children's Learning.* London: David Fulton.

Duffy, T. and Jonassen, D. (eds) (1992) *Constructivism and the Technology of Instruction: a Conversation.* Hillsdale, NJ: Lawrence Erlbaum Associates.

Du Maurier, D. (1938) *Rebecca*. London: Virago.

Durkheim, E. (1957) *Professional Ethics and Civil Morals*. London: Routledge.

Dweck, C. (1999) *Self Theories: Their Role in Motivation, Personality and Development*. Hove: Taylor Francis.

Ebutt, D. (1985) 'Educational Action Research: Some General Concerns and Specific Quibbles', in R. Burgess (ed.) *Issues in Educational Research*. Lewes: Falmer Press.

Eccles, D. (1960) 'Debating the Crowther Report', speech delivered in the House of Commons. *Hansard*.

Elliot, J. (1991) *Action Research for Educational Change*. Buckingham: Open University Press.

Englund, T. (1996) 'Are Professional Teachers a Good Thing?' in I.F. Goodson and A. Hargreaves (eds) *Teachers' Professional Lives*. London: The Falmer Press.

Eraut, M. (2000) 'Non-Formal Learning and Tacit Knowledge in Professional Work', *British Journal of Educational Psychology*, 70: 113–36.

Faulks, S. (2005) *Human Traces*. London: Hutchinson.

Findlay, L. (2003) 'The Reflexive Journey: Mapping Multiple Routes', in L. Findlay and B. Gough (eds) *Reflexivity: a Practical Guide for Researchers in Health and Social Sciences*. Oxford: Blackwell. pp. 3–20.

Fisher, R. (1995) *Teaching Children to Learn*. Cheltenham: Stanley Thornes.

Fox, D. (1983) 'Personal Theories of Teaching', *Studies in Higher Education*, 8(2): 151–63.

Fox, R. (2005) *Teaching and Learning: Lessons from Psychology*. Oxford: Blackwell.

Freire, P. (1970) *Pedagogy of the Oppressed*. London: Penguin Books.

Furlong, J. and Smith, R. (1996) *The Role of Higher Education in Initial Teacher Education*. London: Kogan Page.

Furnham, A. (1988) *Lay Theories: Everyday Understanding of Problems in the Social Sciences*. Oxford: Elsevier.

Galton, M. and Macbeath, J. (2008) *Teachers Under Pressure*. London: Sage.

Gavine, D. (1988) 'Special Educational Needs: Fact or Fiction?', in R. Dale, R. Fergusson and A. Robinson (eds) *Frameworks for Teaching: Readings for the Intending Secondary Teacher*. London: Hodder and Stoughton. pp. 191–200.

Goudas, M., Biddle, S. and Fox, K. (1994) 'Perceived Locus of Causality, Goal Orientations, and Perceived Competence in School Physical Education Classes', *British Journal of Educational Psychology*, 64: 453–63.

Green, T. (1998) *The Activities of Teaching*. New York: Educator's International Press, Inc.

Gubrium, J. and Holstein, J. (eds) (1997) *The New Language of Qualitative Research*. New York: Oxford University Press.

Habermas, J. (1971) *Knowledge and Human Interests*. London: Heinemann.

Haddon, M. (2003) *The Curious Incident of the Dog in the Night-Time*. London: Red Fox Books.

Hammersley, M. (1993) 'On the Teacher as Researcher', in M. Hammersley (ed.) *Educational Research: Current Issues*. London: Paul Chapman Publishing.

Hammersley, M. and Atkinson, P. (1995) *Ethnography: Principles in Practice*. London: Routledge.

Hargreaves, D. (1995) 'Beyond Collaboration: Critical Teacher Development in the Postmodern Age', in J. Smyth (ed.) *Critical Discourses on Teacher Development*. London: Cassell.

Hargreaves, D. (2000) 'Teaching as a Research-Based Profession: Possibilities and Prospects', in B. Moon, J. Butcher and E. Bird. (eds) *Leading Professional Development in Education.* London: Routledge Falmer. pp. 200–10.

Hargreaves, I. (1996) in D. Marquand and A. Seldon (eds) *The Ideas that Shaped Post-War Britain.* London: Fontana Press.

Harris, R. (2007) *The Ghost.* London: Hutchinson.

Hayden, C. (2009) 'Family Group Conferences – Are They an Effective and Viable Way of Working with Attendance and Behaviour Problems in Schools?', *British Education Research Journal*, 35(2): 205–20.

Healey, M. (2005) 'Linking Research and Teaching: Exploring Disciplinary Spaces and the Role of Inquiry-Based Learning', in R. Barnett (ed.) *Reshaping the University: New Relationships between Research, Scholarship and Teaching.* Maidenhead: Society for Research into Higher Education/Open University Press.

Helsby, G. (1995) 'Teachers' Constructions of Professionalism in the 1990s', *Journal of Education for Teaching*, 21(3): 317–32.

Hofstede, G. (1991) *Cultures and Organizations: Software of the Mind.* New York: McGraw-Hill.

Holliday, A. (2002) *Doing and Writing Qualitative Research.* London: Sage.

Holliday, A (2007) *Doing and Writing Qualitative Research*, 2nd edn. London: Sage.

Holstein, J.A. and Gubrium, J.F. (1997) 'The Active Interview', in D. Silverman (ed.) *Qualitative Research.* London: Sage.

Hopkins, D. (2002) *A Teacher's Guide to Classroom Research,* 3rd edn. Buckingham: Open University Press.

Houle, C. (1980) *Continuing Learning in the Professions.* San Francisco: Jossey-Bass.

Hoult, S. (2005) *Reflective Reader: Secondary Professional Studies.* Exeter: Learning Matters.

Hoy, A. and Murphy, P. (2001) 'Teaching Educational Psychology to the Implicit Mind', in B. Torff and R. Sternberg (eds) *Understanding and Teaching the Intuitive Mind: Student and Teacher Learning.* Mahwah, NJ: Lawrence Erlbaum.

Hoyle, E. (1995) 'Changing Conceptions of a Profession', in H. Busher and R. Saran (eds) *Managing Teachers as Professionals in Schools.* London: Kogan Page.

Hryniewicz, L. (2004) *Teaching Assistants: the Complete Handbook.* Ely: Adamson.

Hunt, C. and Sampson, F. (2006) *Writing: Self and Reflexivity*. Basingstoke: Palgrave Macmillan.

Hymans, M. (2008) 'How Personal Constructs about "Professional Identity" Might Act as a Barrier to Multi-Agency Working', *Educational Psychology in Practice,* 24(4): 279–88.

Illeris, K. (2007) *How We Learn: Learning and Non-Learning in School and Beyond.* London: Routledge.

Illich, I. (1970) *Deschooling Society.* Harmondsworth: Penguin.

James, M. (2008) 'Assessment and Learning', in S. Swaffield (ed.) *Unlocking Assessment: Understanding for Reflection and Application.* London: Routledge.

Jarvis, P. (2006) *Towards a Comprehensive Theory of Human Learning.* London: Routledge.

Jarvis, P., Holford, J. and Griffin, C. (2003) *The Theory and Practice of Learning.* London: Kogan Page.

Jenkins, S. (1995) *Accountable to None.* London: Penguin Books.

John, P. (1996) 'Understanding the Apprenticeship of Observation in Initial Teacher Education', in G. Claxton, T. Atkinson, M. Osborn and M. Wallace (eds) *Liberating the Learner: Lessons for Professional Development in Education.* London: Routledge. pp. 90–107.

Johns, C. (1994) 'Nuances of Reflection', *Journal of Clinical Nursing*, 3: 71–5.

Kemmis, S. (1983) 'Action Research', in T. Husen and T. Postlethwaite (eds) *International Encyclopaedia of Education: Research and Studies.* Oxford: Pergamon.

Kemmis, S. and McTaggart, R. (1988) *The Action Research Planner,* 3rd edn. Victoria: Deakin University (1st edn 1981).

Kerry, T. and Shelton-Mayes, A. (eds) (1995) *Issues in Mentoring.* London: Routledge.

Kinder, K. and Earley, P. (1995) 'Key Issues Emerging from an NFER Study of NQTs: Models of Induction Support', in T. Kerry and A. Shelton-Mayes (eds) *Issues in Mentoring.* London: Routledge. pp. 164–82.

Kingsolver, B. (1998) *The Poisonwood Bible.* London: Faber and Faber.

Knight, P. (2002) *Small-Scale Research.* London: Sage.

Kolb, D. (1984) *Experiential Learning.* New York: Prentice Hall.

Kreber, C. and Cranton, P.A. (2000) 'Exploring the Scholarship of Teaching', *Journal of Higher Education,* 71(4): 479--95.

Labour Party Manifesto for the General Election (1997) www.forscotland.com/tracklab/html

Laming, W. (2003) *The Victoria Climbié Inquiry: Report of an Inquiry by Lord Laming.* Norwich: TSO.

Langdridge, D. (2007) *Phenomenological Psychology: Theory, Research and Method.* Harlow: Pearson Education.

Langer, E. (1997) *The Power of Mindful Learning.* New York: Addison-Wesley.

Lave, J. and Wenger, E. (1991) *Situated Learning: Legitimate Peripheral Participation.* Cambridge: Cambridge University Press.

Lawn, M. (1996) *Modern Times? Work, Professionalism and Citizenship in Teaching.* London: The Falmer Press.

Lawton, D. (1980) *The Politics of the School Curriculum.* London: Routledge and Kegan Paul.

Leach, J. (2008) 'Do New Information and Communications Technologies have a Role to Play in the Achievement of Education for All?', *British Educational Research Journal,* 34(6): 783–805.

Lewis, A. and Lindsay, G. (eds) (2000) *Researching Children's Perspectives.* Buckingham: Open University Press.

Lichtman, M. (2006) *All You Need to Know about Qualitative Research.* Thousand Oaks, CA: Sage.

Lincoln, Y. and Guba, E. (2000) 'The Only Generalization is: There is no Generalization', in R. Gomm, M. Hammersley and P. Foster (eds) *Case Study Method.* London: Sage.

Lodge, C. (1998) 'Training Aspiring Heads on NPQH: Issues and Progress', *School Leadership and Management,* 18(3): 347–57.

Lomax, P. (2002) 'Action Research', in M. Coleman and A. Briggs (eds) *Research Methods in Educational Leadership and Management.* London: Paul Chapman Publishing.

Lyotard, J. (1984) *The Postmodern Condition: a Report on Knowledge.* Manchester: Manchester University Press.

MacBeath, J. (1999) *Schools Must Speak for Themselves: the Case for Self-Evaluation.* London: Routledge Falmer.

Mahony, P. (1988) 'How Alice's Chin Really Came to be Pressed Against her Foot: Sexist Processes of Interaction in Mixed-Sex Classrooms', in R. Dale, R. Fergusson and A. Robinson (eds) *Frameworks for Teaching: Readings for the Intending Secondary Teacher.* London: Hodder and Stoughton. pp. 80–90.

Marquand, D. and Seldon, A. (eds) (1996) *The Ideas that Shaped Post-War Britain.* London: Fontana Press.

Marquez, G.G. (2007) *Love in the Time of Cholera.* London: Penguin Books.

Marton, F. and Booth, S. (1997) *Learning and Awareness.* Mahwah, NJ: Lawrence Erlbaum Associates.

Marton, F. and Saljo, R. (1976) 'On Qualitative Differences in Learning: Outcome as a Function of the Learner's Conception of the Task', *British Journal of Educational Psychology,* 46: 115–27.

Marton, F., Runnesson, L. and Tsui, A. (2004) 'The Space of Learning', in F. Marton and A. Tsui (eds) *Classroom Discourse and the Space of Learning.* Mahwah, NJ: Lawrence Erlbaum Associates. pp. 3–40.

Maslin, K. (2001) *An Introduction to the Psychology of the Mind.* Cambridge: Polity.

McCulloch, G., Helsby, G. and Knight, P. (2000) *The Politics of Professionalism.* London: Continuum.

McIntyre, D. (1993) 'Theory, Theorizing and Reflection in Initial Teacher Education', in J. Calderhead and P. Gates (eds) *Conceptualising Reflection in Teacher Development.* London: Falmer Press.

McNiff, J. and Whitehead, J. (2006) *All You Need to Know about Action Research.* London: Sage.

Mendick, H. (2008) 'Subtracting Difference: Troubling Transitions from GCSE to AS-Level Mathematics', *British Journal of Educational Research,* 34(6): 711–32.

Mercer, N. (1995) *The Guided Construction of Knowledge: Talk Amongst Teachers and Learners.* Bristol: Multilingual Matters.

Mezirow, J. (1991) *Transformative Dimensions of Adult Learning.* San Francisco: Jossey-Bass.

Miles, M. and Huberman, M. (1994) *Qualitative Data Analysis: an Expanded Source Book.* London: Sage.

Miller, N. and Boud, D. (1996) 'Animating Learning from Experience', in D. Boud and N. Miller (eds) *Working with Experience.* London: Routledge.

Miller, J. and Glassner, B. (1997) 'The "Inside" and the "Outside": Finding Realities in Interviews', in N.K. Denzin and Y.S. Lincoln (eds) *Handbook of Qualitative Research.* Thousand Oaks, CA: Sage. pp 99–112.

Moon, J. (1999) *Reflection in Learning and Professional Development: Theory and Practice.* London: Routledge Falmer.

Moore, A. (2000) *Teaching and Learning: Pedagogy, Curriculum and Culture.* London: Routledge Falmer.

Morgan, A., Nutbrown, C. and Hannon, P. (2009) 'Fathers' Involvement in Young Childrens' Literacy Development: Implications for Family Literacy Programmes', *British Educational Research Journal,* 35(2): 167–85.

Morrison, K. (1996) 'Developing Reflective Practice in Higher Degree Students through a Learning Journal', *Studies in Higher Education,* 21(3): 317–32.

Moss, P. (2004) Professional Development Master Class, Canterbury Christ Church University.

Nixon, J. (1997) 'Regenerating Professionalism within the Academic Workplace', in J. Broadbent, M. Dietrich and J. Roberts (eds) *The End of the Professions?* London: Routledge.

Olson, D. and Bruner, J. (1998) 'Folk Psychology and Folk Pedagogy', in D. Olson and N. Torrance (eds) *The Handbook of Education and Human Development.* Oxford: Blackwell. pp. 9–27.

Ormrod, J. (1999) *Human Learning.* Upper Saddle River, NJ: Prentice Hall.

Pass, S. (2004) *Parallel Paths to Constructivism.* Connecticut: Information Age.

Perkins, D. (1992) 'Technology Meets Constructivism: Do they Make a Marriage?', in T. Duffy and D. Jonassen (eds) *Constructivism and the Technology of Instruction.* Mahwah, NJ: Lawrence Erlbaum Associates. pp. 45–56.

Perkins, H. (1989) *The Rise of Professional Society.* London: Routledge.

Pole, C. and Morrison, M. (2003) *Ethnography for Education.* Maidenhead: Open University Press.

Popkewitz (1984) *Paradigm and Ideology in Educational Research: The Social Functions of the Intellectual.* London: Falmer Press.

Poulson, L. and Wallace, M. (eds) (2004*) Learning to Read Critically in Teaching and Learning.* London: Sage.

Powell, S., Tod, J., Cornwall, J. and Soan, S. (2004) 'A Systematic Review of How Theories Explain Learning Behaviour in School Contexts', *EPPI Review,* August.

Pring, R. (2000) 'Truth, Knowledge and Power', in R. Pring *Philosophy of Education: Aims, Theory, Common Sense and Research.* London: Continuum. pp. 209–27.

Pritchard, A. (2005) *Ways of Learning: Learning Theories and Learning Styles in the Classroom.* London: David Fulton.

Pye, J. (1988) *Invisible Children: Who are the Real Losers at School?* Oxford: Oxford University Press.

Radford, M. (2006) 'Researching Classrooms: Complexity and Chaos', *British Educational Research Journal,* 32(2): 177–90.

Ramsden, P. (2003) *Learning to Teach in Higher Education.* London: Routledge Falmer.

Ranson, S. (2007) 'Public Accountability in the Age of Neo-Liberal Governance', in B. Lingard and J. Ozga (eds) *The RoutledgeFalmer Reader in Education Policy and Politics.* London: Routledge.

Reber, A. (1993) *Implicit Learning and Tacit Knowledge.* Oxford: Oxford University Press.

Roberts, M. (2003) *Learning Through Enquiry: Making Sense of Geography in the Key Stage 3 Classroom.* Sheffield: Geographical Association.

Roche, J. and Tucker, S. (2007) '*Every Child Matters:* "Tinkering" or "Reforming" – an Analysis of the Development of the Children Act (2004) from an Educational Perspective', *Education,* 3(13): 213–23.

Rogers, C. and Freiberg, H. (1994) *Freedom to Learn.* New York: Maxwell Macmillan International.

Rowland, S. (2005) 'Intellectual Love and the Link between Teaching and Research', in R. Barnett (ed.) *Reshaping the University: New Relationships between Research, Scholarship and Teaching.* Maidenhead: Society for Research into Higher Education/Open University Press.

Rowntree, D. (1988) 'The Side-Effects of Assessment', in R. Dale, R. Fergusson and A. Robinson (eds) *Frameworks for Teaching: Readings for the Intending Secondary Teacher.* London: Hodder and Stoughton. pp. 148–57.

Ruddock, J. and Stenhouse, L. (1995) *An Education that Empowers: A Collection of Lectures in Memory of Lawrence Stenhouse.* Bristol: Multilingual Matters.

Sachs. J. (2001) 'Teacher Professional Identity: Competing Discourses, Competing Outcomes', *Journal of Educational Policy,* 16(2): 149–61.

Salmon, P. (1995) *Psychology in the Classroom: Reconstructing Teachers and Learners.* London: Cassell.

Schön, D. (1983) *The Reflective Practitioner.* San Francisco: Jossey-Bass.

Schön, D. (1987) *Educating the Reflective Practitioner.* San Francisco: Jossey-Bass.

Scott, D. (2000) *Reading Educational Research and Policy.* London: RoutledgeFalmer.

Seger, C. (1994) 'Implicit Learning', *Psychological Review,* 115(2): 163–96.

Seierstad, A. (2002) *The Bookseller of Kabul.* London: Virago.

Sfard, A. (1998) 'On Two Metaphors for Learning and the Dangers of Choosing Just One', *Educational Researcher,* 27(2): 4–13.

Shulman, L. (1987) 'Knowledge and Teaching: Foundations of the New Reform', *The Harvard Educational Review,* 57(1): 1–22.

Shulman, L. (1999) 'Knowledge and Teaching: Foundations of the New Reform', in J. Leach and B. Moon (eds) *Learners and Pedagogy.* London: Paul Chapman. pp. 61–77.

Silverman, D. (1993) *Interpreting Qualitative Data.* London: Sage.

Simon, B. (1988) 'Why no Pedagogy in England?', in R. Dale, R. Fergusson and A. Robinson (eds) *Frameworks for Teaching: Readings for the Intending Secondary Teacher.* London: Hodder and Stoughton.

Simon, B. (1999) 'Why No Pedagogy in England?', in J. Leach and B. Moon (eds) *Learners and Pedagogy.* London: Paul Chapman. pp. 34–45.

Skidmore, D. (2004) *Inclusion: the Dynamic of School Development.* Maidenhead: Open University Press.

Stanovich, K. and Stanovich, P. (1996) 'Rethinking the Concept of Learning Disabilities: The Demise of Aptitude/Achievement Discrepancy', in D. Olson and N. Torrance (eds) *The Handbook of Education and Human Development.* pp. 117–47.

Sternberg, R. (1990) *Metaphors of the Mind: Conceptions of the Nature of Intelligence.* Cambridge: Cambridge University Press.

Sternberg, R. (1998) 'Learnable Intelligence', in R. Sternberg and W. Williams (eds) *Intelligence, Instruction and Assessment: Theory into Practice.* Mahwah, NJ: Lawrence Erlbaum.

Stiggins, R. (1994) *Student-centred Classroom Assessment.* New York: Merrill.

Stronach, I., Corbin, B., McNamara, O., Stark, S. and Warne, T. (2002) 'Towards an Uncertain Politics of Professionalism: Teacher and Nurse Identities in Flux', *Journal of Educational Policy,* 17(1): 109–38.

Sullivan, A. (2009) 'Academic Self-Concept, Gender and Single-Sex Schooling', *British Educational Research Journal,* 35(2): 259–88.

Swann, J. (1999a) 'Pursuing Truth: a Science of Education', in J. Swann and J. Pratt (eds) *Improving Education: Realist Approaches to Method and Research.* London: Cassell. pp. 15–29.

Swann, J. (1999b) 'Making Better Plans: Problem-Based Versus Objectives-Based Planning', in J. Swann and J. Pratt (eds) *Improving Education: Realist Approaches to Method and Research.* London: Cassell. pp. 53–66.

TeacherNet (2009) http://www.teachernet.gov.uk/wholeschool/remodelling/cutting burdens/keysteps/

Thomas, G. and McRobbie, C. (1999) 'Using Metaphor to Probe Students' Conceptions of Chemistry Learning', *International Journal of Science Education,* 21(6): 667–85.

Thomas, R. and Linstead, A. (2002) 'Losing the Plot?: Middle Managers and Identity', *Organisation,* 9(1): 71–93.

Torrance, H. and Pryor, J. (1998) *Investigating Formative Assessment: Teaching, Learning and Assessment in the Classroom.* Buckingham: Open University Press.

Twomey-Fosnot, C. (1996) 'Constructivism: a Psychological Theory of Learning', in C. Twomey-Fosnot (ed.) *Constructivism: Theory, Perspectives, and Practice.* New York and London: Teachers College Press. pp. 8–33.

Usher, R. (1989) 'Locating Adult Education in the Practical', in B. Bright (ed.) *Theory and Practice in the Study of Adult Education: The Epistemological Debate.* New York: Routledge.

Usher, R. and Bryant, I. (1987) 'Re-examining the Theory–Practice Relationship in Continuing Professional Education', *Studies in Higher Education,* 12(2): 201–12.

Walford, G. (2001) *Doing Qualitative Educational Research.* London: Continuum.

Wallace, M. and Poulson, L. (2004) 'Critical Reading for Self-Critical Writing', in L. Poulson and M. Wallace (eds) *Learning to Read Critically in Teaching and Learning.* London: Sage. pp. 3–36.

Warin, J. and Muldoon, J. (2009) 'Wanting to be "Known": Redefining Self-Awareness through an Understanding of Self-Narration Processes in Educational Transitions', *British Educational Research Journal,* 35(2): 289–303.

Watkins, C. (2003) *Learning: a Sense-Maker's Guide.* London: ATL.

Watson, J. (2006) '*Every Child Matters* and Children's Spiritual Rights: Does the New Holistic Approach to Children's Care Address Children's Spiritual Well-Being?', *International Journal of Children's Spirituality,* 11(20): 251–63.

Wellington, B. and Austin, P. (1996) 'Orientations to Reflective Practice', *Educational Research,* 38(3): 307–16.

Wenger, E. (2008) Keynote lecture, Canterbury Christ Church University, Faculty of Education, 'Open Spaces' conference.

Whitty, G. (2003) *Making Sense of Education Policy.* London: Paul Chapman Publishing.

Wilkin, A., Kinder, K., White, R., Atkinson, M. and Doherty, P. (2003) *Towards the Development of Extended Schools.* London: National Foundation for Educational Research.

Willig, C. (2001) *Introducing Qualitative Research: Adventures in Theory and Method.* Maidenhead: Open University Press.

Wilson, E. and Bedford, D. (2008) 'New Partnerships for Learning: Teachers and Teaching Assistants Working Together in Schools – the Way Forward', *Journal of Education for Teaching,* 34(2): 137–50.

Winch, C. (1998) *The Philosophy of Human Learning.* London: Routledge.

Wood, D. (1988) *How Children Think and Learn.* Oxford: Blackwell.

Yin, R. (1989) *Case Study Research: Design and Methods.* Newbury Park: Sage.

Yin, R. (2008) *Case Study Research: Design and Methods,* 4th edn. Thousand Oaks, CA: Sage.

WEBSITES

http://www.behaviour4learning.ac.uk/ – accessed 6 August 2008
http://news.bbc.co.uk/1/hi/education/7462691.stm – accessed 17 June 2009
http://www.educ.msu.edu/cst/annotatedbooks.htm – accessed 4 July 2009

INDEX